THE ARCHITECTURE OF HARRY WEESE

THE ARCHITECTURE OF HARRY WEESE

ROBERT BRUEGMANN   BUILDING ENTRIES BY KATHLEEN MURPHY SKOLNIK

W. W. NORTON & COMPANY

NEW YORK   LONDON

This book was produced with support from the
Graham Foundation for Advanced Studies in the Fine Arts.

For information about permission to reproduce selections from this
book, write to
Permissions, W. W. Norton & Company, Inc., 500 Fifth Avenue,
New York, NY 10110

For information about special discounts for bulk purchases,
please contact W. W. Norton
Special Sales at specialsales@wwnorton.com or 800-233-4830

Manufacturing by KHL Printing
Book design by Abigail Sturges
Production manager: Leeann Graham
Electronic production: Joe Lops

Library of Congress Cataloging-in-Publication Data

Bruegmann, Robert.
  The architecture of Harry Weese / Robert Bruegmann;
building entries by Kathleen Murphy Skolnik.
    p. cm.
  Includes bibliographical references and index.
  ISBN 978-0-393-73193-4 (hardcover)
  1. Weese, Harry, 1915-1998. 2. Architects—United States--Biography.
  3. Architecture—United States—History—20th century. I. Skolnik,
Kathleen Murphy. II. Title.
  NA737.W397B78 2010
  720.92—dc22

  2009052192

ISBN: 978-0-393-73193-4

W. W. Norton & Company, Inc., 500 Fifth Avenue,
New York, N.Y. 10110
www.wwnorton.com
W. W. Norton & Company Ltd., Castle House, 75/76 Wells Street,
London W1T 3QT

0 9 8 7 6 5 4 3 2 1

FRONTISPIECE
Portrait of Harry Weese, probably
taken by Francis Miller for Life
magazine, 1958. Chicago History Museum,
i59241.

CONTENTS

6 PREFACE

8 ACKNOWLEDGMENTS

11 **A LIFE IN ARCHITECTURE**

12 Childhood
15 Getting Started
30 On His Own
45 A Thriving Practice
61 A Slow Fade
74 Some Conclusions

78 **BUILDING ENTRIES**

80 Glen Lake Houses, Glen Lake, MI, 1936–39
84 Tea Wagon, 1940
85 227 East Walton, Chicago, IL, 1956
87 Lillian C. Schmitt Elementary School, Columbus, IN, 1957
90 Johnson House, Chicago, IL, 1957
92 Weese "Studio," Barrington, IL, 1957
96 United States Embassy, Accra, Ghana, 1955–58
100 Northside Junior High School, Columbus, IN, 1960–61
104 Arena Stage Washington, D.C., 1960–62, 1968–72
110 Tangeman House, Muskoka Lakes, Ontario, Canada, 1961–66
114 Hyde Park A & B Urban Renewal Project, Chicago, IL, 1956–63
120 IBM Building, Milwaukee, WI, 1961–66
124 Offices of Harry Weese & Associates, Chicago, IL, 1965, 1976
128 First Baptist Church of Columbus, IN, 1962–65
134 Auditorium Theater Restoration, Chicago, IL, 1964–67

138 Seventeenth Church of Christ, Scientist, Chicago, IL, 1965–68
142 Latin School of Chicago, IL, 1966–69
146 Shadowcliff, Ellison Bay, WI, 1968–69
150 Time-Life Building, Chicago, IL, 1967–70
155 Given Institute of Pathobiology, Aspen, CO, 1970–72
160 Actors Theatre of Louisville, KY, 1970–72, 1990–94
164 Crown Center Hotel, Kansas City, MO, 1968–73
168 Sawyer Library, Williams College, Williamstown, MA, 1975
172 Oak Park Village Hall, Oak Park, IL, 1971–75
176 Metropolitan Correctional Center, Chicago, IL, 1971–75
180 Willow Street Townhouses, Chicago, IL, 1973–76
184 Washington Metro, Washington, D.C., first segment, 1966–76
192 Frederick E. Terman Engineering Center, Stanford University, Stanford, CA, 1974–78
196 Union Underwear Corporate Headquarters, Bowling Green, KY, 1978–80
200 200 South Wacker Drive, Chicago, IL, 1978–81
205 Brown-Forman Distillers Corporation, Louisville, KY, 1979–81, 1987–89
210 Wolf Point Landings, Chicago, IL 1979–81, 1988
216 United States Embassy Housing, Tokyo, Japan, 1979–82
220 Miami-Dade County Transit System, Dade County, FL, 1984

226 BIBLIOGRAPHIC ESSAY

228 CATALOG OF MAJOR WORKS

233 INDEX

PREFACE

In 1978, the year after I arrived in Chicago, I moved into an apartment building at 55 West Chestnut Street on the Near North Side of Chicago. Officially called the John Fewkes Tower, the building had been designed by the office of Chicago architect Harry Weese for the Chicago Teachers Union. Opened in 1967, it was intended as a place for teachers in the system to retire. Units that weren't needed for that purpose were rented out. Although at first glance the twenty-nine-story building was fairly ordinary, not unlike a dozen other postwar buildings nearby, its highly intelligent floor plans and straightforward brick walls gave it a simple integrity that was immediately appealing.

The units, while modest in size, had clearly been planned from the inside out and seemed more spacious than they actually were because of the three-sided floor-to-ceiling bay windows that projected out from the living rooms, catching breezes, framing views of the city, and allowing light to wash over the walls of the apartment. Standing in the bay of my unit, I could look south toward the Loop and west to the spread of the great city toward the horizon. Like the individual apartment units, the public areas were designed with care and attention to detail. On each of the typical floors, the elevator opened into a corridor that was glazed at both ends, creating an entirely different feel from the usual apartment corridor where lights burn twenty-four hours in the gloom. This configuration was possible because of a decision to split the footprint of the building into two blocks and connect them with a core that did not extend out as far as the units. Although a little space that could have gone into the end units was sacrificed, the result was a luxurious sense of light and spaciousness. I felt as though I had all the really important features enjoyed by residents of the most expensive new buildings on Lake Shore Drive at a fraction of the cost and without their unnecessary and distracting architectural embellishments.

I eventually discovered that my reaction was exactly the one Harry Weese had intended. Like many other American cities at the time, Chicago was becoming a city of the rich and the poor. Weese devoted a great deal of his boundless energy to the task of making it once again a place where middle-class individuals and families would want to live. The actual design of 55 West Chestnut had been done by Ben Weese, Harry's brother. Although Ben had a somewhat different worldview and design sensibility than Harry, as was the case with virtually all of the designers who worked in the firm, he shared a common set of ideas about how to build in the city.

The building was deeply rooted in the traditions of Chicago architecture. The bay windows at 55 West Chestnut, for example, could be seen as a kind of homage to the bay windows of the great Chicago office buildings of the late nineteenth century by Burnham & Root, Holabird & Roche, and others. These windows and the simple brick walls allowed the building to integrate seamlessly with the existing fabric of the city around it. At the same time the building reflected an enthusiasm for certain kinds of modern European architecture. The use of the warm-colored brick, the glazed corridors, and a careful attention to human comfort were indebted to the example of Alvar Aalto and other Nordic architects whose work both Weese brothers greatly admired.

Although I had no idea of this at the time, in retrospect I realized that 1978, the year I moved into 55 West Chestnut, might well have been the apogee of the career of Harry Weese. By that time Harry Weese & Associates had completed a long and impressive roster of projects, starting with some small houses in the late 1940s and early 1950s and culminating with the Washington Metro system. Weese had gained national recognition for hundreds of interesting and innovative designs, and had received a considerable number of awards, including the Firm of the Year Award from the American Institute of Architects in 1978. He had also become an important voice in his profession and in his city.

In addition, Weese had materially contributed to the rebirth of large parts of central Chicago. More than perhaps any other well-known designer of his era, Weese was committed to saving old buildings. He bought and redeveloped a good deal of real estate, particularly in the industrial districts immediately around the Loop, and his firm was involved with many of the most important preservation and restoration projects of that era, including the Auditorium Theater, Orchestra Hall, the Newberry Library, and the Field Museum, just to mention some examples in Chicago. With his outpouring of ideas and willingness to speak out publicly against anything that he thought would hurt the city, Weese was known as the "Conscience of the City." In 1978 the Chicago Press Club named him "Chicagoan of the Year."

In the years following 1978, Harry Weese and his firm would continue to work on a great many additional buildings, not a few of them ingenious and skillfully designed. But the momentum was never the same. Weese himself, over the next decade, confronting mounting health problems, became less and less involved in the day-to-day operation of the firm.

Moreover, by the late 1970s, architectural modernism of the kind espoused by Weese and his firm had moved into a temporary eclipse with the rise of the so-called postmodernist movement. And although Weese continued to offer new ideas for civic betterment throughout the 1980s, particularly notions about how the city could reinvent itself through a great world's fair at the central lakefront, by the mid-1980s it was clear that Weese would not play any major role in the design of the fair, and within a few years the fair itself would die in a noisy squabble of competing interest groups. Weese felt increasingly like an unheeded prophet. In 1992 he sold his practice to a group of his employees and pretty much disappeared from view.

By the time of his death in 1998, Harry Weese had become a distant memory for most Chicagoans. Although many people still admired his buildings, they no longer commanded the attention they had received in their own day.

In recent years, however, there has been a marked revival of interest in the work of Harry Weese. From the vantage point of the early twenty-first century, many of the buildings of the postwar decades hold a special attraction as the work of a particularly optimistic moment in architectural history. Architects, especially those in a country emerging from World War II as the greatest economic power on earth, imagined that they could fulfill the dreams of the pioneers of the modern movement and bring modern architecture, good taste, and good design to millions of ordinary citizens. And, indeed, despite the setbacks and the almost inevitable backlash, architects like Harry Weese succeeded in this task to a considerable degree.

For this reason it is not surprising that a group of alumni of the Harry Weese office, along with family members, friends, and clients, had the idea of working on various projects that would celebrate the work of the man and the firm. The first concrete step occurred in 2003 when Doug Tilden, a former vice president at Harry Weese & Associates, met with Kitty Weese, Harry's widow. They agreed that the work of Harry Weese should be better known, and decided to start with a book project. To help them in their venture, they solicited the help of Doug's brother Scott Tilden, who had experience in producing books about architecture. The volume that you have in your hands is the result of the effort they started. It contains an essay on the life and art of Harry Weese, a group of short essays on individual buildings prepared by Kathleen Murphy Skolnik, a bibliographic essay, and a catalog of major works designed by Harry Weese and his firm. However, the work of rediscovering the legacy of Weese is far from finished. This book touches on only a small fraction of the buildings and projects executed by Weese and his firm. Moreover, although the authors consulted a wide range of materials, there is much archival material left to explore. This book is a first, modest attempt to put the entire career of Harry Weese into perspective.

ACKNOWLEDGMENTS

Over the long period that this book was in production, the organizers and authors received a great deal of assistance from many quarters. Listed below, with apologies for the omissions that are all but inevitable in such a large project, are some of the individuals and groups who helped in various ways.

The following former principals of Harry Weese & Associates contributed significant financial support to the book effort and many hours of active participation and assistance: Ben Weese, John F. Hartray, Douglas A. Tilden, and Stanley N. Allan. John A. Buck of the John Buck Company, an important client of Harry Weese's, also provided a sizable gift in support of this book.

The following architectural firms, whose principals worked for or with Harry Weese, also provided financial contributions as well as information: Bauhs & Dring, Architects—Bill Bauhs and Bill Dring; Lisec & Biederman—Michael Lisec and Fritz Biederman; Booth Hansen—Laurence O. Booth; Loggia Architecture—Douglas P. Tachi; and Kathryn Quinn Architects—Kathryn Quinn.

Similar help came from the following alumnae of Harry Weese & Associates: Basil Acey, Wallace Bowling Jr., John B. Buenz, John J. Corley, Ekkehard F. Freese, William B. Gallagher Jr., Luca Gori, Paul Hansen, Karl Hartnack, Joe Karr, Robert Keenan, Margaret G. Kershaw, Carl R. Klimek, Peter Landon, Cy Merkezas, Jerrold R. McElvain, David Munson, Angel Rene Rodriguez, Howard Sackel, Kevin Lee Sarring, Timothy Werbstein, and Mark Zinni.

Over the years, a great many individuals and institutions helped in this endeavor. First and foremost were members of the Weese family, including Harry's wife, Kitty Baldwin Weese, who, sadly, passed away during the preparation of this book; Ben Weese, younger brother of Harry, who provided an enormous amount of information as well as images and documents; and the three Weese daughters, Shirley Weese Young, Marcia Weese, and Kate B. Weese. Scott Tilden played a key role in the formative stages of the book's preparation, engaging an author and publisher.

Among the institutions that helped in the preparation of this book, the greatest debt is to the Graham Foundation—its director Sarah Herda and its board of trustees—and to the Chicago History Museum, which houses the largest collection of Weese materials. President Gary Johnson, Russell Lewis, Rob Medina, Leigh Moran, Bryan McDaniel, Tom Guerra, Justin Huyck, AnneMarie Chase, Lesley Martin, Debbie Vaughn, Le Mar Brazile, Michael Featherstone, Bruce Geraghy, and Martin Nord were especially helpful. At the Ryerson & Burnham Libraries of the Art Institute of Chicago, Mary Woolever was, as always, unfailingly helpful in providing assistance, as was Nathaniel Parks. Thanks also to the Columbus Architectural Archives—Lynn Bigley, Emily Dill, and Rhonda Bollner; the Cranbrook Academy of Art—Marc Coir, Leslie Edwards, and Diane Schmale; the Latin School of Chicago—Craig Noel; the Marcus Center for the Performing Arts—Mark Barnes; the MIT Museum—Gary Van Zante and Laura Knott; the Special Collection Research Center at the University of Chicago; and the Hyde Park Historical Society.

Many friends, clients, and business associates of Harry Weese were willing to talk about the architect and his work. Among these individuals were his attorney Irwin Askow, John Baird, John Buck, Larry Booth, Ben Heineman, John McBride, Jackie Wogan, and Jared Shlaes, who was a goldmine of information about a number of early Weese projects with which he was involved.

Current owners or occupants of buildings designed by Harry Weese were also helpful. Among them were Dan Baldwin, Carol Ross Barney, Craig Dukersheim, William I. Miller, Minfong Gong, Molly Green, Judy and Lester Munson, Len Zaiser, Owsley Brown II and Eric Doniger from Brown-Forman, Jonathan Blythe from the U.S. Department of State, Wanda Snyder and Alexander (Sandy) Spear from the Actors Theatre of Louisville, Amy Dixon from Northside Junior High School in Columbus, Alison Irvin from Arena Stage in Washington, D.C., and Janet Ferrara from the Given Institute in Aspen.

The following photographers and owners of photographic rights agreed to publication of photographs: Hedrich-Blessing, Orlando Cabanban, Balthazar Korab, Adam Siegel, Dietrich Floeter, Steven Brooke, Kim Clawson, Mirte Mallory of Berko Photography, and the McShane-Fleming Studios.

The following former employees of Harry Weese & Associates contributed their recollections of life and work in the office: Basil Acey, Stanley Allan, Kim Clawson, John Corley, Bob E. Bell, Fritz Biederman, Joe Karr, Karl Landesz, Peter Landon, Kevin Cartwright, Lord Roger Cunliffe, Don Dimmett, Bill Gallagher, Ezra Gordon, Karl Hartnack, Jack Hartray, Scott Himmel, Carl Klimek, Marilyn Levy Jonap, Jerry Karn, Joe Karr, Bob Keenan, Margaret Kershaw, William Lipsey, Michael Lisec, Bill McBride, Dave Munson, Hans Neumann, Mits and Barbara Otsuji, Martin Price, Kathryn Quinn, Ronald Pales, Kevin Sarring, Ronald Schmitt, Pat Spillman, Stanley Tigerman, James Torvik, Stephen Truduak, Tom Twohey, George Vrechek, Norm Zimmerman, and Vince Ziolkowski. Valuable information was also obtained from former staff members at *Inland Architect*, including Cynthia Davidson, Nory Miller, and Judith Kiriazis.

Other individuals who contributed to this work include Zachary Schrag, on the Metro system; David DeLong and Sam Roche, on the place of Harry Weese in postwar architecture; Sharon Irish, on Weese's work in Champaign; Robert Sharoff and John Vinci, on Weese's character and creativity; Alice Schlessinger, Devereux Bowly, Bruce Sagan and the *Hyde Park Herald;* Ruth Knack, on Hyde Park A & B; Anne Sylvan, on Weese's unbuilt projects; Richard Wright and Joe Kunkel, on Weese's furniture; Daniele Manni, on the Metropolitan Correctional Center; David Gwynn, on Purity stores; Joan Gand, Diane Gonzalez, and Kathy Huff, for facilitating access to Harry Weese houses; Franklin Gray, on Union Underwear; Richard Eicholz, and Dennis McClendon for his expert help in locating buildings for the catalogue and advice on many other matters.

At W. W. Norton, editor Nancy Green and copy editor Mary Babcock were careful shepherds of the project.

Robert Bruegmann would especially like to thank Leslie Coburn for her work on Hyde Park A & B and Kathleen Murphy Skolnik for her skill, patience, and willingness to devote endless hours to tracking down information, collecting images, and writing and rewriting. He is also particularly grateful to Joe Karr, Jack Hartray, and Ben Weese, the latter a constant help and inspiration as he attempted to find documentation and explain the legacy of his brother. Finally this book would never have appeared without Doug Tilden, the chief force at its inception, who remained at its helm through the years as banker, critic, troubleshooter, and most ardent supporter.

A LIFE IN ARCHITECTURE

CHILDHOOD

Harry Mohr Weese was born on June 30, 1915, in Evanston, Illinois, a well-established upper-middle-class suburb just north of Chicago. Harry's father, Harry Ernest Weese, spent his early youth in relative poverty on a farm near Huntington, Indiana, but through years of hard work and dedication he pulled himself up into solid suburban affluence. After graduating from Northwestern University in 1902, he started a thirty-eight-year career at the Harris Trust Bank in Chicago, working his way up to treasurer before he retired in 1942. In 1914, at the age of thirty-eight, having put himself and his younger brothers and sisters through college, he married Marjorie Mohr. Sixteen years his junior, Marjorie came from a Swiss Mennonite family whose men had a history of itinerant preaching in the Anabaptist tradition. By the time she married, her family was living in Joliet, where her father was the assistant to the president of Illinois Steel Company. She was an elegant and cultivated young woman who went to the public schools in Chicago and graduated from Hyde Park High School before "finishing" at the Southern Seminary in Buena Vista, Virginia. Harry Ernest proposed to her after an opera at the Auditorium Theater.

Harry Ernest and Marjorie's first home was a third-floor apartment at the corner of Washington Street and Ridge Avenue in Evanston. Harry Mohr Weese, their first child, was born in that apartment. He was followed by sister Jane, born in 1916, after which the family moved to a rented house on Park Place in Evanston. There the first two children would be followed by John, born in 1919, Sue, in 1923, and Ben, in 1929. It was a large and bustling household and one where art was a major interest. Perhaps as a result, Harry, John, and Ben would eventually become architects and Jane a fashion illustrator for Lord's department store in Evanston.

From all accounts young Harry was hyperactive, so restless, according to family members, that during the night he would throw off all of his bedding and mattress and end up sleeping on the box springs. During the day he would fidget constantly and chew his tie absent mindedly. He was also highly precocious with a decided talent for drawing and building. The best way to calm him down was to give him some paper and a pencil. The result was an unending series of drawings, "of secret Caribbean islands, pirate coves, self-sufficient with orchard garden, windmill, solar energy, private enclaves," as he would later recall, "also boats and football players."

In 1919, when Harry was still a young boy, his parents moved the clan from Evanston to Kenilworth, a few train stops farther to the north along the lakefront. Kenilworth, founded in 1893 as an ideal family-focused suburban community in a rural setting, was a small place, with a population of just under twelve hundred in 1920, wedged between the larger communities of Wilmette to the south and Winnetka to the north. Sharing a high school, the three suburbs formed a distinct social and economic unit, one of the most affluent and sedate places in the entire Chicago metropolitan area. It was tightly connected to Chicago's Loop by the frequent commuter service of the Chicago and North Western railroad. Every business day Harry Ernest Weese, like many of his neighbors, rode the train into the city and walked from there to his office. Young Harry, like many boys from these communities, learned to take the train into town on his own at an early age.

The Weese house was located at 141 Kenilworth Avenue, the main spine of the village, in a prime location between the lakefront and the center of town. The house was a solid, if architecturally unremarkable, foursquare stucco-covered dwelling set in a neighborhood full of large and handsome homes, a good many of them designed by well-known architects. There was, for example, a house by the famous Daniel Burnham two doors down from the Weeses, and nearby were Craftsman bungalows by the firm of Nimmons & Fellows, and Prairie houses by Frank Lloyd Wright, Walter Burley Griffin, and George Maher. More important than the architecture, though, was the landscape. A great deal of the public and private landscaping had been done by the Prairie School landscape designer Jens Jensen and his followers. Together, the trees in the individual yards and the trees that arched over the streets formed a dense green canopy over this tranquil and prosperous scene, which, once it had filled in, tended to change very little over the years.

Harry Ernest was a tireless advocate for the Protestant work ethic, the value of competition and the virtues of honesty, cleanliness, and good manners. He attempted, with varying degrees of success, to instill these virtues in his children. A surviving childhood document entitled "New Year's Resolutions of Harry Weese," perhaps at least partly composed by young Harry, sets out, on a carefully typed page, lists of resolutions and tasks, the successful accomplishment of which could lead to monetary rewards for Harry or whichever of his siblings achieved the best record. Smoking and drinking were forbidden in his household. Both Harry's parents believed in the value of religion and raised their children in the Methodist church. Harry Ernest was socially and politically conservative and a staunch Republican. His wife, although not usually vocal on the matter, was more liberal and considerably moderated the tone of the household.

Experiencing the panic of 1893 had made Harry Ernest intensely frugal when it came to financial matters. Although he lived in a comfortable and well-appointed house, Harry Ernest tried to remain as self-sufficient as possible. He insisted, for example, on maintaining an extensive agricultural operation in the backyard, growing vegetables, raising chickens, fattening a turkey, and keeping bees. In later life young Harry would recall that as a child he was embarrassed because his family was the only one that kept chickens on Kenilworth Avenue.

Harry Ernest was also a notable advocate of intellectual self-improvement, urging his children to expand their knowledge and explore their talents. Harry Ernest himself had some interest in art. He wrote some doggerel poetry and participated in musicals at the University Club of Chicago, but for him these were only sidelines. Young Harry's early preoccupation with drawing alarmed his father, who was afraid that his son might stray into the low-paying and, to his mind, socially dubious field of art. Harry Ernest took

an active role in a campaign to channel any such inclinations into the more secure and better-paying profession of architecture.

Young Harry attended the Joseph Sears School, which was located a short walk from the Weese house in Kenilworth, and then the New Trier High School just a little farther away, across the border in Winnetka. The local school system, then as now, was ranked among the best in the country, boasting a broad curriculum including unusually robust offerings in theater, music, and the arts. School, like most other things in life, seemed to come easily to Harry. Although he was not always diligent in his studies and was constantly distracted by other activities, he managed, according to his later memory, to graduate in the top ten percent of his class. He read voraciously, moving through the plays of George Bernard Shaw, the poetry of Keats and Shelley, the novels of Charles Dickens, the works of Morris, Blake, and the Fabians, devouring one author at a time, and he played a part in the annual Shakespeare play in the eighth grade.

Beside school there were the usual childhood pursuits. He accompanied his father on hunting, fishing, and golf expeditions—enough of them, Weese later recalled, that by the time he left for college, he was "entirely hunted out and fished out and golfed out." Harry also remembered, later in life, solitary beachcombing along Lake Michigan with his Doberman named Count and playing in the backyard along the "Skokie Ditch" that ran through it. He learned from his grandfather, Horace Greeley Weese (1853–1941), who lived with them for a time, how to keep bees, an activity he continued until he left for college.

Harry also had a knack for making things. He later recalled building huts and tree houses as well as an underground house. His first Scout merit badge was awarded for a bridge built without nails. He apparently got the wood in his backyard by taking branches from wild cherry trees and then weaving them together, securing the whole structure with binding twine. The scoutmaster tested it gingerly at first and then started kicking it vigorously to see if he could break it down. It remained tenaciously intact. Harry also joined the Sea Scouts, dreamed of going to sea in a square rigger, and started making boats at the family's weekend house in Barrington. Long before he went to architectural school, he became interested in prefabricated buildings. He eagerly studied pamphlets issued by the Forest Products Laboratories in Madison, Wisconsin, that described the latest research in the use of plywood in stressed skins and other applications.

Later in life Weese recalled some of his first architectural encounters. Because of an assignment in an art appreciation class, he discovered, as he walked home for lunch, examples of the Greek and Tudor styles, and he quickly learned how to distinguish the Doric from the Ionic and Corinthian orders. In addition to his drawing, Harry started making designs for everything from small objects to entire cities. His first executed design was a monogram for use in embossing letter-of-credit folders for the Harris Trust Bank, where his father worked. The bank officials were happy with the result and agreed to use it.

He soon became aware of two Frank Lloyd Wright houses in town. These elicited an ambivalent reaction. His reservations may have been due in part to Wright's scandalous reputation for abandoning his family and running away to Europe with the wife of a client. However, his more serious reservations seem to have been connected to the way Wright practiced architecture. Harry had heard rumors about the cult-like nature of Wright's compounds in Wisconsin and Arizona and the way Wright exploited young apprentices and generally took advantage of everyone around him. Most important, Harry appears to have disapproved of some of Wright's design features—for example, the consistently broad roof overhangs around houses, even on the north elevations where they couldn't be justified as shading from the sun. He also considered Wright's repetitive use of interlocking geometric forms excessive. As Harry later recalled, during the period when he was growing up, Wright seemed to be more a figure of the nineteenth than the twentieth century and one who allowed romantic associations to compromise his designs.

Early on Harry also developed an interest in cities and urban planning. In a high school paper he developed a scheme for excavating lakes in Barrington and for using the rich black topsoil that was removed for the landscaping of the 1933 fair, which was being built on landfill in central Chicago. Every summer with his family he would visit an uncle on his father's side who lived in Chagrin Falls, outside Cleveland, and who was vice president of the Nickel Plate Railroad. Harry was particularly impressed with his uncle's private railroad car and a series of dams that created little pools on his property. He was fascinated by the manipulation of the landscape and vowed he would do similar kinds of projects. An uncle on his mother's side, the German-born Herman A. Brassert, was head of the firm Freyn, Brassert & Company, an enterprise that constructed steel mills around the world. Poring through his uncle's photo albums of new mills and mill towns fired him with the ambition to build equally grand new works.

In addition to his interests in architecture, young Harry had a considerable talent for music. He started on the piano but later gravitated to the trumpet, then the trombone, and finally the double base, because, as he later recalled, no one else in any group he played in wanted to carry around such a big instrument. He helped to start a musical group called the Holmes-Weese Jazz Band, which played for many of the dances at New Trier High School and elsewhere, and he continued to play in ensembles while he attended architecture school.

Although Harry Ernest Weese was a pillar of the Kenilworth community, serving first as village clerk and then as treasurer, by 1923 he had become concerned that Kenilworth might be too rarified for the proper upbringing of his children. Also, the idea of having his own piece of rural land appealed to him as a way to ensure his family's security no matter what the future would bring. So in 1925 he and a group of friends paid $500 an acre for fifty-three acres at Hawley Woods near Barrington, in northwest suburban Chicago, and there, a few years later, he built a one-story cottage called Hilltop Summer Home on the part of the land that came to him. This was an Aladdin ready-cut house that he erected with the help of local carpenters during a two-week vacation from work. At age nineteen Harry had his first construction experience when he wired the house for electricity and helped build a kitchen addition.

Even though the family had the summer house in Barrington, they liked to take summer vacations elsewhere. About 1921 the family started spending time at Glen Lake, near Traverse City, in northern Michigan. Harry Ernest knew about this part of the world from business visits to Empire, Michigan, where there was a bank affiliated with Harris Trust in Chicago. Although it had a spectacular topography of lakes and enormous dunes, this part of Michigan was in economic distress. The lumber companies had denuded the land of trees, and the soil had been played out after several years of farming. Harry Ernest recognized a bargain when he saw it. His initial idea was to get together some friends from his childhood in Indiana to purchase a large tract on Glen Lake and create a summer colony. Although nothing came of this scheme, by 1925 Harry Ernest had gotten control of one thousand feet of frontage along the lake. At the time he purchased the land there were only a few houses on or near the lake, some of them occupied by local families, others by Chicagoans who came up for the summer. During Harry's school years the Weese family would come up and pitch a tent on the land so that they could fish and hunt. Harry later recalled arriving there in an old Studebaker sedan with a trailer overloaded with luggage.

In 1929 when Harry was fourteen years old, his youngest brother Ben was born. By this time Harry Ernest was fifty-three years old, and young Harry became almost a surrogate father for Ben, particularly in the areas of education and artistic pursuits. When Ben attended Sears School, for example, Harry decided that the art instruction Ben was receiving from his teacher, Miss Robinson, a woman who was then seventy and had been Harry's teacher, was too conservative and was leading to drawings that were stiff and mechanical. So when Ben reached age eight, Harry took on the task of teaching him freehand perspective drawing.

GETTING STARTED

In the spring of 1933, Harry Weese graduated from New Trier High School. He would be attending architecture school at MIT in the fall, but in the meantime, Chicago was hosting a major architectural event, the Century of Progress world's fair. Rather than the classical style seen at the 1893 world's fair or subsequent ones in St. Louis and elsewhere, the Century of Progress was one of the first large-scale demonstrations of modern architecture, particularly the streamlined modernist, or "Art Deco" style that became enormously popular in the United States in the 1930s. After an abortive attempt by Harry and a friend to sail from Kenilworth to the fair on a boat they had constructed, Harry finally did get there, presumably by train or car. What Harry remembered best in later years was Buckminster Fuller's Dymaxion car and a pair of modern houses, the House of Tomorrow of 1933 and the Crystal House of 1934, both designed by the brothers William and George Fred Keck of Chicago.

Later that summer, with a ten-dollar one-way ticket, Weese headed east to Boston on a Safeway bus to attend MIT. His initial destination was Maine, where the MIT architecture department conducted a "summer camp" designed to allow students to get acquainted and to learn land surveying and some basic architectural skills before starting the actual program at "Boston Tech." Although most of the institution had moved to a new campus across the Charles River in Cambridge, Massachusetts, the School of Architecture remained in the Back Bay. It occupied an old building located just off Copley Square, near some of the most conspicuous examples of American architecture of the nineteenth century, notably the great Trinity Church by H. H. Richardson and the Boston Public Library by McKim, Mead & White. Boston was a revelation to Weese. Compared with the wide, gridded streets and relatively recent buildings of Chicago, Boston seemed much older, similar to what he imagined Europe would be like. Weese was delighted by the mile after mile of brick row houses forming a coherent low-rise landscape, broken only by a few church steeples, the skyscraper addition above the old Custom House and the great golden dome of Charles Bulfinch's State House.

Weese found architectural school and some of the curriculum a little old-fashioned. Years later he described the dean, William Emerson, as a "sentimental, nice old guy" who had a lorgnette and wore frock coats. Emerson, who had been heading the architecture program for fourteen years when Weese started, still favored the tradition of architectural education inherited from the Ecole des Beaux-Arts in Paris. This tradition, with its heavy emphasis on historical precedent, clear, often symmetrical site plans, and classically ordered façades, was, at the time Weese entered MIT, under attack by enthusiasts of the new ideas and architectural forms coming from avant-garde European modernist practice. Although there was very little of that work to be seen on American soil, the ideas of architects like Walter Gropius, Le Corbusier, and Mies van der Rohe were creating a considerable stir. The Museum of Modern Art, which had been founded in New York City in 1929 to showcase new art and architecture, had mounted a show on European pioneers of modernism and their American followers in 1931. This exhibition popularized the term "International Style" for the minimal, often asymmetrical and ahistorical style favored by many Europeans.

Many advocates of the new modern architecture were resolutely opposed to what they considered the hidebound ways of the Ecole des Beaux-Arts and were quite unwilling to see any virtue in the older traditions. On the other hand, traditionalists,—for example, one of the Weese's instructors named Mr. Clap—found nothing to admire in the modernist designs they saw in the magazines. According to Weese, Clap insisted that modern architecture was mere paper architecture, based on impossible utopian dreams, and told the librarian to hide all the modernist books. But other professors, including the dean, were more open-minded, and the librarian revealed to the students where the forbidden books were hidden. Like almost all of the architectural students of his generation with any interest in European modernism, Weese eagerly read Le Corbusier's *Vers une architecture*, translated into English in 1927 as *Towards a New Architecture*. One of the things about Corbusier that appealed to Weese, as it did to many young architects at the time, was the fact that the Swiss architect was a painter as well as an architect, and approached architecture as an art. Another was that Corbusier was interested in the design of everything from a small piece of furniture to an entire city and its region.

The first years at MIT were devoted mostly to mastering the rudiments, particularly geometry and a variety of drawing skills, ranging from quick life sketches to elaborate watercolor renderings. Although MIT was the country's foremost engineering school, the training of architectural students in the discipline of structural engineering at MIT, as elsewhere in schools of architecture, was far from comprehensive. The idea was to give students a good intuitive feel for how structures worked and then a few exercises—for example, sizing members for a truss system—so that they would be able to work out the design of simple structures on their own and collaborate easily with structural engineers for larger projects.

At the time he entered MIT, Weese was not really sure of his aesthetic direction, and he gained his footing in this area only gradually. In this process Lawrence B. Anderson, widely known as "LB," was highly influential. Anderson, who had been a student at MIT, joined the faculty in 1933, the year that Weese arrived, and started a career in which he exerted a major influence on generations of students, both through his teaching and through the example of his designs. One important aspect of Anderson's teaching was his way of engaging students with new building programs and materials and with specific sites. Where instructors in the Beaux-Arts system often assigned students programs involving elaborate public buildings for ideal sites, Anderson usually favored new building types for specific locations. Years later Weese remembered doing research for one studio class by visiting George White health care clinics in some of Boston's poorest neighborhoods and interviewing health and social workers. Although Weese recalled that he hardly ever saw Anderson pick up a pencil to correct a student's design, Weese remembered one notable exception. The design problem was to accommodate a handicapped ramp to the front door of a building on a tight site without a sufficient setback to position it unobtrusively. "With one brief scrawl he showed how the stair could go straight and the ramp could stream off to the side breaking symmetry and letting it hang out, so to speak. I do believe that at that moment I was freed from doubt and inhibition as to how to set about solving a problem." During his years at MIT, Weese also got his first experience in an actual architectural office when he worked for architects Robert S. DeGolyer and Walter T. Stockton in Chicago for two months during the summer of 1935.

Both within and outside the classrooms in Boston, Weese made friends who would be important in his later career. For example, one of his roommates was William Hartmann, who would go on to become the partner in charge of the Chicago office of Skidmore, Owings & Merrill. Probably the most important contact was with Ieoh Ming Pei, who was two years behind Weese at MIT. Pei, whose father was one of the most successful businessmen in China, gained a reputation early in architectural school as someone whose charm, ambition, and prodigious talent were likely to take him far. Weese later described him as similar to his architecture, which he characterized as formal and elegant, restrained but powerful. The two students became good friends, sharing ideas on architecture, going to social events, and taking bicycle trips together, often in the company of Ai Ling (Eileen) Loo, who eventually married Pei. The two men would remain friends and professional colleagues throughout Weese's career.

Weese led an active life outside the classroom. He directed the music for the "Tech Show," an annual undertaking at MIT that then traveled to Wellesley and Smith Colleges, and he took charge of the annual architectural students' party his final year. For that party Weese and his fellow students invited Sally Keith, the "tassel queen of Scollay Square" (the reigning honky-tonk district of Boston), to work her magic. She astonished students and faculty alike when she stripped down to little more than a pair of tassels, which she was able to twirl in opposite directions. Weese also gained a reputation as a man about town, someone who was often seen at cultural and social events accompanied by an attractive woman.

While at MIT, Weese drifted leftward politically. This was not unusual and not surprising during the grim years of the Great Depression, when many young people from comfortable backgrounds rebelled against the political and economic beliefs of their parents. Weese's tilt to the left was a cause of considerable concern to his father, but, in fact, the younger Weese was always more "pink" than "red" and less interested in the experience of the Soviet Union than in the Scandinavian "Middle Way" that he had read about in influential books of the day, such as Marcus Child's *Sweden, the Middle Way* of 1936, which advocated a course between socialism and capitalism. Weese's political views did not cause any definitive break with his family or any reluctance on his part to associate with the families of his fellow students, many of whom were affluent and very conservative.

16

glen haven

During his years in architectural school, Weese continued to work on building projects for his family. At the property at Glen Lake, he designed and, with his brother John, helped local carpenters build a log cabin in the summer of 1936. Called Shack Tamarack, it was made of local tamarack logs and was influenced by the traditional rustic resort architecture of the day (see entry.)

In 1936, apparently in a spur-of-the-moment decision, Weese transferred from MIT to Yale University. One of the reasons for this decision was the fact that Eero Saarinen had graduated from there in 1934. Eero Saarinen was the son of Eliel Saarinen, who had brought his family from Finland to America after his second-place design in the

Chicago Tribune competition of 1922 had been greeted with great acclaim. Eero, born in 1910, five years earlier than Weese, had demonstrated in architectural school something of the design talent that would make him a star in the postwar American architectural world. Weese knew Eero's work through the publication of some of his prize-winning designs and decided that any school that had produced a student like Saarinen could teach him something important. The curriculum at Yale was similar to that at MIT and was still based primarily on the Beaux-Arts system. In later years Weese remembered learning about acoustics, illumination, and concrete from professionals who came up from New York City, and he remembered a history

Watercolor of scene at Glen Haven, Michigan, by Harry Weese, 1934. Courtesy of Shirley Weese Young.

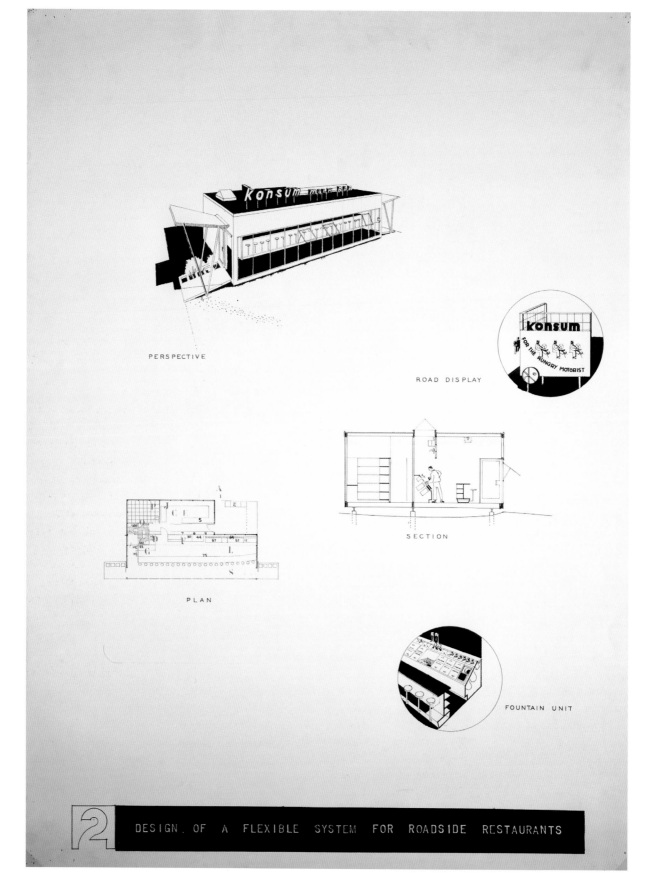

Drawings by Harry Weese for his MIT thesis, "Design of a Flexible System of Roadside Restaurants," Sheet 2, 1938. Copyright MIT Museum.

PERSPECTIVE

ROAD DISPLAY

SECTION

PLAN

FOUNTAIN UNIT

DESIGN. OF A FLEXIBLE SYSTEM FOR ROADSIDE RESTAURANTS

professor named Stevenson who delivered stimulating lectures on the importance of saving historic buildings.

In the summer after his year at Yale, Weese decided to take an extended trip to Europe to study architecture, particularly modern architecture. The trip was inspired in part by a fellow architecture student at Yale who had traveled around the continent on a bicycle every summer for the previous four years, at a cost of only $2.50 a day. Arriving in Europe on the Dutch ship *Staatendam* with George Woodland, a childhood friend, Weese traveled twelve hundred miles through France, Germany, Austria, Scandinavia, and England at a total cost of $500. During the trip he started a series of sketchbooks, a habit he would continue through much of his later career. He was impressed by the way Europeans cared for their land and had created intensely local building traditions using regional stone and other materials. A train trip between Boulogne and Paris inspired the thought that man and nature were in closer contact there than in the United States.

Weese admired the great Gothic cathedrals because of their audacious and highly intuitive structural systems. He found Paris to be noisy and dirty but exciting, and he enjoyed seeing the silvery light falling on the old urban fabric. He also respected the way Parisians lived in high-density neighborhoods during the winter but had summer houses in carefully tended rural settings. He arrived in Paris in time to see the International Exposition of 1937, with its monumental classical German and Russian pavilions confronting each other in an ominous way. He would almost certainly have seen the Finnish pavilion designed by the rising star of Finnish architecture, Alvar Aalto, with its natural materials and warm natural wood furniture, also by the architect. Aalto's work seemed more relaxed and humane to Weese than the austere work of many of the more doctrinaire modernists. As Weese later recalled, Aalto had not let himself be imprisoned by the grid. He was willing to incorporate natural materials and craft traditions, and he "allowed accidents to happen."

Certainly the country that had the most important influence on his later career was Sweden. Primed for this experience by his exposure at MIT to modernist European designs and ideas about the Middle Way, he now saw works by Ivar Tengbom, Sven Markelius, Gunnar Asplund and the sculptor Carl Milles. He was particularly impressed with Asplund's work. It is almost certain that he would have visited the Gothenburg Law Courts extension and the Public Library and Woodland Cemetery in Stockholm, the latter a particularly satisfying amalgam of landscape and building. Weese later remembered Scandinavia as a tremendous revelation and the place where he "first saw modern architecture in actuality." This architecture, he felt, seemed designed for the new social order the small countries of Scandinavia were building, and it involved a "compact with the natural resources, climate and perception of social justice." This idyllic trip was, nevertheless, shadowed by political events on the continent. In Munich, at the end of the trip, Weese came into contact with members of Hitler's youth groups, who would greet him and his friends with the Nazi salute and "Heil Hitler." Weese and his friends would respond with the noncommittal "Gruss Gott."

The trip to Europe was undoubtedly at least as important as the work Weese had done in the classroom in finding his own artistic direction. When, at the end of the summer, Weese returned to MIT for his final year of school and his thesis project, he was no longer a neophyte looking for direction. He had a wide knowledge of contemporary architecture and a clear purpose. His convictions were bolstered by the appearance on American soil of Aalto, who lectured at MIT during two trips he made to the country in 1938 and 1939 and whose buildings and furniture were featured in an exhibition at the Museum of Modern Art in 1938.

A paper entitled "The City," written for a class in March 1938, gives some idea of Weese's views at this period. Curiously enough, for someone who would later champion urban living in Chicago, his verdict on the city was remarkably negative. The great mass of humanity in the city makes individual men lose their perspective, their morality, and their health, he wrote. For Weese, however, the commuter out to the suburbs fared no better because his escape was only temporary. In fact, the only bright spot in the urban picture he painted was the example of Stockholm, which for him represented the antithesis of New York, which he considered doomed. Stockholm apparently might provide the model for a completely replanned and rebuilt American city where wholly new satellite towns and garden cities, each of them protected by inviolable greenbelts, would "hover around the shell of what remains of the old city." But the conclusion was far from upbeat, at least as far as his own country was concerned. "This is not Utopia," he wrote. "It is a possibility. But not in this country for generations, for our clumsy democratic institutions cannot handle the complexities of planning and our people would rather go to the movies."

When it came time for the final project for his degree, Weese knew that he wanted to work on an urban scale. For reasons that are not clear, his thesis committee rejected his first idea, a city for steel mill workers, a subject probably inspired by the pictures he had seen of mills constructed by his uncle's firm. He settled on the design of a chain of restaurants to be built quickly and inexpensively using a system of modular prefabricated plywood elements. The restaurants were highly standardized but could be easily adapted to a variety of local circumstances. Oddly enough, his model was the growing set of restaurants constructed by pioneering chains like Howard Johnson's and the Dutch Mill, which used abstracted historical elements, like Howard Johnson's signature white clapboard, orange roof, and classical cupola, to give the restaurants an easily recognizable image. Weese tried to create the same result deploying a strictly modern vocabulary based on the properties and dimensions of plywood panels. In his thesis he illustrated how the restaurants could be used on sites that he knew—for example, one in No Man's Land, an unincorporated area between Wilmette and Kenilworth close to his childhood home, where county authorities were more likely to allow building innovations than were officials in the straight-laced suburbs around it.

At his graduation from MIT in 1938 Weese received an American Institute of Architects (AIA) medal and a Roche Prize for his work in school, though not the hoped-for traveling fellowship that would have allowed him to go back to Europe. Instead he returned to Chicago and worked over the summer in the architectural office of Burnham & Hammond. While he was in Chicago trying to decide what to do next, he received, unexpectedly, a letter informing him that he had won a fellowship to study city planning for a year at Cranbrook Academy of Art, in Bloomfield Hills, outside Detroit, which was headed by Eliel Saarinen. Oddly enough, for all his interest in Nordic architecture, Weese apparently knew very little about Cranbrook, despite the fact that it had developed a considerable international reputation as a kind of Scandinavian Bauhaus because of the presence of Saarinen and a group of well-known European artists and craftsmen. He jumped at the chance.

In the fall of 1938 Weese moved to Bloomfield Hills. At first he found himself somewhat at sea. He knew no one and there was no curriculum or fixed structure. There were occasional lectures, but otherwise students were free to do whatever they wanted. It was a regime, as Weese later recalled, of "unprogrammed indolence." It was also a somewhat complicated and confusing time for Weese, a "time-out," a break between school and an as-yet-uncertain future. The times were also tense for the world at large as war seemed increasingly likely. As it turned out, this turbulent period would be perhaps the most brilliant one in the school's history as a talented group of faculty members interacted with a stellar cast of aspiring students. Among the faculty were Eliel Saarinen, the director of the school, the painters Wallace Mitchell and Zoltan Sepeshy, the metal artist Harry Bertoia, the sculptor Carl Milles, the weaver Marianne Strengell, and the potter Maija Grotell. In addition, Alvar Aalto showed up at least once as a guest lecturer while Weese was in residence.

The elder Saarinen turned out to be an aloof and remote personality. He spent much of his time in his own architectural office and wasn't often seen. When he did appear, he was stiff and formal—for example, appearing at dinner every night in a tuxedo. There was also some rumbling among the younger faculty, students, and fellows about his presumed sympathy with the more reactionary regimes of Europe. The younger faculty, on the other hand, particularly Mitchell, Strengell, and Grotell, were very approachable. They soon started inviting the students to dinner with them at a local restaurant, the Horse and Hounds.

Among the students were several who would go on to make a major mark on postwar American design. Edmund Bacon, who later became a famous planner in Philadelphia, had arrived at Cranbrook several years earlier. Bacon was working on planning and housing issues in the Detroit area and once took Weese and some of the other students on a trip to the nearby city of Flint, where they got into a confrontation with city officials over public housing policy. Bacon also introduced Weese to the well-known housing expert Catherine Bauer. Ralph Rapson, from Michigan, shared a drafting table with Weese. Rapson, who fashioned himself "le Rapson" in emulation of Le Corbusier, also worked in the office of Eliel and Eero Saarinen, which at the time was located at the school and was involved with a series of pivotal projects, including the Tabernacle Church of Christ (First Christian Church) in Columbus, Indiana; the Kleinhans Music Hall in Buffalo; and the Crow Island School in Winnetka, near Harry Weese's childhood home. Weese helped Rapson in the preparation of the Saarinens' winning competition submission for an art gallery for the Smithsonian Institution in Washington. Although it was never built, publications of the path-breaking modernist design had a major impact on the architectural profession. Rapson and Weese worked together on a number of other projects, including a library in Flint, Michigan, and a library for Smith College in Massachusetts, both apparently actual commissions, although neither was built.

Also at Cranbrook were two other students who would have an important impact on Weese's later career. Benjamin Baldwin from Montgomery, Alabama, two years older than Weese, had earned degrees in architecture from Princeton University and had studied painting in New York City and Provincetown with the pioneering modernist painter Hans

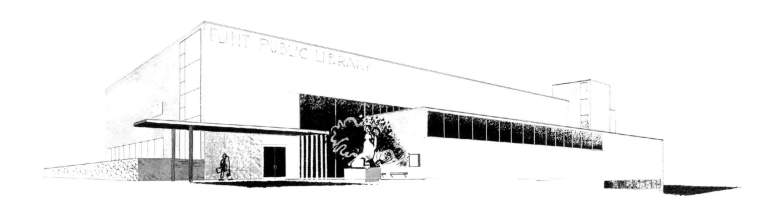

PERSPECTIVE

Hoffmann. Baldwin took an immediate liking to the attractive and congenial Weese. They became close friends and spent a good deal of time together. Charles Earnes was older than the other fellows for that year and had already had ten years of experience practicing in California. At Cranbrook, like Weese and Baldwin, he did very little architecture, instead exploring weaving, ceramics, metalworking, and photography. The transformative experience for him was his work with Eero Saarinen on furniture design. Weese later described Eames as still being in his "Gothic mode" when he arrived at Cranbrook. After his collaboration with Saarinen, Eames came to be convinced of the value of functional modernism. He and his future wife and partner, Ray Kaiser, another student at Cranbrook, would keep in close contact with Weese as they established their highly influential design practice in Los Angeles.

At Cranbrook, Weese finally met Eero Saarinen. At the time Weese arrived, Eero was in New York City, but he came home on weekends. Weese was impressed and perhaps somewhat awed by the slightly older and far more experienced Saarinen. In fact, almost everyone who encountered Eero was struck by his extraordinary intensity, talent, and dedication to work. He seemed determined to do a decade of work in a single year, even going so far as drawing with both hands simultaneously to save time. On a social level, the gregarious and outgoing Weese and the taciturn and often somber Saarinen initially had some conflicts, notably one involving Lily Swann, a young woman who had come to Cranbrook to study sculpture and who would eventually marry Saarinen. Weese, always attentive to attractive women, became altogether too close to Lily to suit Saarinen. Finding Lily and Harry together inside one of the large urns that marked the entrance to Cranbrook, Saarinen challenged Weese to a duel. In the end Weese talked him out of it, reportedly suggesting that they instead go for a walk

Perspective design drawing for library at Flint, Michigan, labeled "Prepared at Cranbrook Academy by Ralph Rapson and Harry Weese," ca. 1939. Copyright Cranbrook Archives.

in the woods, and the three remained close friends until the time of Eero's tragically early death in 1961.

Weese had received his fellowship at Cranbrook for urban planning, and early on he did complete a plan for Chicago's satellite cities of Waukegan, Elgin, Aurora, and Joliet, later remarking that at the time he still distrusted the city center of Chicago. Most of the time he was involved neither in planning nor in architecture but in exploring various craft techniques. With Ben Baldwin and Wallace Mitchell he went to work in Harry Bertoia's metal shop creating furniture and three modern looms. The idea of building the looms was inspired by the woven work of Marianne Strengell and Loja Saarinen, the wife of Eliel. Weese wove enough material to make himself a jacket, which he wore for years afterward and is now in the collection at Cranbrook. He studied sculpture with Carl Milles and Marshall Fredericks, ceramics with Maija Grotell, and weaving with Strengell.

Like many of the students and faculty at Cranbrook, Weese entered a number of competitions, winning at least two. For the prize-winning entry into the Rome Collab-

orative Project, for which he worked with Ralph Rapson, sculptor Donald Gregory, and painter Clifford West, Weese designed the landscape. His most important competition project was for the Productive Homes Contest sponsored by the Independence Foundation. For this competition Weese designed a prefabricated "Productive Garden home" on an acre and a half. The home was intended as low-cost lodging for factory workers on half shifts who would use the other half shift working the land in order to maintain a subsistence living. Weese won one of five awards, each given for one region of the country. As he later recalled, the thousand-dollar prize made him feel so rich he went skiing.

In an article he wrote in the Finnish journal *Form and Function* in the 1980s Weese remembered Cranbrook as "monastic and rarified," an "enchanted place, almost exotic in its rolling landscape—treebedecked and vine-festooned, and with its finely wrought quadrangles of brick, bronze and slate studded with fountains." The major fixed routine every day involved breakfast. The group first assembled to play ping-pong. Weese remembered that it included several very pretty girls, among them Lily Swann, who was the champion player. After breakfast there was work, but there were also plenty of distractions—impromptu touch-football games, outings to Detroit for "fun and mischief," sailing on Walled Lake, cross-country skiing in Bloomfield Hills in the company of automobile moguls who lived nearby, and downhill skiing farther afield at the eastern ski resorts.

After his year at Cranbrook, during the summer of 1939, Weese paid a visit to the New York world's fair, where he was most impressed by the Swedish pavilion of Sven Markelius. During the summer Weese also designed and built two new houses on the family land on Glen Lake. Unlike Shack Tamarack of three years before, these houses, one for his father and one for Richard Pritchard, a friend of the family's, were unabashedly modern (see entry for Glen Lake Houses). In them Weese experimented with opening up the front wall as much as possible by reducing the structure to a minimum and inserting the largest possible pieces of glass. In fact, he pushed his experiment so far that the frame of the Pritchard house proved insufficient to hold the glass in place, and he had to add some reinforcing. But this need to retrofit did not daunt Weese. He had an intuitive sense of structure and, particularly with small frame structures, was quite happy to push his ideas to the limit or perhaps slightly beyond. Then, if something failed during construction or afterward, he had no qualms about inserting a new strut or bolting a diagonal reinforcing member to bring the structure back into alignment. The ultimate measure of structural success was whether the building remained standing. At the houses on Glen Lake he found a way to involve his younger brother Ben, then ten years old, by paying him seven or eight cents an hour to pick up the wood chips at the site.

In late May of his fellowship year at Cranbrook, Weese had received an offer to return to Cambridge to take up a position as a research assistant at the Bemis Foundation, which at the time was experimenting with ways to reduce the cost of shelter using new materials and techniques, such as fluorescent light and plastics. Although the wage was nominal, he gladly accepted the offer, which gave him a chance to work with director John Ely Burchard, whom Weese considered a genius. During his time at the Bemis Foundation in academic year 1939–40, Weese first heard Frank Lloyd Wright speak. According to Weese's later recollection, it was a vintage Wright performance. As Weese described it, Wright strolled across the stage carrying a single lily. After a full minute of silence, he sat down at the edge of the platform with his legs dangling over and pronounced, "What this town needs is a hundred first-class funerals." Despite his annoyance at Wright's performance, Weese approached the great man after his talk to

tell him that he would like to design "Usonian architecture," Wright's term for a moderately priced democratic architecture, but that he couldn't "do it and eat." Wright, according to Weese, had this terse rejoinder: "Then starve." During his year in Cambridge he also renewed his friendship with I.M. Pei, who was then finishing his thesis, a project for prefabricated propaganda centers for China. Weese, in a time-honored Beaux-Arts tradition, helped Pei finish the drawings. He had the opportunity to visit new houses designed by Walter Gropius and Marcel Breuer in Lincoln, Massachusetts.

While still at the Bemis Foundation in 1940, mulling over the choice of staying on the East Coast or returning to Chicago, Weese received a letter from Gordon Bunshaft inviting him to come to Chicago to work at the firm of Skidmore, Owings & Merrill. Weese had known Bunshaft at MIT, where Bunshaft, six years older than Weese, had finished his architectural degree in 1935. Weese remembered him for his blunt talk, large grasp of issues, and design skill. Instead of immediately accepting Bunshaft's invitation, though Weese first applied for a job with the Keck brothers, whose model houses Weese had seen at the Chicago fair in 1933 and whose work on solar design had impressed him. As Weese would later tell the story, George Fred Keck was a crusty old character who looked through the brochure Weese had done at Cranbrook, with its elaborate handwoven fabric cover, and said "Look, I don't need a genius. I just need a draftsman." In the end Weese decided to throw in his lot with Skidmore, Owings & Merrill. As a Chicagoan interested in architecture, he probably would have known of Louis Skidmore and Nathaniel Owings, their work on the 1933 Chicago fair, and the offices they set up in Chicago in 1936 and in New York in 1937.

When Weese arrived at the office in the Monroe Building, he found a small group of designers, including Ambrose Richardson, Brewster Adams, Robert Little, and Matthew Lapota, all working under the direction of Bunshaft. Down three steps from the design studio was the drafting room, where, Weese later recalled, could be found the "evil people who wore green eye shades and sometimes tattoos," and who seemed to be determined to compromise any good designs created by the designers. Weese might have realized from this experience that he did not want to work in a big office with large and somewhat independent divisions within it, that he would only be happy in his own firm and with a small work force completely under his control. Despite Bunshaft's gruff manner, Weese got along with him because he admired Bunshaft's designs. During his time at the Skidmore office from June to December 1940, Weese did some work on a hospital in Petoskey, Michigan,

as well as some projects for the Marshall Field's department store in Chicago, and for Chicago's Charles Stevens Co. store, for which he designed the millinery section.

Although Weese had often returned to Chicago during his years at MIT, Cranbrook, and the Bemis Foundation, he still needed to catch up with the major changes that had taken place while he was gone. First of all, he had a chance to reunite with his family. Weese continued his role of watching over the education of his siblings. He gave sister Sue a subscription to the Boston symphony when she went away to study at Wheaton College in Norton, Massachusetts. He enrolled brother Ben, who was then twelve, in Saturday classes at Moholy-Nagy's School of Design. He also caught up with his brother John, who had gone off to architectural school at Cornell University, but when this experience proved unsuccessful, returned to Chicago to finish school at the Illinois Institute of Technology. This led to work in the office of Mies van der Rohe.

Mies by this time was already a legend. He had been one of the heroic figures of European modernism, a faculty member of the Bauhaus in Germany, and the head of the school immediately before its demise at the hands of the Nazis in 1933. Although Mies had not built much in Chicago by 1940, he was already a major presence in the city. According to Weese's later recollection, Mies "was like a Buddha. He'd sit in his chair . . . and he would pontificate, and we would all be hanging on his words sitting on the floor." Weese was attracted by what he called the "stolid clarity" of Mies's work, the simplicity and the strong technique. "What he taught us was how to build efficiently."

Another important new arrival was the Hungarian artist László Moholy-Nagy. Moholy, who had also been a teacher at the Bauhaus, arrived in Chicago in 1937 at the invitation of a group of Chicago businessmen interested in promoting contemporary design in the city by starting a new school. Although the school they founded was short-lived, in 1939 Moholy opened his own school, which he named the School of Design (after 1944 it became the Institute of Design) with the help of Walter P. Paepcke, director of the Container Corporation of America. Weese apparently met Moholy soon after Moholy's arrival in Chicago, when Weese decided to take a course in visual design from Gyorgy Kepes at the new school. The presence of Mies and Moholy transformed the architectural scene in Chicago. They brought a new cosmopolitan character and firsthand experience of the great cultural transformations of interwar Europe, and they provided a challenge to the existing architectural establishment.

Through Moholy, Weese met another person who came to be important in his professional career. Although

Edward Larrabee Barnes had grown up in Chicago and the Weese and Barnes families knew each other, the two men apparently had not met before Moholy introduced them over dinner at a restaurant. They immediately recognized each other as kindred spirits and remained close friends and colleagues thereafter. Barnes was the final addition to the small group of architects with whom Weese stayed in close touch throughout his career and with whom he was comfortable enough to collaborate and share work. This group included, besides Barnes, Eero Saarinen, I. M. Pei, Charles Eames, and Ralph Rapson.

In addition to the newcomers to the Chicago architectural scene, there was still the looming figure of Frank Lloyd Wright. In 1940 while working at Skidmore, Owings & Merrill, Weese had the idea to take some of his colleagues at the office up to visit Wright. Although Weese had already encountered Wright in Boston, a trip to Taliesin East in Wisconsin or Taliesin West in Arizona was considered a rite of passage for generations of ambitious young American architects. As Weese told the story in a 1988 oral interview, he asked his father if he could borrow the family station wagon to drive up to Taliesin East. His father not only consented but also asked to come along. So into the car piled a group from the office, including the young but already peppery Gordon Bunshaft. Bunshaft, like Weese and many other young modernist architects of the day, considered Wright to be a relic of the nineteenth century. He intended to confront the great man and tell him so face-to-face. In Weese's words, Bunshaft

> rehearsed on the way up how he was going to talk to Frank Lloyd Wright and tell him the truth about himself. He rehearsed it all through. My father thought that was not the right thing to do when you're visiting the great man in his compound. So we came to Taliesin and we got in . . . Wright came out of the drafting room, which was saw-toothed like a factory. A beautiful sun was coming through and the sun hit the back of his head and made a halo out of his white hair. And Bunshaft started to go up and greet him and tell him why he was full of b.s. and was only a nineteenth century relic, but he quailed. He couldn't do it. The next thing I knew my father went up and gave him the Phi Delta grip—Phi Delta Theta. They were both fraternity brothers and went off in a corner and had a long chat.

According to Weese, while Bunshaft sat in the corner rankling, his father got "enough lore out of Wright to entertain us all the way back on the trip in the car."

Watercolor of figure skiing, probably in New England, ca. 1938. Courtesy of Shirley Weese Young.

During his time in Chicago, Weese continued to visit the family compound at Glen Lake, where he was particularly fond of tinkering with his boat, *Popeye*, an experimental eighteen-foot double-ended skiff that he had built with his brother John in 1935. Weese fiddled with it constantly, first working on the centerboard, attaching lead disks to it, then casting a new keel to replace it, and then working on the mast, which he first shortened and then replaced with a remarkable hairpin version. At the memorial service for Weese in 1998, his brother Ben recalled its fate:

> The year was 1940 . . . the day of the big yacht regatta. Harry, dissatisfied as usual with the performance of [*Popeye*] modified it yet once again; this time with a revolutionary double mast. Picture a hoop, like an inverted U, coming down each side to the gunnels, laminated and bent out of thin layers of wood. A double mast joined at the top in an arc. The sail's lead edge was clipped to a cable located where the mast normally would be, the cable running to the apex of the hoop. The design concept: eliminate the conventional mast because it blocks the flow of air over the sail and instead get close to the perfect conditions of air flowing over an airplane wing. So the boat with the revolutionary rig was launched from the lee shore onto the pristine and azure waters of Glen Lake, a group of well-wishers with binoculars trained at the launch point ready to watch its progress. With a fol-

lowing wind, *Popeye* skipped out smartly giving at the same time an almost magical if slightly bizarre appearance. Suddenly out from the protection of the hills behind us there was a fluttering and some jazzy torques. Then the whole arrangement came gracefully pirouetting down on the crew . . . This story explained to me, at the age of ten, the complete Harry: set up a radical, if not impossible task, charm them with a potentially startling solution, confound all the old diehards with a revolutionary modern design, beat the deadline by half a minute and half an inch, then miraculously escape the actual event.

Although its design had clearly failed, Weese was so attached to his creation that he dragged her back to Shack Tamarack, where her decaying body still rests today.

At the end of 1940, in addition to his work at Skidmore, Owings & Merrill, Weese formed a partnership with Ben Baldwin, his friend from Cranbrook. After he had finished his year at Cranbrook in the spring of 1939, Baldwin had moved back to Montgomery, Alabama. In a series of letters preserved at the Cranbrook archives, he described life at Verbena, the Baldwin family home; explained how much he missed Weese; and reminded him that they had made plans to practice architecture together. "I've thought about you so much, Harry and missed you so desperately," began one letter. Another described the architectural work he was doing in Alabama: "It is my whole reason for working—to try to be worthy of working with you." In the fall of 1939 Baldwin left Alabama to return to Cranbrook, where he helped Eliel and Eero Saarinen build an elaborate model for the Smithsonian Institution competition on which Weese and Ralph Rapson had worked earlier that year. In 1940 he moved to Chicago.

At the time of their partnership, in addition to his work for Skidmore, Owings & Merrill, Weese had five commissions of his own. The first was a house for his parents in Barrington, the so-called Red House, down the hill from the Hilltop Summer Home. Built in anticipation of Harry Ernest Weese's retirement from the bank, it was constructed out of salvaged lumber from the Hilltop house. Weese also was working on houses for two aunts in Evanston and an uncle in Barrington, all of them part of a strategy orchestrated by Harry Ernest Weese to jump-start his son's practice, and a house for a high school friend named Alexander Newton. All of these buildings could be described as being modern, in a relaxed, Scandinavian way.

On the strength of these commissions Baldwin and Weese rented the servants' quarters of a house in Kenilworth built by Prairie School architect George Maher and then occupied by his son, Philip Maher, a prominent Chicago architect. In it the two young men opened their office. The arrangement was convenient because it allowed Baldwin to live and work in the rented space while Weese commuted from his parent's house just around the block. With only a limited amount of architectural work, Baldwin and Weese were able to enter a series of competitions, notably the Museum of Modern Art's "Organic Design in Home Furnishings," which was cosponsored by twelve important stores in major American cities. The idea was that, in addition to receiving prizes, the winning designers would be offered contracts with manufacturers. When awards for the competition were announced in 1941, individuals connected with Cranbrook, notably Eero Saarinen, Charles Eames, as well as Harry Weese and Ben Baldwin, walked away with a substantial percentage of the honors. Weese and Baldwin received honorable mentions in two categories, and they were the winners in the category of outdoor furniture. Most of the eight designs submitted by Weese and Baldwin were lightweight, demountable, and transportable. These included a porch cot with a frame of steel tubing and a canvas top held in place by elastic rope, a cantilevered deck chair with a perforated steel seat, a hanging canvas sling seat "cut like a sail," a two-leg outdoor chair made of wrought iron with a slung canvas seat, a wrought-iron table with collapsible legs and a slatted wood top, a wrought-iron table with a glass top, and a table with a polished concrete top and demountable pipe legs. The project that received the most attention was a tubular steel tea wagon that was clearly a translation into metal of a design that Alvar Aalto had executed in wood (see entry). The Museum of Modern Art catalog, documenting the competition, also illustrated a fluorescent desk lamp designed by Weese and Baldwin but not for the competition. Weese subsequently worked with the Lloyd Manufacturing Company of Menominee, Michigan, on a line of furniture based on the competition designs, but the war intervened before any production could begin.

Although the only paying work he had at the time involved furniture and small houses, Weese yearned for projects on an urban scale. As it happened, he had close at hand one of the most spectacular challenges of his day. Chicago at the end of the Depression had an old and obsolete industrial plant and mile after mile of substandard housing. Weese believed that for Chicago to remain vital, it needed to rebuild itself. He soon found himself part of a group of like-minded individuals, including Ralph Rapson, architect Robert Bruce Tague, planner Martin Meyerson, and Ambrose Richardson, formerly a partner at the Chicago office of Skidmore, Owings & Merrill but then at the University of Illinois. These men, together with several other members of the Skidmore, Owings & Merrill firm, started a group called BASIS, modeled after a similar group in San Francisco called TELESIS, which had been founded in 1939 by the British architect Serge Chermayeff and some of his colleagues. The group planned to issue a journal, also called BASIS, that would be devoted to "BASIC" urban issues. Both TELESIS and BASIS considered themselves to be regional affiliates of the Congrès International de l'Architecture Moderne (CIAM), the largely European organization that included the most important pioneers of modern architecture, notably Le Corbusier. Weese prepared a position paper for BASIS in the summer of 1941 in which he described a program for rehabilitating 44 square miles of Chicago's blighted urban fabric. The chief points, including significant changes in landownership rights and taxation, the redesign of large areas as superblocks with cul de sacs, seem to have derived from standard modernist notions of the kind advocated by Le Corbusier.

Although Weese was looking forward to the day when he could create new buildings in the city, he was at the same time intensely interested in old buildings and in history. He was drawn to the great Chicago Plan of 1909, written by Daniel Burnham and Edward Bennett even though many of his fellow architects architects considered it a relic of the City Beautiful movement. He was also eager to try to save old buildings. When he was growing up, he hadn't thought much about preservation, particularly in the city of Chicago. He had been highly critical of the old Public Library in Chicago, for example. Within a year of his return to Chicago, however, his attitude had changed dramatically. As he remembered it,

We were definitely revolutionaries. We wanted to tear everything down and start over. But only for a moment. When we saw what would replace some of those old things we began to think different, some of us. I remember the Public Library in Chicago. It looked like something eligible for destruction but quickly, in fact, almost the next day I began to think otherwise. The idea of co-existence appealed to me. It was European, that there were plenty of places to put new buildings alongside the good old ones. I'm not sure how many others have this conservative pragmatic streak that probably came from my parsimonious father.

However, Weese's explanation does not fully account for his interest in old buildings and preservation. He rebelled against many of the things his father had tried to teach him. In his own life he certainly was not always frugal. His interest in preservation was also not, as it was for many individuals, triggered by nostalgia or worries about the future. Preservation for Weese was tied more to his core architectural values, his desire to find a middle way between the clean-slate urbanism of the pioneer generation of modernists on the one hand and the interest in history and the traditional city that animated many traditional architects on the other. Weese preferred the smaller scale, the quirky, the occasionally irrational—both in buildings and in the larger cityscape—and adapting and reusing substantial pieces of the urban fabric was a way of ensuring that result. Whatever his reasons, Weese soon became one of the most outspoken proponents of preservation among modernist architects. In this belief he felt no conflict. As he later explained, "There are plenty of chances to do modern architecture. . . . There are plenty of parking lots to build on."

It was probably during his time in Chicago just before the war that Harry met Ben Baldwin's sister Kitty. "Tall, slender, reserved and gracious," according to a later newspaper account, Kate "Kitty" Baldwin had been born in Montgomery, Alabama, in 1917, the daughter of a banker. She attended Wellesley college in 1936–37, Briarcliff Junior College from 1937 to 1939, and the University of London, where she studied psychology, from 1939 to 1940, before receiving her Bachelor of Arts in psychology and education from Huntingdon College in Montgomery in 1940. After graduation, Kitty started work as an apprentice in the Children's Clinic at the Johns Hopkins Hospital in Baltimore. This meeting between Kitty and Harry most likely took place during a visit by Kitty to Chicago to see her brother. "I remember the first day I saw him," Kitty later recalled. "I was at his house in Kenilworth, and he came home. I watched him jump over the fence. He didn't come through the gate; he jumped over the fence. And I liked that. It is very funny what attracts you to people." Although there was an immediate mutual attraction, with war looming and the future uncertain, Harry at least was not ready to get married.

In October 1941, three months before the bombing of Pearl Harbor, when Weese decided that he would rather not wait for the outbreak of war and get drafted into the Army, he enlisted in the Navy as a carpenter third class. Learning that carpenters were going to be shipped to Manila, he decided to become a yeoman. This he finally accomplished after first failing a typing test. In January 1942 he applied for an appointment as an officer and, by pulling every string, managed to get assigned to engineering, despite what he described as the Navy's disinclination to allow architects into the Seabees or civil engineering. He entered officer training, taking a "Ninety Day Wonder" crash course, first in South Bend and then aboard the battleship *Prairie State*, which was docked in New York City. For a few years, while Kitty was working in Richmond, she and Harry met at some of the numerous parties that Ben Baldwin threw for his artistic friends in Washington, D.C., where the Navy had assigned him.

After his training, Weese was assigned as the engineering officer of a destroyer, the *Charles F. Hughes*, in charge of keeping the boilers, turbines, pumps, and gyrocompasses running as his ship crisscrossed the Caribbean, Atlantic, Mediterranean, and Pacific over the next three and a half years. Weese's military experience had several important effects on his later career. It reinforced his already long-standing appreciation of the highly compact and efficient design of boats, in this case what he later referred to as the "demandingly and beautifully functional . . . entrails of destroyers." The engineering experience he gained from his training course and the practical experience on the boat also gave him a confidence in his ability to figure out solutions for mechanical problems. In addition, the work allowed him to call himself a professional engineer.

The years aboard ship were both frustrating and useful for Weese. The worst part was the boredom, the endless hours at sea sailing from one point to another. Another problem was a tendency since childhood to chafe at authority of any kind. This trait led to a certain amount of friction between Weese and his commanding officer. On the other hand, he got at least a brief glimpse of several interesting parts of the world, especially at the very end of the war while preparations were being made for the invasion of Italy. His ship put in seven times to the island of Capri on weekends, and on the morning of the invasion of southern France, he saw the spectacular Hotel Latitude 43, which was designed in the early 1930s by the French architect Georges-Henri Pingusson.

Life aboard ship also gave him lots of time to think. In his diary he recorded memories of childhood and thoughts of the future. On the last day of February 1944, memories flooded back in a burst of lyrical description, saturated with sensations evoked by the landscapes of Kenilworth, Glen Lake, and the mountains of New England:

> Sunlight in Mrs. Spicer's garden, wildflowers along the path at Melrose and Warwick [streets in Kenilworth], summer skies and martins, Rex and Count [Weese dogs] on the beach when it is empty, hot wind from the pungent, dusty roadside verdure of cornflower, mullein and sweet clover, the air of Glen Lake, the purity of sails and wind. The snow above the fire trail, white lobed fire and the shadow of one's breath.

More typical were daydreams about the future, often in the form of lists of things Weese wanted to do or to design. One such list anticipated his return to Chicago. It is fascinating both in the way it prefigures Weese's professional career and avocations and in the way it demonstrates his extremely broad definition of design as a tool for an active life:

> The design for a new automobile, furniture design and distribution, a house to live in, how to live in Chicago, to preserve Sullivan's Auditorium, to establish an office, to prefabricate organize and manufacture, to glide, to ski, to sail.

In another jotting, entered on March 16, 1943, he imagined owning a store that would sell objects of modern design, including his own pieces. He described a

> shop gathering together beautiful and useful modern objects . . . Important and anonymous discoveries—subcontracted and assembled pieces of my design; foamed and webbed couch in church pew form, telescoping coffee tables of magnesium or plastic, chests of trays, South American fabrics from Peru, grass matting to a special design from Venezuela, music, restaurant adjacent, movies, bar, a small haven for those interested. [Harry's sister] Sue would be an able administrator of this sort of shop, would she not? . . . There could be a less snooty annex on Wabash for selling low-cost good design in furniture.

While Weese was at sea, Kitty did some work for a master's degree in psychology at Columbia University in New York. She moved back to Alabama in 1944, where she served as a psychologist for the Alabama State Department of Public Welfare until 1945. During the war the relationship between Harry and Kitty deepened through letters, to such a point that toward the end of the war Harry overturned his earlier decision to remain single until the war was over. He and Kitty were married in February 1945 at the Sand Street Gate of the Brooklyn Naval Yard. Weese later recalled that as officer of the day on his ship, he was carrying a forty-five revolver, and that they had their reception at the White Tile restaurant across the street. Harry and Kitty complemented one another well. Harry brought a passionate spirit and restless imagination to the partnership. Kitty brought a mature judgment and measured stability that the frenetic Harry often lacked. "My mother was the quiet anchor to windward," according to daughter Kate Weese.

Even during the war, Weese didn't suspend entirely his architectural career. He drew constantly on every piece

of paper that came to hand, recording ideas for furniture, buildings, and cities as well as what he saw around him. He also entered competitions and managed to send some drawings to *Arts and Architecture* magazine for an article that appeared in the July 1945 issue on the two Glen Lake cottages he had designed. According to his later recollection, he made these drawings on the back of some blueprints for machinery, sent them to the magazine, and saw the issue when it came in a pouch flown over to his ship by the Navy. He also painted a number of watercolors, some of them abstract, and many of them on one of his favorite themes, nude women.

While steaming across the Pacific on his way to participate in the invasion of Japan in 1945, the crew on Weese's ship got news that the atom bomb had been dropped and that the war was over. When his ship returned to California, Weese found Kitty waiting for him with a car. They decided to make the trip back to Chicago into a month-long excursion, perhaps a kind of belated honeymoon. San Francisco with its low wooden row houses and human scale was a revelation and a touchstone to which Weese would

return repeatedly over the years. In Los Angeles they stayed with Charles and Ray Eames in the Eames's Westwood apartment, which had been designed by Richard Neutra. From there they headed east, stopping for a time in the fledgling ski resort town of Aspen, a place to which they would return repeatedly over the years. During their time there they probably crossed paths with Walter Paepcke and his wife, whom everyone called Pussy. The Paepckes, who had been instrumental in allowing Moholy-Nagy to open his design school in Chicago, were also the driving force behind the rise of Aspen as a famous resort in the following decades. Following their trip to Aspen, the young couple made a stop in Montgomery, Alabama, to visit Kitty's family before returning to the Chicago area, where Harry was reunited with his own family.

While Weese had been away in the Navy, much had changed at home. In 1942 Weese's father had retired from his job at the bank. Weese's parents, together with youngest son Ben, had moved to Barrington for the duration of the war. Living in the Red House that Harry had designed in 1941, they had hunkered down, creating their own Victory

Garden, growing fruit and vegetables and raising goats, sheep, and chickens as Ben finished high school.

After the war there was also a new feeling in the architectural world. The United States had done relatively little building during the decade and a half of depression and war. Weese later described the feeling he had that the situation was like a coiled spring just ready to be released. The war had brought many people together and showed what could be done when everyone was united toward a purpose. Now, he felt, it was time to tackle problems on the home front.

Before tackling these problems, Weese still had to decide once again whether he would stay in Chicago or move east. In 1940, when he faced a similar choice, he knew his decision was a temporary one. This time it was likely to be permanent. The choice was not immediately clear. Although Chicago had long had a vigorous architectural scene, the heart and soul of the American architectural establishment was on the East Coast. Along the railroad line between Washington, D.C., and Boston were clustered many of the country's most important architectural institutions, from the headquarters of the American Institute of Architects in Washington to major schools such as Princeton, Columbia, Yale, Harvard, and MIT. The Northeast had also been the site for many of the most important early examples of architectural modernism by architects such as George Howe, William Lescaze, Edward Durell Stone, Walter Gropius, and Marcel Breuer. The undisputed center was New York City, where so many of Weese's classmates, friends, and colleagues had chosen or would soon choose to practice.

Weese, however, had deep personal and professional roots in Chicago. He also had the feeling that Chicago was an excellent place to explore the challenges facing the American city. Weese saw in Chicago a place that was falling apart at the seams and requiring urgent attention from architects and planners. Despite his early skepticism about central Chicago, by the time he had returned in 1946 he was enthusiastic about living and working there. Throughout his career, his office and residence would always remain within walking distance of the Loop.

Perhaps Weese also figured that he was more likely to stand out in Chicago than in the more crowded field of New York. In 1946 only a handful of people were doing significant modern design in the city. Notable among these were George Fred and William Keck, the Bowman brothers, Paul Schweiker, Andrew Rebori, and Mies van der Rohe. All of their practices were small. Then there was Skidmore, Owings & Merrill for whom Weese had worked in 1940. The war years had provided tremendous opportunities for the energetic and ambitious Nathaniel Owings and he seized them, winning for the firm a number of large government commissions, including the design of the entire town of Oak Ridge, Tennessee, one of the secret cities created by the military to manufacture the first atomic bomb. This war work brought Skidmore, Owings & Merrill important contacts in government and industry and allowed them to develop the kind of architectural and engineering expertise they needed to do jobs on the largest possible scale.

For the near term, Weese decided to return to Skidmore, Owings & Merrill. By this time Gordon Bunshaft had returned to New York, but Weese's old roommate at MIT, Bill Hartmann, had come to the Chicago office, and Weese knew many of the other members of the firm. Weese was happy to get more experience with a large practice, but he knew that this was temporary. He warned Nat Owings at the outset that he was only interested in a short-term job because he knew his goal was to open his own office as soon as he was able. It is not clear what Weese did at Skidmore, Owings & Merrill in the brief period he was in that office after the war, but within a year he was ready to strike out on his own.

ON HIS OWN

Already during his years at MIT, Harry Weese had had a plan for opening a furniture store and gallery that would also double as a salon for individuals interested in modern design, and his wartime diaries took up this theme more than once. He also figured that a store might provide some income that would allow him to start his own practice. The idea suddenly took concrete form in early 1947 after Kitty and Harry attended a party at the apartment of James Prestini, an industrial designer at Moholy-Nagy's Institute of Design. When conversation turned to the pent-up demand for modern furniture and design, the subject caught the attention of Jody Kingrey, a vivacious young woman originally from Minnesota whom the Weeses had just met. Kingrey had been passionate about modern design from an early age, and after getting a job at Watson & Boler, a Chicago design store, she had tried, unsuccessfully, to convince the owners to sell modern furniture. Together, Harry, Kitty, and Jody agreed that they would open such a store, one that would sell inexpensive modern designs directly to the public rather than through the traditional wholesale system, where everything was sold through the intermediary of architects and interior designers.

Although none of the three had had any experience selling modern design, they felt that they had other important qualifications. Jody Kingrey had actual sales experience. Kitty had learned a good deal about design from her brother Ben. Harry had witnessed firsthand the flowering of the modern design industry in Europe during his 1937 trip and had spent a good deal of time working with textiles, ceramics, and wood in the workshops at Cranbrook. Through Moholy-Nagy, he and Kitty knew many of the designers in Chicago, and through Kitty's brother Ben they were well informed about the art scene and emerging artists nationwide.

The three partners called their new venture "Baldwin Kingrey" and approached their parents for loans, asking each pair of parents to contribute $3,000 toward their first $9,000 of merchandise. Harry traveled to the East Coast to meet with Alvar Aalto, hoping to secure the Midwest franchise for Aalto's line of furniture. Aalto turned out to be highly enthusiastic. He was eager to have outlets for his furniture in the United States, and owing to the ravages of war in Finland, he was desperately in need of hard currency.

Harry and Kitty found the perfect place for their store one evening while walking from the railroad station back to their apartment on Superior Street. The Diana Court (Michigan Square) Building on Michigan Avenue between Ohio and Grand streets was a sophisticated design of the 1920s by architects Holabird & Root, perhaps the most successful large architectural office practice in Chicago during the boom period of the interwar years. The building had a series of shops on the ground floor along Michigan Avenue that also extended around the corner to Ohio Street. Baldwin Kingrey signed a lease for a space with about a hundred feet of frontage at 105 East Ohio.

Weese set to work designing the shop. For signage he devised a set of three-dimensional rectangles, projecting at an angle from the top of the shop front, each rectangle carrying one letter of the store's name on the two outer faces so that the letters were visible from either direction along the street. Below the signage, the large plate glass windows of the shop framed display cases with glassware, jewelry, and ceramics and vivid room-like settings with furniture, decorative objects, and art. Weese solved the problem of storage space by excavating below the shop, an operation that was accomplished outside business hours and without the permission of the building's owners.

During the first few years, Weese, working with his first employee, Donald Dimmitt, a young student at the Institute of Design, perfected a series of display techniques that would allow maximum visibility and minimal distur-bance of the plaster walls. These included glass shelves supported by thin metal poles and minimal horizontal wall moldings from which to hang items. Weese also did the advertising for the store, reducing images of the objects to black-and-white, then cutting them out and floating them on the page. All of these techniques created a novel and dramatic image for the store. The core of the store's offering was Aalto's Artek furniture, manufactured in Finland and shipped in knocked-down form directly to Navy Pier in Chicago, where Dimmitt would collect it, bring it to the shop, and assemble it in the back room. Over the years came jewelry by Harry Bertoia; wooden bowls by James Prestini; textiles by Alexander Girard, Angelo Testa, and Baldwin-Machado; glass by the Venetian company Venini; and furniture by Borge Mogensen, Kaare Klint, Bruno Mathsson, and Charles and Ray Eames. Weese too designed a set of furniture, one he called Baldry, which included pieces that he devised to fill obvious gaps in the product lines otherwise available—for example, a convertible sofa bed, slat bench, demountable storage units, and a series of floor and table lamps.

Opening day was a great success. Many people stopped by to get a close look at furniture that was normally unavailable to ordinary consumers. In fact, opening day was all too successful. The proud proprietors were delighted when the operator of a Chrysler Plymouth dealership on Wacker Drive walked in, looked around, and proceeded to buy out the entire stock for his showroom; but at the same time they were disconcerted since it completely depleted their inventory, and they knew it would take weeks to get new stock into the store.

Over the next decade Baldwin Kingrey became a fixture in the Chicago art, architecture, and design scene. The partners made a series of trips to Europe to check out the latest design trends and sign contracts for furniture and decorative objects. They also featured work by a great many local designers and artists. The shop served as a salon for Chicagoans interested in modern design and, because of Chicago's mid-continent location, for architects and designers stopping in Chicago as they traveled across the country by railroad or airplane. There was even a brief attempt to open a branch in Minneapolis, but this venture quickly proved abortive, apparently in part because the person chosen to run it, a friend of Kitty's, lacked experience.

Baldwin Kingrey was not the first store to sell modern furniture. Aalto had opened a store in Finland to sell his Artek furniture. Modern furniture, particularly office furniture manufactured by major furniture companies such as Herman Miller, was available to architects and decorators through dealers in places like the Merchandise Mart.

Baldwin Kingrey store, ca. 1952. Ferenc Berko photograph. Scan courtesy of Richard Wright.

It was also not the first to sell directly to consumers. The Swedish company IKEA, for example, which was founded in 1943, added a line of furniture to its offerings in 1947 at almost exactly the same moment that Baldwin Kingrey opened. But Baldwin Kingrey was the most conspicuous example in America of the postwar trend to allow consumers to buy modern design directly from retailers, and it was a precursor of establishments like architect Benjamin Thompson's Design Research, which opened in 1953 in Cambridge, and somewhat later, the even more successful Crate and Barrel. In a sense, it might be argued, the store was, like many of the things that Weese thought of, ahead of its time. It pioneered ideas that other people would later take and roll out on a much larger scale.

In the back of Baldwin Kingrey, Weese set up his office, which he called "Harry Weese, Architect & Engineer" (sometimes just "Harry Weese Architect"). At the beginning it was a very small operation and in some ways a family affair. Weese invited his brother John, who had returned from the Army in 1946, to help in the office and with the shop. John remained for two years before joining Skidmore, Owings & Merrill in 1949. Harry also found a place for brother Ben. Although from a young age Ben had been exposed to architecture through his older brother, he originally had no intention of going into the field. He even wrote an essay in high school on this theme, perhaps in part to reassure his father, who was skeptical about the prospect of one son making an adequate living in architecture, let alone all three sons. Of course, as Ben later realized, the very fact that he felt it necessary to write the essay should have tipped him off, not to mention the elaborate cover, which was composed of architectural elements that he had cut out from *Architectural Forum*. Still, when he entered Harvard College in 1947, his intention was to study sociology and philosophy. While in Chicago during the summer vacations he helped his brother by unpacking crates delivered from Finland and assembling furniture.

Clearly anticipating that his practice would pick up significantly, Weese felt that he needed a partner. Apparently the first person he turned to was Edward Larrabee Barnes. Barnes would have been a logical choice for Weese. The two men had had a similar background and a similar design sensibility. Like Weese, Barnes had been raised in the Chicago area, was socially well connected, and had deep artistic connections in the city through his mother, the well-known writer Margaret Ayers Barnes. He had attended Harvard, where he got his undergraduate degree in 1938 and a master's in 1942. Like Weese, he served in the Navy during World War II, then worked briefly for William Wurster in San Francisco and for Henry Dreyfuss, the industrial designer, in Los Angeles. In June 1947 Weese wrote a letter inviting Barnes to return to Chicago to start a partnership that would involve not only the practice of architecture but the development of prefabrication ideas, housing and city planning. In the end Barnes decided not to return to Chicago but instead moved to New York to establish his own practice. As each of their offices grew and prospered, the two men maintained a cordial relationship and collaborated on a number of projects.

As is the case with a great many architects, most of the first commissions for the Weese firm involved small residential projects for family members. One of these was a house for his own family in Barrington in 1948, called "Water Tower House" because it was built immediately adjacent to an enormous municipal water tower. In it Weese experimented with a lightweight steel structure with radiant floor heat based on the model of the ancient Romans and a curious hinged counter that could be pivoted open or shut to gain more space in the kitchen area. Nearby, at the speculative "Yellow House," he used panels made of a lightweight foam concrete pumped into forms made of steel mesh. After drying, the panels were lifted into place to create a quickly erected and inexpensive structure whose exterior walls had an intriguing nubby texture. In 1950–51, through Chicago architect Larry Perkins of the well-established firm Perkins & Will, Weese got commissions for three houses in Champaign, Illinois, for faculty members at the University of Illinois.

Baldwin Kingrey, drawing for advertisement for the store by Harry Weese, ca. 1950. *Courtesy of Richard Wright.*

With plenty of time on his hands, Weese continued to enter competitions and design furniture. Together Harry and John Weese entered the Jefferson National Expansion competition for St. Louis in 1947. They didn't win, but they got first-stage recognition, and Harry at least had the satisfaction of seeing his friend Eero Saarinen garner top honors for the spectacular arch, which would eventually be built, opening in 1965. He designed at least one home for popular shelter magazines of the time. A "Low Cost and Modern Home" was published in the spring 1949 edition of *Popular Home*. In 1948 he received a $6,000 grant from the Museum of Modern Art to do some research on low-cost furniture at the Armour Research Foundation in Chicago. In his final report for that project, Weese described a modular bookcase unit that could be folded up after manufacture for easy shipment and then reassembled at the final destination. He soon had some of these bookcases made for sale at Baldwin Kingrey.

A great deal of Weese's time and energy in the early years of his practice was aimed at obtaining large-scale urban projects. When Weese returned to Chicago after World War II, he found that the state of the city was even more dire than when he had left in 1942. The city, he told a reporter for the *Chicago Tribune* in 1951, was falling apart at the seams. He said that he was going to Europe to sit on park benches in the storied public squares of historic cities in England, Sweden, Finland, and Switzerland. The intent was to discover how Chicago could reinvent itself for a new era. "If we did less consuming of highballs and chasing of golf balls, perhaps we could build the city beautiful of our dreams," he stated. Weese obviously intended to be polemical. In fact, the trip to Europe was probably primarily a buying trip for Baldwin Kingrey, and Weese was interested in far more than sitting on park benches. He spent a good deal of time studying the housing, transportation, and other systems of these cities. But in describing it for the press, Weese, above all, hated to be boring or pedantic. He favored the bold proposal, the unexpected gesture as a way of galvanizing support for the thorough-going, large-scale, methodical work that he knew was necessary.

Getting work in large-scale urban design was not easy, but in 1947 he managed to get a job as consultant to the Chicago Plan Commission for a design for a proposed new civic center on Wacker Drive between Madison and Van Buren. Nothing came of this project. From 1949 to 1953 he was a member of the Urban Renewal Committee of the Metropolitan Housing and Planning Council. In 1952 Weese and his colleagues unveiled a group of spectacular projects for the revitalization of the city in an exhibition called "Chicago Tomorrow" at the Conrad Hilton Hotel. The effort had apparently been initiated by Charles Blessing, head of the Chicago Plan Commission. Although Blessing was unable to convince his own department and the city to endorse the bold and controversial projects, and the hoped-for private funding was not forthcoming, the American Institute of Architects agreed to sponsor it as part of a Centennial of Engineering celebration.

Based on the available evidence, Weese was the driving force in the design of the proposals, which were done with the help of six students at the University of Illinois and their professor, Ambrose Richardson. The proposals included a dozen or more satellite cities to be located between existing suburban railway suburbs; a "strip city"

of new cultural, civic, business, and housing along the newly created Congress Street Expressway leading west of the Loop; a slum clearance project for twenty-six square miles of land around the Loop; new transportation facilities, including an intermodal water, rail, and truck terminal near the mouth of the Calumet River; an international airport near the Indiana state line; and two large islands located two miles off the shore of Lake Michigan.

It was the latter project that got the most attention. These islands, which would have extended from Montrose Avenue, some seven miles north of the Loop, to Fifty-first Street, about six miles south of the Loop, would have provided land to house a half-million Chicagoans. The idea was not new. In 1909 the Burnham Plan had proposed a series of islands parallel to the existing shoreline that would shield it from lake storms, provide space for recreation, and create a sheltered lagoon between the islands and the shoreline. One small piece of the Burnham scheme was actually carried out. Northerly Island, the landfill created for the 1933 world's fair, was to have been the northernmost link in the chain of islands that would have extended down the south lakefront. However, owners of lakefront property successfully blocked any further development. The idea resurfaced again in the 1940s when British experts suggested a floating airport in the lake.

The new element in the AIA scheme was to place the islands two miles offshore so they would have little negative impact on existing lakefront property. In fact, landowners might have welcomed the prospect of having their properties front a great protected bay. The idea for the 1952 project, as Weese explained to the *Chicago Tribune* in an article on September 12, 1952, was to create twenty-five miles of new shore land for recreation purposes and twenty-six acres of new land for housing and retail development. The cost to create the landfill and the tunnels and bridges needed for access, he argued, would be no more than the cost of buying land for urban renewal and demolishing the buildings on it. Together, he hoped, urban renewal of the core as well as the new land on the islands would revitalize a center that had been eroded by blight and chopped up by urban freeways. This dual approach might allow the central city to compete successfully with the suburbs for middle-income families. Over the years he would return again and again to ideas he first put forward in 1952, particularly the idea of islands in the lake.

The island project also appealed to other people. It surfaced in the city's draft for a master plan in 1958, and it continued to have a life of its own for decades until a growing interest in the environmental movement and a growing skepticism about landfills in general weakened public support. In the end, none of Weese's visionary projects of the 1950s were built.

One substantial commission from the late 1940s and early 1950s that did get built was a Chicago Housing Authority project called Loomis Courts. For this commission Weese served as design architect associated with the long-established architectural firm of Loewenberg & Loewenberg, which had an expertise in housing and probably supplied much of the technical support and contact with the client. Two talented young architects worked with Weese on the project: John van der Meulen and Brewster Adams.

Van der Meulen was born in Michigan in 1913, received his architectural degree from the University of Michigan in 1938, and worked in Chicago since 1945, teaching at Moholy-Nagy's Institute of Design and practicing with Ralph Rapson. Van der Meulen and Rapson had designed the Gidwitz house on Woodlawn Avenue in Kenwood on the south side of Chicago, which on its completion in 1937 attracted a great deal of attention as one of the most conspicuous and highly regarded modern houses in Chicago. Brewster Adams had come from the University of Illinois and Skidmore, Owings & Merrill, where Weese probably met him. There was no formal partnership between the three young architects; they worked together in the kind of loose arrangement that was common in architecture schools.

The buildings at Loomis Courts, which opened in 1950, were seven-story structures with elevators opening onto outside galleries, which, in turn, gave access to the front door of the units. Despite differences of opinion between Weese and the city's housing authority and its administrator, Elizabeth Wood, most observers considered the structures successful. Unlike many other tall public housing projects in the city, they were restored in recent years rather than torn down. In many ways, the most important thing this experience did was to give Weese an important lesson in the problems of housing generally. He joined a growing chorus of discontent, not just with the architectural decisions being made for public housing but with the program as a whole. His most cogent diagnosis was made in a letter to Jane Jacobs, who at the time was an editor at *Architectural Forum*. In that letter, apparently never published but preserved in the Weese papers at the Chicago History Museum, Weese argued that building large projects on superblocks resulted in "single purpose warrens which by design are permanently indigestible on the private market." He argued against superblocks and proposed dispersion of smaller units of housing closer to places of employment. He also called for "protective col-

Perspective drawing for islands in the lake scheme, probably early 1950s. From *Inland Architect*, September 1957.

oration" of these small clusters of buildings so that they could more easily evolve toward private ownership over time. Like many housing advocates, he suggested that the housing be broadened to include more families with higher income, and he recommended subsidized conversions and rehabilitation, rather than wholesale clearance, to extend the life of declining areas.

This letter shows that Weese, even at the outset of his career, was surprisingly moderate in political stance and pragmatic in outlook. Where many housing reformers were dubious about the private sector providing housing for anyone except the wealthy, Weese had a healthy respect for what the real estate industry could do in remaking cities. He also had little of the disdain for home ownership exhibited by many of the more radical housing advocates who worried that ownership was a trap and left families vulnerable any time there was a downturn in the economy or a family crisis. Furthermore, he broke with many public housing advocates in his rejection of the idea that residents of close-in slum areas should necessarily be rehoused in public housing on the same site or nearby. In this case, his concern wasn't so much about the residents or the housing itself but about the economic vitality of city centers. As someone passionately devoted to the idea that the city centers needed to expand and become more vital by attracting affluent citizens, he considered it "folly to clear the most valuable prime urban land (close-in slum) and perpetuate it as low income ghetto strangling the heart of the city and wasting its economic potential." He advocated, instead, making prime slum sites available for the "highest and best use." For the displaced residents he suggested a direct subsidy so that they could find their own living quarters in market-rate housing.

Weese started off the 1950s with a small practice but with every expectation of major work. He was, after all, a well-trained architect, with expertise in design at all scales from furniture to urban planning, excellent social and professional connections, a winning personality and handsome appearance, and, by no means least important, an intelligent and devoted wife. By the early 1950s, moreover, it had become clear that the American economy had shaken off the woes of the Depression and scarcities of the war years and was starting to boom.

In the early 1950s Weese thought again about taking on a partner. About 1953 he turned to Ralph Rapson, his friend from Cranbrook. Rapson had stayed in Bloomfield Hills to work with Eliel and Eero Saarinen for a while, then moved to Chicago, where he became head of the architecture department at the Institute of Design and established a practice with John van der Meulen that would produce the highly acclaimed Gidwitz house. In 1946 Rapson had accepted a teaching position at MIT, but in the early 1950s he had taken a leave of absence to go to Europe to work, again with John van der Meulen, on several landmark designs for American embassies. When Rapson decided to return to the United States, Weese suggested that there were remarkable opportunities for the two of them if Rapson would move back to Chicago and join him in practice. Rapson instead chose to return to MIT and eventually ended up in Minneapolis, where he established an important practice and served for many years as dean of the School of Architecture at the University of Minnesota.

The largest group of commissions in the 1950s followed a modest meeting with the head of an Indiana company who wanted to build a small group of houses. J. Irwin Miller was the great-nephew of the founder of the Cummins Engine Company of Columbus, Indiana. He graduated from Yale in 1931, joined the business in 1934, and by 1950 became head of the firm. Before taking over the firm, however, Miller had a major encounter with the art of architecture. In the 1930s Miller's parents took the lead in building a new church for their congregation, the Tabernacle Church of Christ, later the First Christian Church, of Columbus. After several false starts in their selection of an architect, Mrs. Miller decided to follow up on a lead someone had given her about Eliel Saarinen. To her chagrin Saarinen declined the commission. At that point, her son offered to travel to Chicago to convince the great architect to reconsider. He was ultimately successful, and Saarinen designed the church, which was constructed in 1939–42.

During one of the trips Eliel Saarinen made to Columbus to discuss the design of the structure with the church's building committee, Irwin Miller entertained Eliel's son Eero and Charles Eames, both of whom had accompanied the elder Saarinen. The three men fell to talking about architecture, which clearly fascinated Miller, and he and Eero Saarinen became lifelong friends. The design of the First Christian Church, with its bold modern lines and splendid craftsmanship, was hailed almost instantly as a landmark in the development of modern American architecture. Widely described in the professional and architectural press, it put the otherwise unremarkable small town of Columbus, Indiana, on the American architectural map. In so doing, it confirmed Irwin Miller's belief that architecture was a powerful tool not only in making more satisfactory communities but also in attracting business. Although Eero Saarinen would go on to design additional buildings for Irwin Miller, including a house in Columbus and a house in the Muskoka Lakes region of Canada, his office soon became so busy that he begged off on some of the smaller jobs and instead suggested that Irwin look up his friend Harry Weese in Chicago.

As Weese later recalled it, Irwin Miller was a member of a committee the mayor of Columbus had set up to build some new rental housing that could be used as an incentive to lure the brightest and most capable young people, many of them freshly graduated from Ivy League schools, to a small midwestern town. In that capacity Miller had asked Eero Saarinen and his friend Douglas Haskell at the *Architectural Forum* for some recommendations for an architect. From their suggestions Miller and the mayor compiled a list and went to interview a number of architects. In the early 1950s they came to Chicago, and visited at least three offices, including those of two older modernist practitioners, Morgan Yost and George Fred Keck, and that of the young Harry Weese. When they arrived at his very modest office at 612 North Michigan, as Weese later recalled, there was only one good chair to sit in. So he borrowed another and he remained standing. The two visitors from Columbus must have been impressed because Weese soon became involved with a series of commissions for Columbus that would stretch out for at least fifteen years. The first of these, the one that had been the reason for the trip to Chicago, was the Columbus Village apartments, which were finished in 1954. This in turn led to commissions for two schools, the Lillian C. Schmitt Elementary School, finished in 1957, and the Northside Junior High School, finished in 1961 (see entries), and, directly through Irwin Miller or indirectly through institutions in which he was involved, buildings for the Cummins Engine Company, a skating rink, a golf club, two branch banks of the Irwin Trust Company, and the First Baptist Church, which was finished in 1965 (see entry). Farther afield there was the Tangeman House in Muskoka Lakes region of Ontario, designed for Miller's sister and finished in 1964 (see entry).

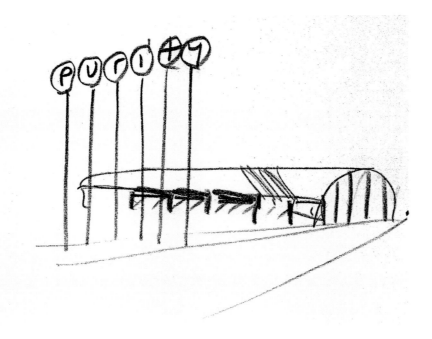

Perspective sketch of
prototype for Purity stores,
probably early 1950s.
Chicago History Museum.

The early work that Weese did in Columbus for Irwin Miller also had other important consequences for both men. For Miller, it reinforced his enthusiasm for the benefits of good modern architecture. From his experience working with Eero Saarinen and Harry Weese in the early 1950s, he devised a remarkable program for Columbus in which the Cummins Engine Foundation would encourage institutions in town to invest in good modern design by offering to pay the architectural fees if that institution was willing to hire an architect from a short list of architects the foundation considered innovative. The result was a long string of commissions in Columbus from that day to this from some of the most famous architects in the country.

For Weese, the work in Columbus also cemented a relationship with landscape architect Dan Kiley, who, like Weese, did a large amount of work in Columbus over many years. Kiley, together with fellow Harvard classmates Garrett Eckbo and James Rose, had been widely heralded, even while at Harvard, as pioneers of modern American landscape design. Weese had always had a strong interest in the land and landscape, and in Kiley he found a kindred spirit. Both favored a direct, modern approach to problem solving, and both were playful and highly intuitive, even impulsive, in their approach to design, grasping a problem as a whole, laying out the entire scheme, and then entrusting younger members of the office with the task of working out the details.

In addition to the work in Columbus, Irwin Miller steered other commissions to the Weese firm, particularly those involving prototypes for standardized buildings,

which had been the subject of Weese's thesis at MIT. For the Cummins company, the firm designed dealerships in twenty-four states, Mexico, and Canada. For the Purity company, a chain of grocery stores in which Miller had a major interest, Weese designed thirty-four stores between 1953 and 1962, mostly in California, all of which were based on a standard kit of parts that could be deployed in various combinations for varied programs in different locations but still produce a strong brand identity.

Together the commissions coming directly or indirectly from J. Irwin Miller provided a steady stream of work for the Weese office during the 1950s and allowed it to grow in size and capacity.

By the early 1950s both Baldwin Kingrey and the architecture office had become sufficiently busy to justify the hiring of additional employees and the leasing of space for a separate architectural office. In 1951 Weese leased space at 612 North Michigan Avenue, just north of Baldwin Kingrey and the Diana Court Building. Weese's first permanent employee, Charles Hogan, a draftsman with fifteen years of experience, did not stay long in the office, but Pat Y. Spillman, who had earned his bachelor's degree in architecture from Texas A&M before going on to study urban planning at Yale and receive a master's degree in architecture from Harvard, worked in the office from 1951 until 1959. At that time he moved to Dallas to start what would soon become a successful practice there. Another key hire, in 1954, was Hans Neumann, who had attended Darmstadt Technical University in Germany before moving to Chicago in 1953 and working briefly at Holabird &

Root. He stayed at the Weese office for ten years as head of the drafting room and production in the office.

In 1954 the loose organization of Harry Weese, Architect & Engineer, turned into a more formal arrangement with the arrival in the office of Brewster Adams and John van der Meulen. Both men had worked with Weese on earlier projects, notably the Ottawa Bank in Holland, Michigan, completed in 1948, and Loomis Court, mentioned earlier. In the early 1950s van der Meulen left Chicago to practice briefly with Eero Saarinen, where he had a hand in the design of Kresge Auditorium and the Chapel at MIT, two spectacular pieces of modern design. He then moved to Europe to work with Ralph Rapson on the design of several important American embassies. Adams probably continued to work at Skidmore, Owings & Merrill during this period. In any case, in 1954 both men entered the Weese office as senior designers. Around this time, the name of the firm changed from "Harry Weese, Architect & Engineer," to "Harry Weese & Associates."

By the mid-1950s the office had grown to employ half a dozen people. In addition to the architects, there was a secretary, Frances Fox, who had the task of trying to maintain order in an office that could charitably be described as nonhierarchical, democratic, and loosely organized. Weese had always had something of a negative attitude to authority or discipline of any kind, and the office reflected that. Given the mounting work and the fact that he was away from the office a great deal, for both business and personal reasons, it was always something of a struggle to keep everything running.

Two of the most interesting projects that came into the office in the 1950s were urban renewal projects associated with Weese's old friend I. M. Pei. Southwest Washington, D.C., and Hyde Park, A and B in Chicago were two of the largest in the country, and they gave Weese a chance to explore what could be done to attract middle-class citizens back to a city. The main contract for both was held by the flamboyant developer William Zeckendorf, head of Webb & Knapp, an established real estate development firm in New York City that Zeckendorf had revived. Pei at the time was working for Zeckendorf.

When it came to ideas about the city, Weese and Pei represented a new generation of architectural modernists. The great pioneers Walter Gropius, Mies van der Rohe, and Le Corbusier, among others, were still very much alive after World War II and, if anything, more influential than ever, but there had been a growing dissatisfaction within the ranks of younger architects, particularly in Europe. The younger generation, notably Peter and Alison Smithson in Britain and Aldo van Eyck in the Netherlands, had grown impatient with grandiose schemes to create universal solutions to human problems and the idea of massive towers rigidly lined up in rows. They wanted instead to create an architecture that was more responsive to the individual, to specific locations, and to the existing building stock. Pei and Weese were clearly on the side of the younger generation.

For the Washington project, Weese was influential at an early stage in the planning, particularly with the idea that he shared with Pei that the plan should consist of some highly traditional building types such as row houses and some new building types, particularly apartment towers. However, at a certain point, Zeckendorf brought in other planners and Weese pretty much bowed out. His exposure to Southwest Washington did have one happy consequence, however. It led to his commission for the Arena Stage theater (see entry).

For the Chicago project, called Hyde Park A & B (see entry for Johnson House and Hyde Park A & B), Weese's influence was more pervasive and continuing, although it is a little difficult to know exactly what the Weese office did and what the office of I. M. Pei did, since the two men shared so many ideas and so much of the early planning work was done by a team composed of employees from both offices. What they accomplished was to insert into an old fabric a web of new townhouses, a shopping center, and a pair of tall apartment buildings that, except for the latter, was clearly intended to maintain the scale and texture of the community.

The Washington and Chicago urban renewal efforts, like those around the country, were controversial. For many observers even the sensitive interventions by Pei and Weese were too drastic, destroying perfectly good pieces of urban fabric. There soon developed a widespread perception that urban renewal was actually a scheme for urban removal, meaning the removal of poor and minority residents in favor of more affluent families. There was also unhappiness in many cities with the new architecture, particularly when it involved large modern buildings inserted into the tightly woven structure of older neighborhoods. However, cities were in deep trouble after World War II and some major new initiatives were probably needed to convince the middle class to stay in older neighborhoods. The Southwest Washington and Hyde Park A & B projects did accomplish this goal, and the designs of I. M. Pei and Harry Weese, particularly the elegant row houses, have been considered successful reinterpretations of traditional urban building types. Seen today with their mature landscape, these urban renewal efforts blend in remarkably well with the older urban fabric that surrounds them.

Where the work for Irwin Miller was relatively low profile, and the urban renewal projects were slow-moving team efforts and controversial, the commission to design the U.S. embassy for what would soon become the newly created African nation of Ghana (see entry) was a solo effort and very high in profile. When it was released to the public, Weese's scheme—with its tapering columns lightly touching the earth, double roof and temple-like symmetry, its fusion of traditional African materials and motifs and Western technology—attracted a great deal of attention and served as an important early notice to the public at large that Harry Weese was a young architect to watch. The process of design for the embassy at Accra provides a good illustration of Weese's working methods. After spending a few days studying the site, researching local conditions, and contemplating the program, Weese sank into his seat on the return flight, and as the plane flew west with the sun, he worked out the entire design for the building in his head, setting out the plans, elevations, and most of the details on paper napkins, air sickness bags, or whatever other paper he could get his hands on. From all accounts, Weese was prodigious in his ability to push aside every other matter, concentrate on the design task at hand, and imagine the entire structure in three dimensions, worked out down to the details. Even drawing as quickly as he could to get the entire conception onto paper this could mean working for eight or twelve hours straight. The burst of energy was sometimes followed by a period of withdrawal from the project and relaxation, often involving the consumption of alcohol.

The architects in the office, as they started the process of translating the boss's quick calligraphic sketches into a finished design and working drawings, were often astonished by the amount of detail contained in the sketches. Nevertheless, Weese did allow a considerable amount of leeway for the designers in his office to suggest changes and improvements. They would work up some drawings during the day and, before they left for the evening, pin them to the wall or leave them on their desk. Very early the next morning Weese would come in, take his red pencil, and mark up the drawings. One of the side effects of the way Weese worked was his impatience with the time it took to make architecture. After he worked out the design in his head, he resented the slow process of design development and actual construction.

A 1956 commission for an apartment building at 227 East Walton (see entry) represented a step up in the scale and complexity of commissions. Kitty had convinced Harry that he should undertake, with playful reference to the Soviet Union, a Five-Year Plan. The idea was that at least every five years, Harry should try to get involved with another major building type. This reinforced his desire to avoid being typecast as a specialist in a given kind of program. For Weese architecture was about continuous exploration, and one of the best ways of doing that was constantly attacking new problems. That made it much harder to settle into a routine or to develop a set of rules or norms that could easily be applied to the next project.

The apartments at 227 East Walton also represented Weese's first major attempt to buy and develop property on his own account. This practice was somewhat unusual in the profession at the time, and it was not looked upon favorably by the American Institute of Architects. The AIA's position was that the architect was a professional, like a lawyer or doctor, someone who should act as a neutral advisor in money matters and whose advice could be relied on because, as a professional, he had no personal financial stake in the outcome of any decisions made. Although many architects over the years disregarded the AIA's strictures, it was rare in the postwar years for an architect with high artistic aspirations to do so. Weese, however, found real estate development irresistible. He loved finding and buying land and working out development projects that could make the land pay. He also had a restless nature and propensity for risk taking as well as a taste for expensive living, all of which made real estate speculation attractive. Finally, and by no means least important, being his own developer allowed him to escape the restraints imposed by clients.

By the late 1950s, Harry Weese was poised to begin two decades of work that would gain for him and his office great critical acclaim. One important event of these years was a trip, probably about 1955–56, that Weese and Eero Saarinen took to the Greek islands. The two men renewed the friendship that they had kindled at Cranbrook, communed with some of the greatest buildings of classical antiquity, and undoubtedly compared some of what they saw with the first fruits of their own fast-rising careers.

The years 1956 and 1957 saw a substantial change in the office as it grew and matured. In 1956 it was moved from 612 North Michigan to 104 South Michigan Avenue, where it would remain for five years. The next year saw the arrival of Harry's younger brother Ben. Ben's decision to join the practice did not come easily or quickly. He entered Harvard College in 1947 firmly determined not to become an architect. Never as personally ambitious or socially outgoing as his oldest brother, he was highly suspicious of the profession. In his mind, architects, despite protestations to the contrary, were largely driven by aesthetic issues, whereas he was more interested in questions of social justice. During his years in college he acted on these impulses by attending the Cambridge Quaker meeting and working with settlement houses in East Boston. Despite his misgivings, however, a visit with his brother to Cranbrook in 1949, where Ben met Eliel and Eero Saarinen and some of the most eminent young architects of the day, helped change his mind. He announced in a letter to his brother during his junior year that he was switching his studies to architecture. However, even after making the switch and graduating in 1951, he was not clear that he wanted to be a practicing architect. In the meantime, he returned to Chicago to work over the summer for three months in Harry's office.

In 1952, facing the prospect of being drafted, Ben declared himself a conscientious objector and went to work for the Church of the Brethren, which sent him to Europe for two years, most of which he spent in a West German reception camp for refugees fleeing from the Eastern Bloc to West Berlin. This experience radicalized him even more, created a definite conflict with his family, particularly his highly conservative father, and further called into question his participation in the architectural profession, given its apparent preoccupation with expensive buildings for wealthy people. On the other hand, while he was in Germany he had the chance to see a great deal of architecture, mostly in the North German Hanseatic cities such as Hamburg and Lubeck. He was particularly drawn to vernacular buildings because they allowed him to think about architecture in a way that seemed far removed from the preoccupations of high art, more attuned to the needs of ordinary human beings, and more immediately responsive to the demands of topography and climate.

On his return to the United States, Ben spent another nine months working in his brother's office, where a number of projects for Columbus, Indiana, and the urban renewal projects in Hyde Park were underway. He then went back to Harvard for two more years to earn a master's degree in architecture. At Harvard the major influence on him was not anyone in the School of Architecture but Eduard Sekler, a professor of visual art at the Carpenter Center for Visual Arts. Seckler, a gentle, thoughtful man, was interested in the way that social concerns drove aesthetic considerations. It was also important for Ben that Seckler was equally at home with the world of Cistercian monasteries and the pages of *Architectural Review*. Ben finally came to the conclusion that architecture could be about both rarified stylistic matters and social justice. After finishing with his coursework, he was awarded a scholarship to spend a summer at Fontainebleau, where he did some studio work,

sang in a choir directed by Nadia Boulanger, and looked at new architecture. On his return to the United States he worked part-time for The Architects Collaborative (TAC), a firm founded in Cambridge in 1945 by Walter Gropius and seven younger colleagues, before Harry called him back to Chicago.

In Harry's office Ben quickly found his own niche, typically working on smaller-scale housing and institutional buildings rather than larger commercial work. Fortunately for Ben, Harry, while interested in stylistic matters and often quite perplexed by Ben's social and political views, had a wide-ranging and catholic attitude toward architecture, and Harry himself was interested in vernacular buildings and historic architecture. Because Ben was his brother and had worked for him on and off for many years, Harry was willing to allow Ben considerably more autonomy than anyone else in the firm. Ben's early projects in the office—for example, the Northside Junior High School in Columbus, Indiana (see entry), or a group of townhouses in Hyde Park—were usually quite distinct from other work in the office, simpler and more closely related to vernacular architecture, often more direct in their translation of program, and more austere in their forms.

A 1957 *Inland Architect* article provides a glimpse of the structure of the firm at the time. It included a list of twelve men and five women who worked in the office. Harry Weese, of course, headed the list. Under his name were those of Brewster Adams and John van der Meulen. By 1957 it had probably become clear to both Adams and van der Meulen that they were never going to become partners, and they would not remain long thereafter. As heavily as Weese depended on them, he relished even more the flexibility and control he enjoyed as sole owner, and in the end he was not willing to compromise his autonomy by taking on partners, at least not design partners. Although the departure of van der Meulen and Adams undoubtedly caused problems, their places were quickly taken by other talented architects, many of them quite young and unlikely to stay for more than a few years. When most employees left the Weese firm, the split was amicable. The departing architects, after a convivial send-off lunch at Weese's favorite eating place, Ricardo's, typically found excellent positions in other offices or established practices of their own. In fact, this cycling of individuals through the office became such a tradition that "HWA," the acronym for Harry Weese & Associates, came to be known by wags in the office as the "Harry Weese Academy."

If Weese were going to take on a partner, it probably would have made sense to have one whose skills were tech-

nical or in the business end of the profession, particularly someone who might have brought some order to the financial side. At least at one point, Weese started talks with Jack Train, who at the time was working in the Skidmore office, about taking him on as a managing partner rather than a designer. As usual, nothing came of these talks. In the end, the pattern that developed was that Weese would find one or more people whom he could depend on to deal with specific issues involving the running of the office. The strongest characters turned out to be the ones connected

with technical matters. Ezra Gordon, who had received his architectural degree from the University of Illinois in 1951 and who had previously worked at Pace Associates, would play a major role in the firm during his tenure there, from 1956 to 1961. Eventually his place as an overseer of technology and construction would be taken by Jack Hartray. In addition to the technical expertise in the firm, Weese regularly tapped outside experts—for example, Frank Kornacker, who did the structural engineering on a number of projects in the 1950s.

Kate, Kitty, Marcia, Shirley, and Harry Weese at the "Studio" in Barrington. ca. 1970. Arthur Siegel photograph. Print courtesy of Shirley Weeese Young.

The failure to find a partner or even a strong business manager meant that as the office grew, the organizational problems grew with it. Because he needed a fairly large office to do work on the scale to which he aspired, and because he was so often distracted and away from the office, he relied heavily on his employees, often young and inexperienced, but he was never really willing to cede enough authority to allow the office to develop stable operating procedures or a sound business plan. William Wurster, a friend of Weese's and dean at the University of California at Berkeley, put it this way when he introduced Weese before a lecture in October 1958: "He's a true American tinkerer type. First you try something—refine it for a period—then discard it when its limitations become apparent." This approach might have been quite acceptable in a small firm, but by the end of the 1950s Weese was starting to build a substantial office. As Ezra Gordon would later recall, despite Weese's frequent claim that he was committed to meeting programs and budgets, the "spark of inspiration" was unfortunately, quite often "financially irrational." His brother Ben described Harry's approach to issues involving money as the "anti-business plan."

Very little of this was visible to anyone outside the office. Almost everyone Weese encountered in the first decades of practice found him to be an attractive and charming personality, so persuasive that he could convince them to do things that they never would have agreed to with anyone else. He seems to have gotten along with all kinds of people, from individuals with the most modest backgrounds to his numerous wealthy friends from Barrington and Lake Forest.

By the end of the 1950s, Weese had attracted a good deal of attention among his peers in Chicago and farther afield. Perhaps the best early assessment of his work appeared in an article devoted to Weese in the May 1957 issue of *Architectural Review*, the major British architectural journal. It stated that "Weese's reputation at the moment is something of an Architect's Architect—not a well-known figure to even the magazine-reading public, but enjoying the wholehearted respect of his fellow practitioners." American magazines also started following his career. In September 1957, *Inland Architect* magazine devoted four pages to the work of the Weese office.

The general magazine-reading public learned about Weese in a large spread in *Life* magazine published on October 6, 1958, which featured descriptions of several house designs by him accompanied by large color illustrations. *Life*, then at the zenith of its popularity, would have brought the Weese name and the Weese design aesthetic into millions of American homes. In addition to the illustrations of unbuilt-house designs, the *Life* article had a photograph of one building that had been built—the so-called Studio in Barrington, built in 1957 as a weekend house for Weese's own family on land that Weese received from his father when Harry Ernest decided to retire to Florida in the early 1950s (see entry).

In the magazine illustration the photogenic architect is standing in front of the house in a characteristically jaunty outfit, without a sports jacket but with a dress shirt and a signature string bow tie. According to family members, this tie was probably one of several he owned, all made of beautiful silk and possibly purchased during his trips to Finland.

With its diminutive scale, unexpected structural gymnastics, and whimsical layout, the Studio seems more like a game, a challenge to be met, than any kind of rational solution to a program. It was a little like the experiments with the houses at Glen Lake. Weese's first impulse was to subvert the apparently logical way to do something and then see how he could resolve all of the problems brought on by the initial decision. This was a characteristic response to rules or restraints of any kind. "We try to break the rule," Weese later said. "If you can't break the rule you're going to wind up in the same place as everybody else because they're all working in the same way, constrained by the same things."

As the practice expanded in the late 1950s, Weese's one-man campaign to improve Chicago went into full swing. He worked vigorously against the building of the original McCormick Place, Chicago's convention center, on the lakefront because he believed that this land should be left open for recreational purposes. He derided the new low-pressure sodium vapor lights being installed in the Chicago region, holding up what he considered to be the attractive old Lake Forest gas lamps by comparison. Many of Weese's opinions directly contradicted traditional notions of "good taste." He had high praise, for example, for the way the Eisenhower Expressway crashed right through the middle of the old post office to create a dramatic entrance to the Loop. This design move, he believed, was an example of why it was frequently necessary to "break the rules" and do the unexpected to create new and interesting design solutions. This philosophy led him throughout his career to attack design guidelines and other attempts to legislate good taste.

Most of his commentary focused on how the city could retain its population and increase its livability while maintaining or even increasing its density. In an important essay he contributed to *Architectural Record* in July 1958, called "Housing Patterns and What Makes Them," he contrasted what he considered the banality of much of urban America, constrained by zoning and a host of other regulations, with the more humane and varied European urban regions, such as those found in London and the Nordic countries. In the article he skewered American suburbs with their low density, lack of focus, and absence of greenbelts. He instead proposed new versions of the kinds of structure he had designed for Hyde Park A & B—row houses, two-story "maisonettes" or single-family units that could be stacked together at densities of up to forty units per acre. He believed that in the city center some high buildings were probably necessary, but his preference was for relatively low structures so that the city could maintain its green canopy and most citizens could have a direct connection with the land. Most people, he believed, would prefer to live "within tree-top height." The city, he felt, needed to find "some proper coexistence between cliff dwelling and suburbia" if it was going to survive as a place for all kinds of Chicagoans.

He even had good words for the lowly mobile home or trailer, which almost all "right minded" architects and planners of the day disliked and which, because of the vociferous complaints of the trade unions, was outlawed within the city limits. But for Weese, as for his near contemporary Paul Rudolph in New York, prefabricated mobile structures were a way to provide a great deal of housing at low price and at high density, and if they were tucked away on the fringes of greenbelts or forest preserves, Weese believed, they would not negatively impact existing neighborhoods. "The mobile home should be made respectable," he wrote, "for it is an honest answer to the needs of transient workers, newlyweds, certain older persons, and those who simply do not like to settle down for long."

While Harry's architectural practice was getting off the ground and Kitty was busy at Baldwin Kingrey in the 1950s, the couple was also starting a family. Daughter Shirley was born in 1949, followed by Marcia in 1951 and Kate in 1955. When Shirley and Marcia were babies, the family lived in an apartment on East Superior Street, but before the birth of Kate they moved to 1315 North Astor Street. They subsequently moved to a coop apartment at 1235 North Astor. The daughters attended the Latin School, which was a short walk from the apartment.

For the girls Weese was a loving presence even if he was usually preoccupied with work or away on business. They soon became aware that architecture was never far from his mind. Craving an audience for his work, he would call his daughters in to his studio behind the kitchen to look at a drawing he was doing at home, or he would invite them to come down to the office or suggest they accompany him to visit a site of architectural or urban interest—for example, a gravel pit, construction site, or slum on the south side of Chicago. When he was in town Weese would casually invite visiting architects over to the house, often on the spur of the moment, for dinner. Somehow Kitty always found something to serve them. Some of these architects, such as I. M. Pei, visited frequently; others, like Alvar Aalto, only rarely.

Throughout the year there were trips. Within the city these were often bicycle excursions to visit Ben Weese and his wife, Cindy, or other firm members. During the summers the family spent much of its time in Barrington, first at the Water Tower House and after 1957 at the Studio. Harry would commute back into the city each day by train. Every summer they would also drive up to Glen Lake to spend two weeks visiting with Harry's parents and the extended family. In winter the family went to ski in Aspen. At first they usually stayed at the Hotel Jerome, but in 1968 Kitty bought an old Victorian house near the center of town. She purchased it without telling Harry, using money she had made on her own. At first he was disgruntled, particularly since he had created dozens of schemes over the years either for buying land and building

a house of his own design or for buying an existing building like the Hotel Jerome and remodeling it, but he soon threw himself into the process of making the house comfortable for the family. No matter how far away they were from the office, however, architecture and real estate were never far from Weese's mind. He would draw wherever he was and, particularly while he was in Aspen, remain constantly on the lookout for sites he could develop or redevelop.

The playful, risk-taking attitude visible in Weese's architecture also characterized his life away from the office. Most people outside his family responded positively to his casual even daredevil attitude. Unfortunately, it also had its downside. He terrified his mother and wife by driving to the very top of great sand dunes in Michigan or to the edge of precipices in Aspen. On a number of occasions, Weese's sailing mishaps put other people at risk. The casual attitude extended to his professional practice. During the construction of the Studio in Barrington, for example, the vertical walls were so lightly braced that when Kitty and the girls were having a picnic at the site, a gust of wind against the enormous flat vertical surface easily toppled the bracing, and the entire wall came crashing down, hitting Kitty, breaking her jaw, and narrowly missing the children.

Weese's unlimited curiosity also put him at risk. While exploring a construction site at Barrington one night, he didn't realize that a plastic sheet looking like it lay on solid ground was actually covering an excavation for a basement. He fell through the plastic and landed head first, breaking his collarbone and fracturing his skull. Doctors gave him only a 40-60 chance to live, but he survived the accident, apparently without any permanent damage. When a major storm approached in Barrington, and Kitty headed for the basement, Harry would run to the balcony to watch. Or when he saw something interesting while he was driving, he would frequently drive off the road to take a look, even when he was driving a low-slung city car in the mountains, with a result that the car would often get stuck.

Luck seemed to follow him. Very rarely did his mishaps cause any lasting damage. Daughter Marcia tells the tale of one family automobile trip from Chicago to Barrington. The car was a light blue Jaguar X6 with a red leather interior, one of several stylish but highly temperamental Jaguars owned by the family over the years. At some point during the trip the brakes failed. According to Marcia, her father never got flustered. Shouting to his wife and daughters, "Hang on girls," he swerved the car off the road, over an embankment, under a billboard, and down a ravine, finally coming to a stop at a gas station.

A THRIVING PRACTICE

By the early 1960s, Harry Weese, now in his mid-forties and with an impressive string of commissions behind him, had established a national reputation. This was confirmed in 1961 when the American Institute of Architects named him a member of the College of Fellows, clear recognition of the esteem in which he was held in the profession. Because architecture has long been a profession dominated by the elderly, he was still the quintessential young architect destined for great things.

In 1961 the office moved from South Michigan Avenue back up to North Michigan Avenue, to the top floor of a two-story building at 140 East Ontario Street, on the corner of North Michigan. As Karl Hartnack, who worked in the office from 1964 to 1969, later recalled, "It was all very informal. Everyone was young. I had been hired by Hans Neumann who was then second in command. During my second or third week someone asked me if I had ever met Harry. I hadn't. Harry was out of town a lot. Harry was the very friendly 'older guy,' just over 50. Everyone else was between 30 and 35." As the commissions continued to come into the office, Weese leased additional space in an annex nearby on Erie Street.

The year 1961 also saw the addition to the staff of Jack Hartray, who was born in Evanston, attended Cornell University, and cut his teeth in the large Chicago firms of Skidmore, Owings & Merrill, Holabird & Root, and Naess & Murphy. The Murphy office was known for its minimal modernist designs in the mode of Mies van der Rohe. These designs, particularly those in steel and glass, required a high degree of technical precision if they were to work at all. Hartray became known as a master of the craft of building. He was also one of the wittiest men in architecture, someone who could defuse a tense situation in an instant with a perfectly timed comment so hilarious that everyone stopped to laugh. Weese especially valued this trait, as he placed a very high value on social grace. For Hartray the job would offer a chance to grow. In the Murphy office, practices had become somewhat codified. There were standard solutions to many of the standard problems. In the Weese office, on the other hand, there was no such body of practice to rely on. This was in part because Weese had come out of a different and more eclectic tradition, one that included earlier modernist architects in Chicago and Nordic architects such as Alvar Aalto. It was also because every time things started to settle into a pattern, Weese could be counted on to break the mold. Hartray could see

that working at the Weese office would present ample challenges.

"The Murphy office," Hartray recalled, "was like High Episcopalian Church, and then, off on the edges, you had the Unitarians and the Christian Scientists. There were Bud Goldberg and Harry and Ed Dart—they were the people who were recognized as being talented, but they were considered really kind of weird by the IIT [Illinois Institute of Technology] mafia, where everything was settled and everyone knew exactly what they were going to do. Harry and Goldberg and Ed Dart kept doing these things that didn't really fit it." Hartray went on to compare designing buildings in Weese's office with boat building: "In sailing when you design a sailboat you make a group of compromises. At no point do you ever have a structure that is really rigorously statically determinate, where all the forces come together at points and everything is really rigid. With Harry there was always a little bit of bending, where the structure was a little soft. There was always a little flaw which you could work around."

Weese apparently recognized that he needed someone with the technical skill of a Jack Hartray, particularly since he knew that Ezra Gordon was about to leave the office, but he hesitated. According to Hartray, the Weese office at the time was filled with very young designers, many of whom came from abroad. They were passionate about architecture and thrilled to be working in the office of a designer as interesting as Harry Weese, but they often had limited experience and even less command of English. This created an exciting and stimulating atmosphere, full of energy, but one that could become dangerously disorganized with large-scale or highly complicated commissions. Weese was torn. Although he wanted the technical expertise, he feared any kind of rationalization or standardization of design. As Hartray later recalled, "It was sort of a children's crusade . . . Harry could suggest almost anything and they'd go crashing off and do it." In the end, the desire to take on bigger work settled the issue. After a long courtship, Weese finally agreed to hire Hartray.

The early 1960s saw a substantial buildup in the size of the office. In 1963 Robert E. Bell joined the office. Bell, who had studied architecture with Louis Kahn at the University of Pennsylvania in Philadelphia, would work at the Weese office from 1963 to 1968 and again from 1980 to 1984. This hire reflected Weese's rising interest in the work of Kahn, who had come to national prominence in the late 1950s with a set of buildings at the University of Pennsylvania, where Kahn rigorously sorted out the "served spaces" such as the office interiors from the "servant spaces" such as the stairways, elevators, and air shafts. For a few years a number of the buildings from the firm showed the strong influence of Kahn—for example, the science center for Beloit College of 1968, with brick utility shafts that marked the exterior surfaces. Equally important to the office was the addition of Robert Reynolds, who was hired about 1964 on the recommendation of Serge Chermayeff, who knew Reynolds from the Graduate School of Design at Harvard. Reynolds, from all reports, was a prodigious design talent and, like Weese, a master at conceptualizing in three dimensions.

In 1964 Stanley Nance Allan came aboard. Allan, who received his bachelor's degree in architecture from the University of North Carolina in 1948 and his master's degree in architecture from Harvard in 1953, had twelve years of experience at Skidmore, Owings & Merrill. He would have a long career at Harry Weese & Associates, first in Chicago, then as head of the Washington office, and after 1978 back in Chicago as president and later chairman of the board of the firm. Allan's strong suit was management, and he played a key role in keeping the office from spinning out of control. Finally, Marilyn Levy (later Marilyn Levy Jonap) joined the office in 1964 as Weese's secretary. She played a large role from that date until her retirement in 1992, keeping track of Weese's personal and office affairs. In addition, the firm often used outside contractors for specific tasks, particularly involving structural issues, mechanical equipment, and interior design. For the latter, in the 1960s the firm often turned to Dolores Miller, who worked first on her own and then later with her husband, Walt. With Hans Neumann, Ben Weese, Jack Hartray, a stable of eager young designers, and support staff on board, as well as reliable consultants, the Weese office was about to move into its peak period of achievement, one that would last over a decade.

Almost everyone associated with the office during these years remembers it as an exciting place. Many employees have memories of coming into the office very early and seeing Weese with drawings he had obviously been working on all night, for once he had an idea he had to get it down on paper as quickly as he could before the thought disappeared. As Weese himself later recalled, "A true designer can have it all figured out in his head, because he can visualize three dimensions and he can figure it out in the middle of the night and turn on the light and sketch it out with a few lines." Or as Jack Hartray remembered it,

Harry seemed to see everything at once, and he saw it all immediately and at all of the possible scales. He would see the landscaping and the site plan and the changes in the regional highway system and things of that sort, but

he'd also see the hardware details and all of the little stuff at the same time. And he would usually put it all on one drawing. And then you'd spend three months sorting it all out and getting it onto the right sheets so the contractors could understand it.

On another occasion he observed,

Harry's eye was directly connected to his fingertips and pencil. And it did not pass through any rational process on the way. And so he saw things immediately and drew them. If Harry went out to look at a building site, he would see the building there. It was just as clear as any kind of computer simulation. That took about twenty seconds; he did not have a long attention span. It usually took about twenty minutes to draw what he saw, and from that time on the project was behind schedule. He kept wondering; why isn't it out, why haven't we built it?

The work of the early and middle 1960s was quite diverse. The commission for the Arena Stage theater in Washington (see entry) was the kind of commission Weese liked best. The client was an energetic, decisive woman, an attractive one at that, and the building was a new type to learn about. On its completion, the theater was a major success in both architectural and theatrical circles and eventually led to commissions for several dozen other theater venues across the country. Among the other commissions of those years were the carefully scaled Old Town apartments on Eugenie Street in Chicago, 1961; the Jens Jensen Elementary School, with its monumental tower, on the city's West Side, 1962; a handsome and comfortable library for the Morton Arboretum in west suburban Chicago, 1964; a dramatically sited and highly complex house for Irwin Miller's sister in the Muskoka Lakes in Ontario, 1964 (see entry); and an ingenious low-cost office building in Milwaukee, 1966 (see entry).

Somewhat unexpectedly for an architect who was a resolute and unapologetic nonbeliever, two of the most successful buildings of the first half of the 1960s were churches. For the first one, St. Thomas Episcopal Church in Neenah, Wisconsin, Weese was asked to build a new sanctuary for an older church that had burned. In response, he fashioned a dramatic space contained within two great warped surfaces framed with heavy timber, finished on the inside with wood decking and on the outside with slate and shingles. The result was very much like an inverted keel of a great wooden ship, but quite asymmetrical. Near the prow of this ship on the exterior he placed an enormous

FACING PAGE
St. Thomas Episcopal Church, Neenah, Wisconsin, view of interior, ca. 1963. Photographer unknown.

brick tower. Curiously, this commission, undoubtedly one of the most striking and unexpected of all of the architect's buildings, was not well publicized by the firm or in magazines, and it remains little known. It was perhaps the closest that the Weese firm would get to the highly sculptural work of Le Corbusier. The church also recalls the sinuous lines of Eero Saarinen's TWA Terminal at Idlewild (now Kennedy) Airport, the Ingalls Rink at Yale, and some of the sinuous structures of Felix Candela in Mexico.

Something of the same spirit but with completely different results can be seen in the First Baptist Church of Columbus, Indiana (see entry). The main spaces here evoke both medieval churches and great inverted boat hulls. In this case, however, the elements that appear somewhat arbitrary and personal in Neenah have been toned down in favor of what, at least at first glance, is a more rational and more conventional scheme. In retrospect the medieval illusions at the First Baptist Church might be seen as an important predecessor to the literal reuse of historic forms that would become a key feature of the postmodern architectural movement of the 1970s. Literal pastiche was certainly not the intention of Weese, however, and even a quick glance at the disjunction between the sober, rectilinear plan and the highly exuberant section reveals a complex and even somewhat discordant dialog between modern requirements and the great architectural tradition. The reason the building has seemed to later observers to prefigure the postmodernism of the 1970s was because Weese, unlike the vast majority of his contemporaries, felt no need to consciously avoid forms that would evoke specific architectural monuments of the past.

In addition to its churches, the office received quite a few commissions from colleges and universities, many of which would be designed by Ben Weese. One particularly important cluster of buildings, at Drake University in Des Moines, was an expansion of the earlier work on campus by Eero Saarinen. Ben Weese also did a substantial amount of work at Cornell College in Mt. Vernon, Iowa.

The burst of commissions in the early 1960s soon attracted attention. In 1963 *Architectural Record* devoted a substantial article to the work of Harry Weese & Associates. It included documentation of a dozen designs then in progress at the office, including the First Baptist Church of Columbus; the Illinois Center for the Visually Handicapped in Chicago; the Cornell College residence halls and Drake University Arts Center; a project for the redevelopment of the Cincinnati Riverfront; and the Beloit College science building. The magazine quoted the architect: "Human nature is the constant factor. We have had the same sensory equipment for a million years, albeit a bit dulled and jaded currently. The joy and the stimulus in architecture is the discovery of fresh combinations of old ingredients appropriate to present problems. Faced with the choice, I would rather be right than contemporary." Weese appears to have spent considerable time and energy getting his designs published in foreign publications. In the mid-1960s, articles appeared in the *Manchester Guardian, Edilizia Moderna, Bouwkundig Weekblad, Deutsche Bauzeitung, L'Architecture d'Aujourd'hui,* as well as journals published in Sweden, Poland, and Russia.

In 1964 Weese was awarded the $1,000 Brunner Memorial Prize in architecture from the National Institute of Arts and Letters. This put him in excellent company, as he was inducted with, among others, Ben Shahn, the artist, and Lillian Hellman, the dramatist. It meant that he joined an illustrious group of previous architectural laureates, many of them his friends, including Gordon Bunshaft, Paul Rudolph, Edward Larrabee Barnes, Louis Kahn, and I. M. Pei. Weese promptly put the $1,000 into his boat fund.

In 1966 the office made its final move, this time to a loft building at 10 West Hubbard Street that Weese had remodeled into a striking light-filled working environment (see entry). Unlike the previous locations, all of which were considered to be "good addresses," on or immediately off Michigan Avenue, the Hubbard Street location was in a decidedly unfashionable area, a faded industrial zone several blocks west of Michigan Avenue. And unlike the previous offices, all of which had been rented, this one belonged to Weese. He set up a company called the 10 Hubbard Corporation, of which Harry owned ninety percent and Ben Weese ten percent, to purchase the five-story building at a cost of $135,000, or less than $3 per square foot. After renovations the architectural firm moved into the top two floors, while sheet metal shops, a company that packed candied fruit for Marshall Fields', and other light industrial and warehousing spaces occupied the lower floors.

The renovation of 10 West Hubbard demonstrated some of Weese's attitudes about preservation. He was by no means a purist. He didn't necessarily believe, as some preservationists did, that the preservation of a building, even an important architectural landmark, precluded modern interventions or dramatic alterations. On the other hand, his view of what should fall into the realm of preservation could also be considerably more expansive than that of many preservationists. He had a particular fondness for the timber-framed loft buildings that still, in the 1960s, comprised the basic building type in a wide swath that surrounded three sides of the Loop. Their simple structure and great open spaces made them an ideal laboratory for trying out new design ideas. Their construction also led to a new kind of aesthetic. For visitors used to the slick corporate offices favored by many of the larger Chicago architectural firms, the exposed brick walls and chunky wooden columns and beams of the Weese office must have been a considerable surprise, at least until the aesthetic became so common it turned into a cliché.

Buildings for Weese's own use (like 10 West Hubbard), were almost always quirkier than those he built for others. Journalist Nory Miller caught the spirit in an article in *Inland Architect* in 1972:

> The entry way is a Dadaist's dream of ambiguity and visual playfulness. A short hall (painted white on one side and black on the other) opens into an apse-like space (where black and white walls reverse) encircling a white brick shaft. And, just for fun, where the wall is white, the trim is black; and where the wall is black the trim should be white—but it's not, it's black too. In addition, there is no hint of elevators or stairs . . . A low hung sign says Harry M. Weese & Associates [*sic*], so you look around. To the left of the brick shaft you find an utterly unannounced elevator. And right would have worked too, for the elevator opens both ways.

Once in the elevator, visitors soon realized that the cab had a plastic top that provided a full view of the elevator shaft and all the elevator equipment, dramatically illuminated by a skylight at the top. As the elevator rose, the tunnel above appeared to get larger and the light levels increased. At least by the 1970s, this experience was heightened by sheets of silver Mylar that lined the walls of the elevator shaft. As the elevator ascended, these surfaces rippled slightly in response to the air movement caused by the cab and created an unearthly shimmering surface.

The highly informal workspace mirrored the atmosphere in the office, which was extremely casual. Many of the employees rode to work on bicycles, storing them in a bicycle storage area on the ground floor. While everyone was expected to work hard during office hours and often well into the evening, there was plenty of time for fun. One of the office rituals was lunch at nearby Ricardo's restaurant, which was so heavily patronized by Weese and his employees that it became a kind of office annex. Weese would often take clients and anyone who happened to be nearby to lunch there. Over the years these lunches stretched out longer and longer as the consumption of cocktails increased.

Newly hired employees were almost always struck by the informal office routine. Bill Dring, who was in the office from 1963 to 1974, described a typical scene:

Harry was the most creative person I have ever known. He was creative not just with the big things, like his buildings, but with all of the small everyday things. Once, just after I started at the office, I came in very early on a Sunday morning to get some things done. I heard a noise and went to investigate. It was Harry with their Dachshund "Corbu." I startled Harry as much as he startled me, and in an effort to defuse the situation, he said he would show me one of Corbu's tricks. He reached into the waste paper basket and pulled out a two-page letter. He tore the sheets top to bottom, then tore a thin, curved strip about an inch wide. He then told Corbu to sit, which he did, presenting a lovely vertical aspect ratio. He stuck the two strips into the dog's mouth making huge fangs. On further command, Corbu growled like a dragon.

Still, with the larger office, some of the informality disappeared. As Karl Hartnack, in the office from 1964 to 1969, recalled,

> When we moved to Hubbard Street a lot of the closeness experienced at Ontario Street was gone. There were suddenly more people. Instead of the 25 people that had occupied the Ontario Street office, the group from the "annex" was added and there was space for forty drafting tables and offices for approximately 10 people directly adjacent to the atrium.

Hartnack continued with a description of how Jack Hartray managed the office's casual atmosphere:

> Jack was always calm, objective, and always had the right solution for any problem. I think that Jack Hartray's presence and role in the office let Harry be who and what he was. Jack had a solution for everything. This was in the late '60s and there were not as many lawyers around then as there are now. Things may have been easier.

During the late 1960s, as the number of commissions increased and the office grew, there were, as usual, quite a few arrivals and departures among the staff. In 1968 Bob Reynolds departed the office to take up a position at DMJM (previously Daniel, Mann, Johnson & Mendenhall) in Baltimore and, shortly after that, a position at the giant engineering and construction company Bechtel. At Bechtel he soon became chief architect in charge of projects worldwide and was in a position to steer some work to his former employer. The year 1969 saw the arrival of landscape architect Joe Karr. Karr graduated from the landscape program at the University of Illinois at Urbana-Champaign

South Lower Campus,
Humanities Building,
University of Wisconsin
at Madison, 1970. Robert
Bruegmann photograph, 2007.

in 1960, studied at the University of Pennsylvania with the famous landscape architect and pioneer environmentalist Ian McHarg, and worked with Dan Kiley at Kiley's office in Charlotte, Vermont. While working for Kiley, Karr had regular contact with the Weese office, involving landscapes Kiley had designed for Weese buildings, such as the First Baptist Church of Columbus and the Performing Arts Center in Milwaukee, as well as the spectacular south garden of the Art Institute of Chicago, where Kiley had done the design and Weese provided help with architectural detailing and local supervision. In 1968 Weese made Karr an offer to move to his Chicago office with the proviso that Karr could also do other work on his own. Karr agreed and moved into a space on the fifth floor of 10 West Hubbard Street shortly

thereafter. Having Karr in the office strengthened further Weese's already substantial interest in landscape.

The amount of work in the Weese office during the late 1960s was prodigious. The largest group of commissions was a set of buildings for colleges and universities. These included buildings for Cornell College in Mt. Vernon, Iowa; Reed College in Portland, Oregon; the University of Colorado at Boulder; the Rochester Institute of Technology in Rochester, New York; the University of Illinois at Chicago; the University of Vermont; and Beloit College in Beloit, Wisconsin. There were also two new junior college campuses, one at Benton Harbor, Michigan, the other for St. Louis. The St. Louis campus has been well maintained over the years and provides a good example of the robust architectural forms coming out of the office in the late 1960s as well as a highly sensitive landscape design by Karr. For the Latin School of Chicago the office provided a handsome new building at North Avenue and Clark Street that managed to squeeze a substantial program into a tight urban site (see entry). In Milwaukee the firm did an impressive performing arts center. Important restoration projects included work on the Auditorium Theater (see entry), Orchestra Hall, and the Field Museum, all in Chicago.

In addition there were some special challenges. One was Shadowcliff, a spectacular glass-walled rectangular box suspended high above Green Bay near the town of Ellison Bay, Wisconsin (see entry). Another was a set of houses for Air India in Bombay, the challenge being to provide quarters for members of different castes. Weese was particularly proud of the fact that he convinced the client to create one set of buildings with separate entrances so all the groups could share the same building without throwing a direct challenge to their social customs.

A group of three commissions at the very end of the 1960s provide some indication of the range of the Weese office at this time. For the Time-Life company (see entry), he completed his first tall business building in central Chicago. In this building Weese was able to introduce some innovative design ideas—for example, a two-level elevator and a cladding system of enormous metal panels that speeded construction. The simple rectangular configuration of the Time-Life Building brought it as close in appearance to the work of Mies van der Rohe as anything Weese ever did, but Weese, never one to follow closely in the footsteps of anyone, gave the building quite a distinct personality by making the exterior more robust and three-dimensional than most buildings in the Miesian mode, and by using two striking new materials, a gold-tinted glass and the rugged self-weathering steel called COR-TEN. Weese would later describe a dream he had where Mies was smiling at his Time-Life Building. True to form, however, once Weese had explored that aesthetic he would more or less abandon it to try other approaches.

For the Seventeenth Church of Christ, Scientist (see entry), Weese attempted to take advantage of a dramatic but demanding triangular site where Wacker Drive bends at Wabash Street to follow the course of the Chicago River. He imagined an auditorium in the form of a great semicircular Greek theater raised up one level above grade, with Sunday school classrooms below, offices behind, the whole composition enclosed in a sweeping concrete wall facing the intersection. This building garnered an award from the Chicago chapter of the American Institute of Architects on completion and a prestigious twenty-five-year award in 1997.

A third commission, an academic building and museum making up the South Lower Campus at the University of Wisconsin at Madison, completed in 1970, is arguably just as impressive, but it has not fared as well in critical opinion. Occupying a key site at the very core of the campus, this building is a vigorous six-story concrete structure that completely filled its site to accommodate a large and complex program. At the same time, the architects tried to make it fit in with its neighbors by maintaining cornice lines and employing limestone panels as cladding. Although the Elvehjem Art Center has always had admirers, the Humanities Building has come in for a good deal of criticism in recent years for being, according to its critics, too big, too heavy, too detached from the street. Current plans call for its demolition.

The negative appraisal of the South Lower Campus complex was well in the future in the late 1960s, however. At that time almost everyone would have agreed that Weese's career was in full swing. By far the most important commission the firm received in the 1960s, indeed the commission that would eventually become the most important of Weese's career, was the rapid transit system for Washington, D.C., the Washington Metro (see entry). This was clearly an exceptional opportunity for any architectural firm. In most work of this kind in recent years the major functional decisions are made by transportation engineers, with the participation of architects largely confined to elements considered to be more or less purely aesthetic. In the case of Metro, because the system was for the nation's capital, responsibility for the design was to be shared by the engineers and the architects.

Planning the Metro was a long, difficult process involving a great many players who had very different ideas about the way the system should work and look. The biggest challenge to Weese in his efforts to establish a unified design came from the engineers who argued, quite reasonably from a functional point of view, that while the great vault envisioned by Weese made sense for the deep stations, which would be tunneled, it made little sense for the stations much closer to the surface, which would be built in an open cut. They suggested that there should be different types of stations for different situations as there had been at the Bay Area Rapid Transit (BART), the other great American subway system of these years.

From that day to this, there has been disagreement over what happened next, who gets credit for bringing back the idea of the great vaulted space and the single design for the entire system. People in Weese's office are adamant that Weese's original vision ultimately triumphed. Other observers have suggested that members of the Commission of Fine Arts, especially the powerful and pugnacious Gordon Bunshaft, by then head of the New York office of Skidmore, Owings & Merrill, deserve at least some of the credit. In retrospect, it seems safe to say that what was built was largely what Weese had initially envisioned and that he and his office deserve most of the credit for maintaining the integrity of that vision over the many years the system was under design and construction.

There is little disagreement about the success of the design. From the day the initial segment of the system opened in 1976, architectural critics and ordinary citizens alike have marveled at the great coffered spaces, the fine durable materials, and the meticulous detailing of every object in the system. While some of these elements, particularly the somber colors and graphics, now have something of a period look to them, the basic architectural elements hardly seem to have aged at all. They are at once modern in the way they are stripped of every superfluous element and reduced to basic geometries, and at the same time classical in their scale and elemental relationship with the human form. As much as any piece of postwar American architecture, they appear timeless. Although Weese was not solely responsible for the Metro, it was his vision and his ability to guide the project through the difficult years of negotiation that led to the system as we see it today. The Metro alone would be sufficient justification to rank Harry Weese as one of the most significant figures in the history of American architecture.

In 1976 Harry Weese had finally completed a major structure that received worldwide attention. Weese seemed to be well positioned to enter into the most productive phase of his career. Few people today, however, even those greatly admiring his work, would say that the projects during the years that followed fulfilled this promise. In fact, the Metro system was such a powerful monument that it tends to make the later career of Harry Weese seem anticlimactic. It isn't that there weren't important later commissions. There were many important buildings, entire new transportation systems such as the one for Miami, even entire new towns such as the one at Riyadh. It is that no subsequent commission would ever have quite the symbolic importance or the potential for demonstrating a control of form that was possible in Washington.

In some ways one of the best testimonies to the high hopes observers had for him is the fact that today so many people think of Weese as a great talent whose career, like that of his friend Eero Saarinen, was cut short at an early age. But Saarinen died in 1961 at the age of fifty-one, while Weese was sixty-one years old in 1976 and continued to be active in his practice for at least another ten years. This perception of a career cut short has stuck because it is so hard to imagine a satisfactory encore to the Washington Metro.

While work on the Metro was going on, Weese continued to offer to anyone who would listen copious advice about architecture, planning, the future of cities, or a great many other topics, some of them seemingly quite remote from his own areas of expertise. As he came to be better known, he had more and more opportunity to weigh in on these issues in public. His opinion, like his architecture, was never entirely predictable. He clearly believed himself to be part of the camp of progressive reformers. At least in the 1960s he was willing to advocate fairly radical means to achieve his urban goals, suggesting, for example, that all urban land ought to be municipally owned so that every family could have "a crack at owning a party-wall house with a garden and a garage." This was exactly the kind of program that he had designed for his Hyde Park urban renewal scheme, and it was the kind of house that he eventually chose to inhabit in Chicago.

On the other hand, he was willing to argue against some of the ideas held dear by many of his peers, particularly the ones with the most Utopian views. He did not argue that automobile use should be discouraged, particularly among poor people, because he believed that it opened up job opportunities. Nor did he believe that it was wrong to differentiate standards of housing for families at different income levels. This, for him, was simply common sense because otherwise it would drive up the cost of low-income housing to the point where little of it would get built. Given Weese's extremely eclectic mode of thinking, it is difficult to say whether these were merely pragmatic responses to conditions as he found them or an indication of a slide to the right politically.

Weese's attitude toward architectural or design control was ambivalent. He remarked in a piece in the *AIA Journal* in 1961 that design controls seemed to work very well in certain cases—for example, on Park Avenue in New York or along the streets of the Chicago Loop, where zoning codes promulgated in the 1910s and 1920s had led to a certain regularity of the cornice line, creating an impressive effect. On the other hand, he noted that it was possible to achieve even better results where rules were suspended, citing Rockefeller Center and Lincoln Center in New York and Courthouse Square in Denver by I. M. Pei as examples. The great question, he believed, was how to achieve order without excessive control, how to get a unified, coherent effect without sacrificing the individuality of the architect. It was a question that would occupy him for the rest of his career, perhaps in part because this balance between spontaneity and order seemed to echo a central problem in his own architectural design.

Because of his highly inventive turn of mind and the unpredictability of what he might say, Weese became a favorite speaker at public and professional events. A speech at the San Francisco Planning and Urban Renewal Association in January 1961 provides a particularly good example of the way he thought about cities. This speech, first of all, provides evidence on how much Daniel Burnham, who had done a major plan for San Francisco immediately after the great earthquake in 1906, was on his mind. Weese, however, started with the assumption that San Francisco in his day, unlike in Burnham's day, was already a mature city, one that had been built in previous generations, and that the task ahead was not to rebuild it but instead to perfect what was already there.

There followed a torrent of provocative suggestions, many of them on themes that would recur throughout his later career. He proposed to diminish the impact of the automobile by housing them off the streets so they were out of sight, with parking on the streets available only at highly priced meters. He proposed that some of the most important urban arteries, including Market Street, Columbus Avenue, and Van Ness, be turned into rivers of trees. He recommended halting the advance of the elevated expressway then under construction along the Embarcadero and reclaiming the waterfront. He also recommended building no more automobile bridges across the bay, proposing instead more ferries and public transportation. He suggested the cataloging of all historic buildings and landmarks, maintaining the cable cars, and restoring old sailing ships. He also favored, very much in the spirit of Burnham, the creation of more focal points, including a great public place at the center to pull the design of the city together. A great many of these ideas, adapted to slightly different circumstances, he had already proposed for Chicago.

Back in Chicago, Weese had a chance to put some of his ideas into practice. He played a key role in the restoration of Adler and Sullivan's magnificent Auditorium Theatre (see entry). For Weese this was not just an architectural masterpiece; it had strong personal connections too. It was here, after an opera, that his father had proposed to his mother, and it had been familiar to him from trips into the city as a child. While aboard ship during the war he had started to daydream about how to preserve the building. When Weese finally got a chance to take on this task, he operated in characteristically pragmatic fashion. By insisting on doing just what was essential to get the building's doors open, Weese was able to carry out the renovations for

a sum that the owners were able to raise, leaving additional work for later. Even so, the firm was successful in cleaning or remaking a great deal of the spectacular ornament design by Louis Sullivan, allowing the interior to glow once again. Eventually other parts of the restoration were completed.

His work on the Auditorium alone would have been enough to make Weese a hero in Chicago preservation circles in the 1960s, but he did much else. Harry and Ben Weese stood on the picket lines at Louis Sullivan's Garrick Theater. This building ultimately came down, but the battle to save it really started the organized preservation movement in Chicago and attracted the attention of a number of influential journalists, notably Ruth Moore at the *Chicago Sun-Times*, Paul Gapp at the *Chicago Tribune*, and M. W. Newman at the *Chicago Daily News*. There was a victory in the battle to save Glessner House, the great stone mansion designed by H. H. Richardson on Prairie Avenue on Chicago's Southside Gold Coast. Both Weese brothers had long admired the Glessner House, and their opinion was confirmed during a tour of the city Ben Weese had given Alvar Aalto in 1961. According to Ben, Aalto didn't even get out of the car to see Mies' Crown Hall at the Illinois Institute of Technology, but he stood rapt in the street in front of the Glessner House and spent an hour studying the building inside and out. As Harry Weese later recalled, he and his brother Ben made a pitch to Philip Johnson for a donation to save the house while the three were walking briskly down Fifth Avenue in New York. Johnson pledged $10,000. The Weese brothers then pledged $10,000 of their own money and secured funds from friends such as John Entenza of the Graham Foundation, Bill Hartmann of Skidmore, Owings & Merrill, and Larry Perkins. The sale took place in December 1966, and bit by painful bit, the house was restored and filled with paying tenants, including the Chicago chapter of the American Institute of Architects. An organization modeled on some suggestions put forward by Harry Weese, and named the Chicago School of Architecture Foundation, was founded to maintain the structure. Ben Weese became treasurer, then chairman, then president. He finally left the year the Kenilworth Garden Club decided to have a benefit there, figuring that by this point he had done his job.

In the early 1970s family life for the Weeses changed substantially. During the preceding years the daughters finished high school and left home to go to college, Shirley to Sarah Lawrence and then the Rhode Island School of Design (RISD), Marcia to Bennington College, and Kate to Cranbrook and RISD. By 1970 Kitty Weese decided that, with the children out of the house, it was time for her to go back to work. She hadn't worked since 1957,

when she sold Baldwin Kingrey, but in 1970 she started an interior design practice with her friend Jackie Green (later Wogan). The two women called it "Design Unit," apparently a reference to the practice that Kitty's brother Ben had founded in New York City in 1948 and had called Design Unit New York. Kitty operated out of the offices of Harry Weese & Associates and was mainly involved in the design of commercial interiors, including many of the firm's projects, particularly office space in the Sears Tower commissioned by Ben Heineman, the redoubtable head of Northwest Industries for whom Weese had designed Shadowcliff. Daughter Marcia spent some time working in the practice starting about 1980.

In the mid-1970s Harry and Kitty moved to a row house, one in a group of four he had developed in what he called a "private urban renewal scheme," on Willow Street in the city's Old Town neighborhood (see entry). The idea for redeveloping a parcel in this faded but gentrifying neighborhood was based in part on the experience of his brother Ben. In 1957 when Ben started working at the Weese office, he bought and renovated a Victorian house dating to the 1870s in the 2100 block of Hudson Street in the Lincoln Park neighborhood just to the north of Old Town. Originally a substantial single-family house, it had been turned into a rooming house during the neighborhood's long decline in the early twentieth century. Ben turned the upper floors into an apartment for his mother, who was on her own after the death of Harry E. Weese in 1956, and turned the lower floors into a garden apartment for himself.

This experience led Ben to propose another project. Just south of his house was a large urban renewal project that involved clearing substantial areas of modest housing and replacing it with new, more-upscale structures. Ben proposed a small project at the corner of Larrabee and Dickens Street that he wanted to be more affordable than the rest of the renewal effort so that it could help preserve a mix of incomes in the neighborhood. When that project didn't go forward, Ben had little interest in further real estate development, but in the process he and his brother had created a business entity called "Larrabee Dickens" that Harry Weese ended up using for a variety of real estate deals and other purposes. The set of four houses on Willow Street, a variant on the urban row house formula that Harry had been exploring since the 1950s, was one result. Each of the four units was customized for a specific owner. The unit that Harry built for himself and Kitty would serve as the Weese home until health problems would force Harry to leave. Kitty remained in the house until her death.

During these years Harry Weese had the means to indulge many of his hobbies. The most expensive of these was boating. In the late 1960s he bought a "Rancher 41," a forty-one-foot sloop designed by the English boat designer Alan Gurney. When *Periphery* arrived from Britain, Weese started racing in earnest, particularly in the famous Mackinac Race between Chicago and Mackinac Island. Later boats included *Isosceles* and *Cumulus*, the latter a joint design of Weese and Britton Chance, a professor of biochemistry at the University of Pennsylvania and well-known sailor and boat designer. Like *Periphery*, *Cumulus* became a familiar sight in the harbor and in boat races. Weese would often leave work and go directly to Belmont Harbor, where he would join Kitty and sometimes the girls for a picnic dinner out on the water. On many sailing also involved a good deal of drinking.

Cumulus was involved in one of Weese's most spectacular mishaps. On July 23, 1975, it ran aground and sank two hundred yards off East Grand Traverse Bay Lighthouse, oddly enough, very close to the Weese summer compound at Glen Lake. The eleven crew members were safely evacuated by a Coast Guard helicopter and rescue ship as well as two civilian vessels. When the boat was put back into service, Weese refused to replace the original sails. Deeply stained by oil when it sank, they served as an emblem of the near disaster.

As the architectural firm continued to expand in the 1970s there was an effort to maintain the same informal atmosphere it had when it was smaller. As before, Weese would go through periods of intense concentration on a given project and then long periods when he was distracted by other matters. However, when he was in town, he continued to pay close attention to the work in the office. Kevin Cartwright, who served as receptionist in the office in 1972–73, remembered that during this period Weese often rode to work on a fancy collapsible Italian bike. She also remembered an occasion when Weese and Jack Hartray decided to go riding along the lakefront after some serious drinking. As Cartwright remembers the story, Weese fell into the lake, and they both were fined.

A major interruption of office routine in the middle of the 1970s was a serious fire in the Hubbard Street building on December 31, 1974. The owner of the recording studio on the third floor, who was in financial difficulty and was apparently also being sued by Weese for his failure to provide sufficient sound insulation for his recording studio, had stuffed his suspended ceiling full of insulation in order to deaden the sound transmission to the floor above. In the process he covered over the sprinkler heads, insulating them from the fire that broke out in his recording console. (The fire department labeled the blaze suspicious but was unable to prove arson.) Weese was at his house in Aspen during the early morning hours of January 1, 1975, when a call from Chicago alerted him to the fire and the extensive damage to his office. According to his daughter Shirley, Weese was at first quiet, then angry, but within a short time he took pencil in hand and sketched out a new expanded office that would occupy the top three floors of the building instead of the two it had previously occupied. He decided to leave exposed the charred beams to bear testimony to the fire in the new, enlarged office that emerged from the ashes.

In the early 1970s Weese continued to be active in civic organizations and to address a flood of suggestions, criticism, and commentary to elected leaders, heads of businesses, and ordinary citizens. Although the topics were often different from those of previous years, his larger goals never changed. They always revolved around the role of architecture and design in creating a better living environment for all citizens. In 1970 he typed up a set of points that he labeled "My Philosophy," which serves as a good summary of many of the things he had long believed:

> The physical environment determines the quality of a large part of our life. It is more than individual buildings.

In most respects landscape is more important than architecture.

In the exterior world the public sector is more important than the private.

The things we own in common are the measure of civilization and what we preserve of these is the civilization.

The separation of man from nature is distorting values and is producing less human people. Man doesn't need to be separated from nature.

Profit making must be subordinated to the responsibilities of producing environment.

Nature is design.

Weese continued to advocate saving old buildings. By 1973 he had become so identified with this cause that *Time* magazine devoted an article in the July 23 issue entitled "The Landmark Man," to his activities. "Every building is a landmark until proven otherwise," was one of his most memorable formulations. He also continued to criticize things he didn't like. He decried what he considered the wasteful pattern of low-density suburbia with its freeways and big houses. He continued to agitate for a relatively high-density central city that would be attractive to middle-class residents. He pushed for more effective public transportation—for example, new regional transit lines that would connect the suburbs together and a set of new lines on the underused rail land surrounding the Loop. He called for a new airport far south of the city, in Kankakee, with a new high-speed rail line that would speed passengers from the airport to the Loop, then tunnel under the central business district to emerge at Clybourn and Western Avenue, from which point it would continue to O'Hare.

At the same time, he disparaged the views of many prominent urban thinkers—for example, in a speech in Great Falls he lashed out at "ekistics, arcology, dymaxion, pseudo-scientific Habitat" as irresponsible romanticism. Of course, the architects in the crowd knew exactly who he was referring to—Constantinos Doxiadis, Paolo Soleri, Buckminster Fuller, and Moshe Safdie—some of the best-known contemporary commentators on the design of cities. In the earliest years of the 1970s, his criticism was usually done in this way, without naming names and somewhat tongue-in-cheek.

One measure of the interest many people had in Weese's ideas is the frequency with which he was asked to serve on the board of civic organizations. He played leadership roles with Chicago's Openlands Project, the Metropolitan Housing and Planning Council, the Mayor's Committee for the Preservation of Chicago's Historical Architecture, and the Chicago chapter of the American Institute of Architects, to which he was elected president in 1975. At the state and national level he was asked to serve on the Creative and Visual Arts Advisory Panel for the American Revolution Bicentennial Commission, the Task Force for the West Front of the United States Capitol, Governor Richard Ogilvie's Commission on Financing the Arts in Illinois, President Nixon's Citizens Advisory Commission on Environmental Quality, and President Johnson's Citizens Advisory Committee on Recreation and Natural Beauty. In 1974 he was named to a six-year term on the National Council of the Arts, a significant honor he shared that year with, among others, two icons of the American cultural scene: Van Cliburn, the pianist, and Jerome Robbins, the choreographer.

Given the high esteem in which he was held and the way so many of Weese's ideas were entering the public mainstream, it is surprising that a tone of disillusionment started to creep into Weese's public pronouncements by the middle of the 1970s. Perhaps this was in part due to a sour national mood caused by problems with the economy, the oil crisis, and the bitterly divisive aftermath of the events of the late 1960s and the Vietnam War. But it is hard to escape the impression that there were also more personal causes for the increasingly strident criticisms Weese made of fellow architects and fellow citizens. Observers at the time noted that when he was speaking to a group, he usually delivered even his most stinging criticisms with a smile and, often, a playful epilogue that seemed to lighten the mood. The words captured in print appear to suggest a darker side.

An October 1974 interview with *Commerce* magazine provides a good example. He found little to cheer in the economy during those years of the oil crisis and inflation. No one was building, he said, because of skyrocketing land values and high interest rates. He described environmental roadblocks at every turn and red tape from what he called the "safety lobby," presumably citizen groups dictating new building standards. He noted the loss of ten percent of the city's population between the last two census tallies and predicted that new suburbs would soon become slums. One recurring theme for Weese was the permissiveness of society, the way the constraints of earlier periods had loosened to cause chaos both in society and in design. He repeatedly decried what he considered a decline in design standards because of clients with too much money and

Perspective sketch of shopping center for new town near Riyadh, Saudi Arabia. From *Inland Architect*, February 1976.

architects unwilling to impose discipline. He was appalled by the way materials were being cheapened—for example, the way rosewood, which was once a luxurious material, could now be bought as a thin veneer encased in plastic. He also decried the political climate, saying that good men had been willing to serve as public officials in the 1950s but that the situation had changed much for the worse in the years since. He started to become more personal and emphatic in his criticisms of fellow architects. Whereas in the past he had often made witty remarks about buildings he didn't approve of, by the mid-1970s these attacks often turned vitriolic and personal. Oddly enough for someone at the peak of his career and influence, he increasingly described himself as a loner.

Nevertheless, important work continued to come out of the Weese office. At the Sawyer Library at Williams College, for example, Ben Weese responded to the energy crisis by designing an energy-efficient building with internal light courts and sun protection, which made it possible to do without air-conditioning (see entry). Other work in the early and middle 1970s included designs for the Crown Center Hotel in Kansas City, 1973, with its spectacular indoor garden (see entry); the inexpensive but spatially complex Given Institute of Pathobiology in Aspen, Colorado, 1972 (see entry); the Actors Theatre of Louisville in Kentucky, 1972, with its new stage set behind a restored gem of the American Greek Revival style (see entry); the Mercantile Bank Building in Kansas City, 1974, with its innovative water-filled columns; the highly theatrical waterside library for the new campus at the University of Massachusetts in Boston, 1975; the Oak Park Village Hall, 1975, obviously heavily influenced by Alvar Aalto (see entry); and the Metropolitan Correctional Center (William J. Campbell U.S. Courthouse Annex) in Chicago, 1975 (see entry), one of the few jails in American history to become an architectural landmark.

One project undertaken during this period involved the creation of an entire new town near Riyadh in Saudi Arabia. It was not only one of the largest projects ever completed by the firm but also among the least known.

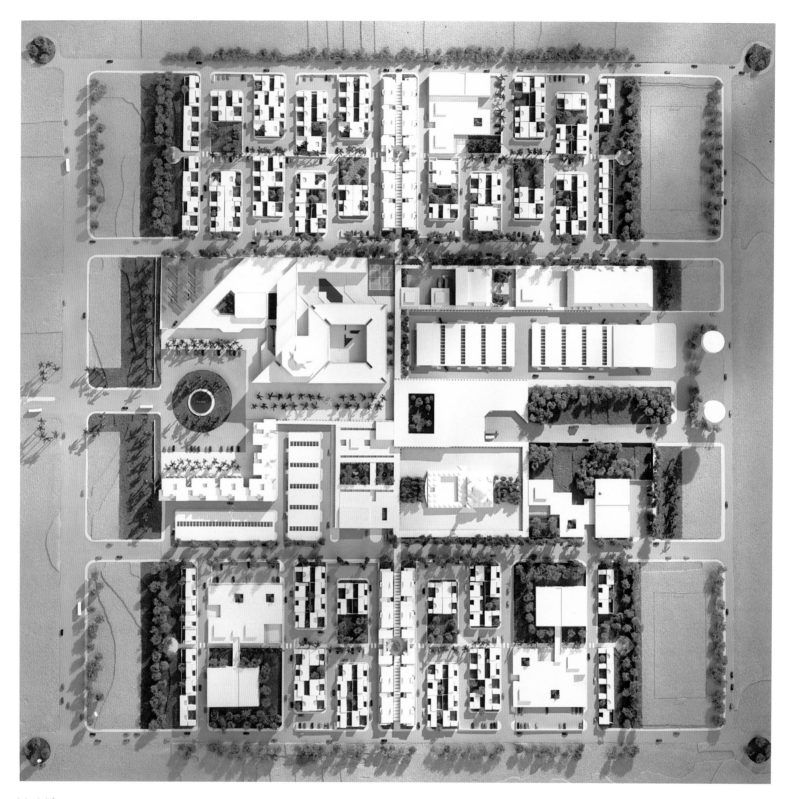

Model for new town,
Riyadh, Saudi Arabia,
ca. 1976. 40679-A, Chicago
History Museum.

As a result of a dramatic increase in oil prices in the 1970s, a number of Middle Eastern countries started a building boom, often hiring European or American builders and architects to help them. The Saudi government wanted to build a new airport near Riyadh, so it turned to the giant American engineering and construction company Bechtel, where former Weese employee Bob Reynolds was in charge of architecture and was able to play a key role in securing for the architectural firm the contract to design a new town to service the airport. Ben Weese was the primary designer of this huge project, which involved a master plan for an entire city of thirty thousand airport employees, at first mostly Europeans, but eventually replaced largely by Arabs. The commission also presented difficult questions about building in the desert and, like the one for the embassy at Accra, about conceiving an architecture suitable for a non-Western country. Because of government concerns about privacy, very little information and few pictures have ever been released, making it difficult to judge this highly ambitious project.

As the firm grew, various members started to specialize in different building types—for example, Norm Zimmerman with hotels, Mike Lisec with theaters, Bill Bauhs with a variety of others. Of all the members of the firm, Ben Weese had the most autonomy. He continued to work on housing and institutional design. Some of his most conspicuous achievements during these years were apartment buildings, including Lake Village East in Chicago and the John Knox Home in Norfolk, Virginia, both finished in 1974. In both cases he tried to break down the box-like forms that had characterized most of the firm's previous residential buildings. Working from the interior outward, he devised plans that maximized the space of the units and the amount of daylight admitted, while minimizing exterior perimeter by chamfering the corners of the building. This strategy produced highly faceted structures that not only achieved a high ratio of interior space to exterior perimeter but also multiplied the number of corner apartments, enhanced views, and broke down the scale of the building.

In the middle of the 1970s Harry Weese increased the scale of his forays into real estate development. Whereas earlier in his career he had dealt with single buildings—for example, 227 East Walton in the mid-1950s and his own office at 10 West Hubbard in the 1960s—in the 1970s he took on an entire district. His project in the South Loop held out not only the promise of freeing him from clients but also the possibility of considerable profit, which was increasingly important to Weese because of the mounting costs of his boats in Chicago and Michigan, his homes in

Chicago, Barrington, and Aspen, and vacations in Europe and elsewhere. In addition, he probably considered his real estate dealings as both an intellectual challenge and a civic act. He had long argued that the city needed to be able to compete with the suburbs for the middle-class families that were fleeing the center in such great numbers during the postwar decades, and he became increasingly interested in the preservation of the city's stock of solid but under-used old buildings. Buying neglected industrial buildings in close-in locations and renovating them for residential use seemed to fulfill all of these aspirations. It confirmed his commitment to the city and his status as an "urban pioneer," the media's characterization of upper-middle-class individuals and families who stayed in the city during the 1970s, when many large American urban areas faced unprecedented economic and social challenges. And once again, the considerable challenge involved in buying property in a city with a declining population must have made the proposition even more attractive.

He fixed his sights on a stretch of Dearborn Street in the South Loop that had been the heart of the Chicago printing industry. This stretch of street, extending from Congress Street in the north to the Dearborn Street station in the south, was an expanse of bulky loft buildings that had been mostly abandoned by the 1970s. Weese called a friend, the talented young architect Laurence Booth, to go down to take a look. Booth was enthusiastic as well. Knowing that they needed more real estate expertise, Weese turned to his longtime friend John Baird, with whom he had worked on 227 East Walton at the outset of his career, and Ivan Himmel, who had collaborated on the Euclid Square project in Oak Park, which involved the reuse of parts of a Frank Lloyd Wright apartment building. They also enlisted the help of Theodore Gaines, a lawyer who owned several of the most important properties in the district. The first name for their project was "Dearborn Park." Unfortunately that name was taken by the Chicago 21 Corporation, the group doing a large new development just south of the Dearborn Street terminal. They settled on "Printers Row."

The group started with the Transportation Building, a twenty-two-story structure built in 1911 that the partners planned to turn into apartments. This would have been enough of a project to keep most people busy, but once Weese got an idea into his head, he ran with it. He was so sure of the success of the new Printers Row district that he was willing to risk his own money, much to the consternation of his friends and family, especially his wife, Kitty. He decided to buy for himself the Donahue Building, a structure at the southernmost end of that stretch of Dearborn

Perspective sketch of
Printers Row, Chicago,
probably late 1970s.
From firm brochure.

heavy-timber structures for residential purposes, and a substantial portion of the Donahue had this kind of construction. All in all, it was a hugely risky proposition.

Somehow it all worked out. The blessing of Chicago's mayor, Richard J. Daley, apparently smoothed the way for changes in the building code to permit heavy-timber residential lofts, and against all odds, Weese managed to buy the necessary piece of land and overcome most of the rest of the problems. His goal was to replicate a practice he had seen in the SoHo district in New York, where building owners had started renting out raw space to artists. Between 1979 and 1983 Weese spent just over a million dollars bringing the building up to the point where he could sell space for $6 per square foot. The large open spaces, exposed brick, and whitewashed columns in the lofts of artists such as Vera Klement and Nancy Berryman were novel in Chicago and attracted a great deal of attention in the media. Other units were spun off to architecture students at the University of Illinois at Chicago Circle, who used them as a kind of fraternity and crash pad, and part of the ground floor space was taken by Bill and Marilyn Hasbrouck, proprietors of Prairie Avenue Bookstore, the city's most important outlet for architectural books, after they agreed to move their store from nearby Prairie Avenue. Soon the price for raw space had risen to $40 a square foot, and Weese started making money.

The Donahue and Transportation buildings were by no means the end. Weese next convinced his partners, now called the South Dearborn Renovation Associates, later Community Resource Corporation, to buy the fourteen-story Terminals Building because, he insisted, it was a bargain. Once that was done, as John Baird later told the story, "We told him to stop for a while. No more." But Weese had already gotten enthusiastic about the eight-story Rowe Building. "Harry, don't do it," Baird recalls telling him in 1976. "I already have," Weese replied. He took one floor of the building and convinced a number of friends and fellow architects to take other floors. In the end Weese, his partners, and their allies controlled virtually the entire frontage of Dearborn Street from the station at Polk Street to Congress Street.

By the mid-1980s the district had become a solid success, with hundreds of apartment and condominium units and a group of thriving businesses. A lot of people made money on South Dearborn Street, including some of Weese's business associates and some of the people who bought raw space at extremely low rates in the earliest years of the development. Weese himself made over one million dollars on Printers Row, according to the later recollection of George Vrechek, who helped manage Weese's firm and

Street. He put $20,000 down toward the $150,000 purchase price. Larry Booth agreed to put in $5,000 because, as Booth later recalled, "Harry told me his wife, Kitty, would kill him if he bought it alone."

It was not clear exactly what Weese originally intended to do with the Donahue Building. He later told George Vrechek, who managed the firm's finances for many years, that he thought that the Chicago Transit Authority (CTA) was going to buy the property for a bus turnaround. But it soon became clear that the CTA was not going to do that. Weese eventually decided that he would convert the building to residential use. That decision raised many issues. Unlike the Transportation Building, which was tall and narrow, and therefore ideal for residential conversion, the Donahue had a big floor plate. It was burdened by substantial back taxes and had a leaking roof and obsolete boiler. Worse yet, a key piece of land under the middle of the building had been rented on a ninety-nine-year lease and was controlled by a bank in California. Even if all of these problems could be overcome, the city code at the time forbade the use of personal finances. Printers Row vindicated Weese's belief that Chicago could revitalize a derelict district and turn its underused architectural heritage into a vibrant new community. It provided a beacon of hope in a city that was struggling to keep afloat in turbulent economic times.

A SLOW FADE

By the middle of the 1970s many outside observers probably thought the Weese office had hit its stride and everything was working admirably. By then the firm had a staff of 140 with offices in Chicago, Washington, and Miami. It handled a large amount of work, most of it with a very high level of design. All of this was done without any of the elaborate organization and hierarchy that characterized other large firms, such as Skidmore, Owings & Merrill. Instead the organization of the firm remained informal, and it continued to depend to a great extent on Weese himself. As Jack Hartray later put it, "It all worked because he controlled the process in a positive, energetic, but congenial manner. His charismatic nature flowed into the sketches—a kind of raw talent, alive with ideas. He was endlessly restless; always shifting ahead to a new idea for a new client; and leaving a huge amount of the work to be done by others."

Beneath the surface there were problems, however. Ben Weese recalls feeling that there was just too much work in the office and that in the rush to the next project the architects were starting to cut corners and neglect clients. Harry himself seemed to be increasingly erratic, distracted from the work at hand by personal matters and unable to maintain the kind of concentration he had demonstrated earlier. He failed to prepare adequately for meetings and even insulted potential clients on job interviews. Members of the firm remember a number of commissions that should have come their way but were sabotaged by gratuitous comments by Weese. Moreover, some damaging rivalry cropped up between the head of the firm and younger designers.

A big part of the problem was related to alcohol. Drinking, which early on seemed to help Weese overcome shyness, sparkle in social settings, and lubricate his creative processes, soon became a crutch. He felt that he needed it to deal with clients and to maintain his creativity. Lunch at Ricardo's, which had always included a cocktail, soon became the effective end of the business day for him. After lunch he would often retire to his private loft space above the fifth floor to take a nap and draw, finally leaving the office for home by 4:00 or 4:30. Of course, in this period,

Weese, who usually arrived at the office by 6:00 in the morning, had already put in a full day's work.

None of the problems in the office were immediately apparent to outsiders. Drinking, including heavy drinking, was considered part of the routine for many of the most successful architects of the era, and it was not something most people were willing to discuss as long as it remained under control. However, by the middle of the 1970s it had become a definite issue within the firm.

There was also the long-standing problem of organization and succession at the firm. In the mid-1970s Weese decided he needed to create a different structure for the company, one that would allow more participation in decision making and profits and that would allow the firm to continue on after his eventual retirement. He devised a scheme whereby some of the senior members of the firm, notably his brother Ben and Jack Hartray, could buy into it. This had the great advantage of providing Weese with much-needed cash for his own personal activities, but it didn't actually result in much sharing of leadership because he was never willing to relinquish his majority position.

As soon as other members of the firm came to have a direct stake in its profitability, they became more worried than ever about many of the financial decisions Weese was making, particularly those related to real estate. Over the years some of his investments had paid off handsomely. His real estate activities along Printers Row and in Aspen were lucrative. Others did not turn out as well. Although his instincts were often sound, he had a tendency to buy before the market was ready. When he was using his personal money, it was mostly Kitty who worried. But because his personal finances and those of the firm were so tightly connected, when he gave other members of the firm an equity position, they too became concerned. Most of his senior architects were interested in practicing architecture and were uneasy about real estate speculation.

When it became clear to everyone that there were no solutions in sight for these internal problems, an exodus of some of the most talented members of the staff began. The first to depart was Jack Hartray, in 1976. He went on to play a significant role in association with Larry Booth and his partner Jim Nagle. The next significant departure was Ben Weese, in 1977. As he later recalled, he left because of business problems, the lack of a realistic succession plan, and the personality changes in his brother. Ben started his own firm, Weese Seegers Hickey Weese, with his wife, Cynthia, and two former employees of Harry Weese & Associates, Tom Hickey and Arnie Seegers. Between 1977 and 1983 a number of other key employees would also depart.

With the departure of so many important figures, there was a pressing need for a further reorganization of the office. Perhaps the most significant step was the hiring of George Vrechek in 1977. Vrechek, who had been an accountant with Arthur Andersen and had been auditing the firm's books for several years, came aboard to run the financial side of the business. In 1978 Stanley Allan took over the presidency of the firm.

Surprisingly, given the length of service of some who left, the departures were, for the most part, amicable. During these years, Weese usually maintained the good humor and gracious demeanor that had made him such a charming personality in the office. He was willing to have his brother take clients with him to start his own office, for example. And although the loss of so many seasoned staff members had a significant downside in the long term, in the short term it was merely the latest chapter in a long story in which Weese could always count on some of the brightest young talents in the architectural world to knock his door, spend a few years there, and then leave to start their own office or move elsewhere. He spoke about the relief he felt of being unchallenged at the helm again and surrounded by mostly young employees "because they're more easily influenced, hopeful, appreciative."

Kathryn Quinn, who worked in the office from 1977 to 1979, was one of those young people. She later remembered the office as a gathering of fun-loving individuals. In her opinion, the Weese office attracted a specific kind of architect, one who was comfortable with a high degree of informality and experimentation and one who was interested in both hard work and hard play. She was surprised to be invited, despite her lowly status in the office, to the legendary lunches at Ricardo's with Weese and project managers, and she enjoyed the camaraderie of the office softball games and the rally that followed at the Twin Anchors pub near Weese's home in Old Town. Weese, already in his sixties, took an active part in these activities, managing during one outing to tear a bicep while playing softball. This view of the firm as an informal, highly creative place was clearly a major reason why it was selected for the American Institute of Architects Firm of the Year Award for 1978, one of the most significant honors available to architects in the United States.

Important work continued in the late 1970s and early 1980s. There was the Thomas Roberts House in DeKalb, Illinois, 1976, with its almost Japanese-looking timber framing and stucco-covered infill panels; the low-lying but expansive First National Bank in Albuquerque, 1976; the extensive urban renewal scheme and new municipal

building in Middletown, Ohio, 1976; the tall, very thin 1100 Lake Shore Drive apartment building in Chicago, 1979; the ground-hugging corporate headquarters for Union Underwear on a large open site southeast of Bowling Green, Kentucky 1980 (see entry); the gleaming white office tower at 200 South Wacker Drive in Chicago with the adjacent Quincy Park along the Chicago River, 1981 (see entry); the remodeling of a distillery building into offices for the Brown-Forman company in Louisville (see entry); the United States Embassy Housing in Tokyo with its striking white stucco panels and black neoprene joints, 1982 (see entry); and the Miami-Dade County Transit System, 1984 (see entry). During these years work from the office continued to surprise by its novelty. Where most observers might have expected a high-tech solution for the Frederick E. Terman Engineering Center at Stanford University, 1978 (see entry), for example, Weese instead turned in exactly the opposite direction, proposing a building of heavy-timber construction with stuccoed infill panels and windows with big movable shutters like barn doors. The result was surprisingly sympathetic to the earlier buildings on the campus and provided a warmer and more welcoming environment than many of the postwar buildings on the campus.

Not every commission turned out as well. One of the ironies of the AIA Firm of the Year Award was that it came one year after what was, by many people's estimation, the most unfortunate project ever undertaken by the firm, the commission that eventually became the Marriott Hotel on Michigan Avenue. The site was a prime lot occupied by the Diana Court (Michigan Square) Building, ironically the building that had housed Baldwin Kingrey and where Weese had started his practice. With its spectacular central court and fountain by Carl Milles, this building, designed in the 1920s by the well-known firm of Holabird & Root, was one of the most elegant and beloved structures in Chicago. The original design had included a base and a tall tower, but by the time of the stock market crash in 1929, only the base had been completed. Given that the foundations and structure were built to accommodate a much taller structure and that the North Michigan Avenue corridor had boomed in the postwar decades, it seemed like a golden opportunity to redevelop the site at a much higher density.

At first there was optimism that the architects could devise a scheme to preserve the old building and create a new structure on top. When it became clear that this wasn't going to work, there was still the possibility of saving the most important interior feature of the old building, the Diana Court. However, when the Marriott Corporation took over the project, it brought in its own architects, who

Civic Center, Middletown, Ohio, 1979. Hedrich-Blessing photograph, HB40831-C2, Chicago History Museum.

pushed to do something much closer to the usual Marriott formula. Although the Marriott people eventually came back to Harry Weese & Associates, by this time the program was pretty well set, and although the steel skeleton of the old building was re-used, the idea of saving even the court had disappeared. As Weese told Rick Kogan, who wrote a major story on the architect for the February 18-19, 1978, issue of the *Chicago Daily News' Panorama* magazine, "I had an uneasy feeling about working on what had been Diana Court, and once I got involved it was quite a struggle. It's very hard to control a very successful hotel chain. I wanted to set the monster back a little so it wouldn't obliterate the sky. That was done." However, that

still left a bulky, unrelieved slab. Weese hoped he could at least soften it by painting the structure in two colors. But even this was eliminated. "No go. Gargantua prevailed," as he put it. In an August 1989 television interview with John Callaway, he described the resulting building as "something of a dog."

Two of the most interesting projects of the early 1980s were unbuilt schemes. The first was a design submitted in a 1980 competition for a library in Anchorage, Alaska. It involved a structure that would not rest on the ground but instead would float free in a pond so that it would be isolated from the shocks of earthquakes and could turn toward the sun, maximizing precious daylight hours during

Perspective rendering of
Marriott Hotel on Michigan
Avenue, Chicago, ca. 1977.
From firm, brochure.

the long, dark winters. This scheme earned a place among the five finalists.

The second, a series of designs for super-high buildings, represents one of the oddest twists in the entire Harry Weese story. Weese rarely had a good word to say about really tall buildings. Although he designed some higher buildings in his career, this didn't happen often, and he once stated that he would never live or work in one. Seventeen stories was his limit, he proclaimed. Never one to tie himself down by consistency, this same Harry Weese in the 1960s wrote a note to his colleague and friend, the architect Minoru Yamasaki, designer of the World Trade Center Towers, praising his designs for their technical and design competence. "If we must go one hundred stories high, this is the way to go!" he wrote.

So perhaps it was not really surprising that in the early 1980s he collaborated with Charles H. Thornton from the engineering office of Lev Zetlin in New York on schemes for structures that twisted as they went up, allowing them to resist wind loads internally in a way that was analogous to the system seen in tall television towers that are held in place by exterior guy wires. He went public with some designs for a 210-story building, almost twice as tall as any building then standing. One of these schemes involved seven segments, each 30 stories high, separated from the next segment by an open trussed section that would allow the wind to pass through. It was to have a 2,400-room hotel, its own sewage treatment plant, a mental hospital, 800 condominiums, and several restaurants and would sit on an elevated railroad line. The building was never built, but for a few years Weese was deeply involved in promoting very high structures, and the model for one of these projects hung in the atrium in his office for years afterward.

The most conspicuous of all the planning schemes of the late 1970s and early 1980s was one for the completion of the Federal Triangle in Washington, D.C. The Federal Triangle had been designed as a grand, coordinated classical ensemble south of Pennsylvania Avenue between the Capitol and the White House. By the end of the 1920s the majority of the complex had been built to the designs of some of the country's most accomplished architects. However, money had run out before some parts had been completed, notably the parts that would have required demolition of a group of important earlier buildings on the site. The result was an incomplete scheme, some large vacant lots used for surface parking, and several buildings with temporary and unsightly brick walls that no one had intended to remain in place for long.

By the late 1970s, when the federal government was finally ready to complete the triangle, tastes had changed. The classical style of the 1920s buildings was widely considered old-fashioned, and there was a new interest in historic preservation and a mounting resistance to demolishing the earlier buildings on the site in order to complete the 1920s scheme. This created a considerable planning challenge: how to finish the complex so that it not only created continuity with the classical buildings of the 1920s but somehow integrated the earlier buildings as well. The General Services Administration (GSA) launched a competition. In 1978 Harry Weese & Associates was one of three firms invited to submit a design for the second round of the competition. In 1979 the GSA declared the Weese office design the winner. After several further rounds of revisions, the final scheme by the GSA and the Weese office was announced in 1983. It proposed the construction of two large buildings to fill in the missing pieces of the design as well as the finishing off of all the truncated wings in the classical style. What was most striking about the design was its deference to the 1920s plan and to the classical architectural style of that era at a time when these buildings were still unpopular.

Winning the Federal Triangle competition ought to have been a cause for celebration at Harry Weese & Associates. Instead it was a hollow victory at best. Within the Washington office, where the design was largely developed, there had been disagreements from the beginning about the direction of the design. As usual, several members of the office worked up proposals. In ordinary circumstances, eventually one would be chosen and the office would throw its energy behind developing that proposal. However,

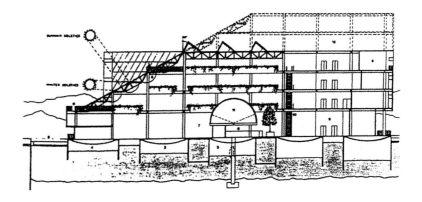

Section of Anchorage Library competition project, 1981. *Chicago History Museum.*

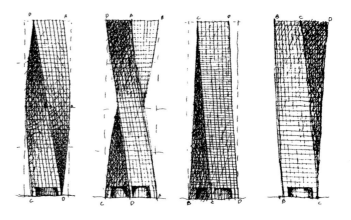

Elevation studies for super-high building, 1982. *From Inland Architect, January/ February, 1982.*

because Weese rarely visited the Washington office, the staff there, led by Jerry Karn, had worked pretty much on their own initial scheme which was the one submitted to the GSA. Weese was apparently never happy with the direction the design was taking. He considered it Karn's scheme and worked up his own plan—a massive single block bisected by a diagonal and perforated with three circular courtyards. In the meantime, in Washington, the approvals process was going forward on the scheme prepared by the Washington office. To everyone's astonishment, after all the approvals were in place and the Washington office's scheme was pronounced the winner on national television, a letter signed by Harry Weese appeared in the *Washington Post* on May 1, 1983, stating that the master plan attributed to the Weese office was not, in fact, the plan preferred by Harry Weese

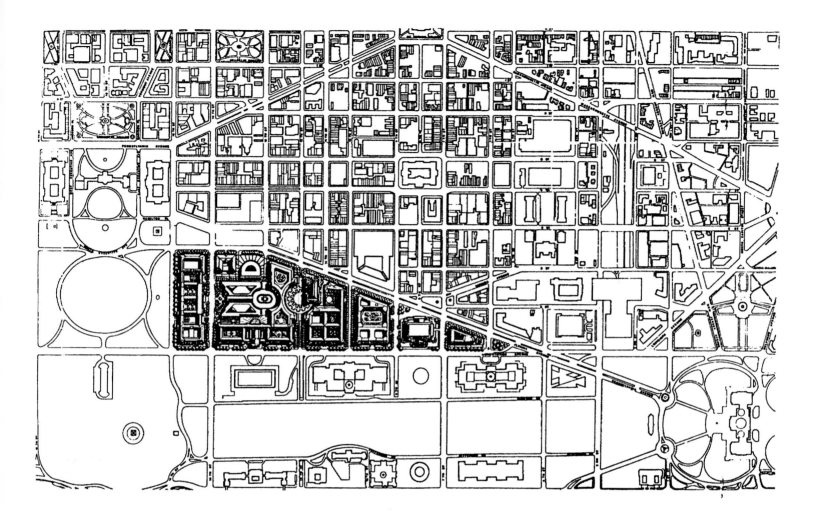

Site plan for Federal Triangle final scheme, Washington, D.C., 1982. From *The Master Plan for the Federal Triangle*, 1982.

& Associates. Although the Weese firm did no further work on the Federal Triangle, the master plan by the Weese office marked an important step in the rehabilitation of the reputation of the original plan for the Federal Triangle, and it probably better embodied Weese's preservation ideals than the architect's own scheme.

As the 1970s gave way to the 1980s, Weese shifted more and more of his energy away from architectural work into public campaigns of one kind or another. In part this was a way for him to avoid dealing with institutional clients and committees, a process he found to be more and more disagreeable. In part it reflected his desire to follow in the footsteps of Daniel Burnham and to move from architecture and single buildings to planning, public policy, and the city as a whole. Where earlier in his career he wrote an occasional letter to a public official or the editor of a newspaper, during the late 1970s the volume of his writing, whether in letters or editorials, grew dramatically. He found some new targets to attack, and he

was buoyed by the prospect of some very large-scale new projects, among them an idea to create a new Burnham plan for Chicago.

From the late 1970s through the mid-1980s, Weese would generate new ideas faster than anyone could assimilate them. It is a little difficult to know how to characterize these ideas. He was certainly no longer the young, radical idealist of his college days. Although he once stated that he was really an anarchist, in fact an acquaintance of many years was probably closer to the mark when he described Weese as a conservative with a liberal vocabulary. In a speech for the series Bright New Cities in 1976, he started with an homage to Daniel Burnham and then unleashed a barrage of new proposals. He suggested raising Lake Shore Drive to the level of Buckingham Foundation to allow pedestrians access to the lakefront under the road and to allow for the development of commercial establishments below the level of the roadway. The stores would be hidden from the main part of the park but would animate

looking west thru
the NAVY pier at civm

Hv 77

ferris
wheel

Perspective drawing of
scheme for Navy Pier,
Chicago, 1977.

the entire area by drawing people all the way to the water's edge. He also called for the revitalization of Navy Pier and for the remaking of Wabash Street—repaving it, roofing it over with glass, and making it pedestrian-only every day from noon until midnight. This would, he said, create a great public arcade at the center of the Loop.

In his 1978 interview with Rick Kogan of the *Chicago Daily News*, he talked about planting the city's alleys with grass and trees, creating urban wildlife sanctuaries, flooding the Midway Plaisance, constructing low-rise apartments on Goose Island, boarding up the existing McCormick Place and building a new underground convention center west of the Loop, preserving the Cabrini-Green Housing project but making it more humane, and creating for Chinatown, oddly enough, a small Mt. Fuji. He also revived his islands-in-the-lake idea but now proposed that they run from Wilmette in the north to the Indiana state line. The scale of these projects suggested that the example of Daniel Burnham was increasingly on his mind. He told Kogan

that in the next two years he would write a book called "*Burnham Revisited.*"

During the late 1980s he also spent a great deal of time thinking about one of his favorite hobbies, sailing, and pushing a plan for a floating marina north of Navy Pier. He had long been an advocate for retaining Navy Pier and remodeling it as a place for recreation, and it was in no small part through his efforts that the complex was put on the National Register of Historic Places in 1979. He was, however, not pleased when he saw some of the plans the city drew up for the Pier in the early 1980s. He argued for having a big private developer, such as Walt Disney, Great America, Marriott, or James Rouse, come in and create an urban amusement park, complete with a great Ferris wheel and streetcars that would extend out to the end of the pier. For the marina he organized a not-for-profit corporation that, he proposed, would build the marina and lease it out just long enough to recover the costs. Then, according to his plan, ownership would revert to the city. Weese drew up the plans, found the investors, and was convinced that the city was on board with his scheme, which, he argued, would create a valuable public facility at no cost to taxpayers. He even spent $100,000 of his own money to build some floating docks as an example. However, after he floated them in place and tied them to Navy Pier, the city told him that not only was it not prepared to approve his plan, but he would have to remove the docks.

Weese also continued his preservation activities. Most dramatic was his bid to save the Loop elevated system. Many city leaders had long considered the elevated track circling the Loop to be obsolete and a blighting factor for the streets over which it ran. They proposed the construction of a new subway that would replace the elevated structure, allowing them to demolish it. There were a great many advocates for the new subway but also many opponents, who argued that the $4 billion it would cost could be better spent elsewhere. Into this battle stepped Weese, who agreed with the critics that the money could be better spent elsewhere—for example, on a new riverbank line along the existing right-of-way from the Merchandise Mart to Midway Airport or a new lakefront line. He also advanced an argument that took a great many people by surprise. "Let's Spare Chicago's splendid L" was the heading for an opinion piece by Weese in the August 27, 1978, edition of the *Chicago Tribune*. In this essay Weese argued that the elevated track was not a blighting factor but rather an historic structure, much like the cable car system in San Francisco. He argued that if properly cleaned, repaired, and outfitted with welded rails and new cars with divided axles and sound-absorbent rubber-mounted car bodies, the elevated system could be a great asset for the city and a tourist attraction.

He then moved to put the structure on the National Register, a step that left many observers sputtering with anger. In the end Weese failed in that bid, but so did the backers of the subway system, so the elevated structure has remained. It is not clear how much of this was due to Weese's actions and how much to simple economics, but it is fair to say that Weese's intervention played a big role in enlarging Chicagoans' conception of historic preservation and their appreciation of the "L." Weese used a similar tactic to try to stop demolition of Soldier Field, the grand stadium built immediately after World War I to plans by architects Holabird & Roche. Even though Weese agreed that Soldier Field usurped prime parkland along the lakefront and should not have been built there in the first place, he argued that since it was there and since it was such an important monument, it should be retained. In the end, Weese won that battle, although some people would say he

ultimately lost the war because although the stadium was saved, it was topped by a huge glassy addition constructed 2001–03.

In the late 1970s, Weese finally found the powerful ally in City Hall that he had not had while Richard J. Daley or his successor, Michael Bilandic, was mayor. Even before Jane Byrne was unexpectedly elected mayor in 1979, Weese had served as her most important informal consultant on matters of architecture and urban design. This continued after Byrne was elected. She came to Weese's office every other Monday morning to attend a meeting hosted by Weese and city architect Joe Fitzgerald. It was a heady moment for Weese, but it did not last long. Soon Byrne was turning to other advisors, and despite his ceaseless activity and the occasional victory, Weese felt even more marginalized than before. In a story on Weese in the *Chicago Daily News' Panorama* magazine in 1978, journalist Rick Kogan observed that Weese was aware that he had not changed the face of Chicago the way some of his colleagues in the large architectural firms had. Kogan added that Weese was starting to become resigned to the fact that he might not get the chance. "I'm a man 10 years ahead of his time that never comes," he quoted Weese as saying. Weese added in a tone that was new for him, "Most of my friends are tycoons but they won't touch me with a 10-foot pole."

For a while Weese could take consolation in the fact that he seemed to be making progress on his largest and most important civic undertaking. Nothing in his career engaged Weese more than the proposed Chicago world's fair of 1992. He must have felt that he had been preparing for this event all his life. He had been throwing out ideas and making plans for various parts of the city since the 1940s. The world's fair seemed to be the logical next step for him, as the 1893 fair had been for Daniel Burnham, a step that would allow Weese to move beyond his architectural practice into a much larger role as planner and civic leader and to reshape his city.

Weese had been doing designs for a 1992 fair since at least the mid-1970s. He eventually convinced a core group of people, including Harvey Kapnick, John Baird, and Marshall Bennett, to join in the effort. It wasn't so much the fair itself that excited him and his colleagues, but the prospect of using the fair to create some massive improvements in Chicago's built environment, particularly the creation of some basic new infrastructure and an upgrading of the central lakefront. From the beginning, Weese had the idea of a fair that would be centered on Grant Park and Daniel Burnham's great east-west axis along Congress Street. It was to be the catalyst for a major remaking of

Chicago's central area, a remaking heavily based on the old Burnham Plan.

In a piece he wrote for the April 1980 issue of *Inland Architect* titled "Beyond Burnham," he laid out a thirteen-point program for revitalizing the city by completing the Burnham Plan. In the article he called for

> Creating islands in the lake to form nine new lagoons for boating,
>
> Realigning Columbus Avenue and the Outer Drive to create a one-way pair and raising the Outer Drive to create a commercial arcade under it,
>
> Building a conference center at the Coast Guard station on the north side of the Grant Park yacht harbor to match the aquarium and planetarium to the south,
>
> Creating a polder northeast of the filtration plant and southeast of Meigs Field to serve as the location of the major buildings of the 1992 world's fair
>
> Restoring Soldier Field,
>
> Expanding McCormick Place by the elimination of the Arie Crown Theater and the extension of glass to the outer edge of the structure,
>
> Linking all lakefront projects with transit,
>
> Building a new port of Chicago at Iroquois Landing at the mouth of Lake Calumet,
>
> Revitalizing the inner-city parks and recreation areas,
>
> Building a crosstown transit/highway corridor extending from the Edens Expressway on the north to I-57 on the south,
>
> Creating new Riverfront and Lakefront transit lines,
>
> Completing the expansion of O'Hare airport, and
>
> Remaking and colonizing the Chicago River with riverbank neighborhoods.

Over the next few years Weese worked tirelessly on his plans for the fair. It kept him upbeat during a time of increasing challenges.

One of these challenges involved some major changes in the world of architecture. The modern movement, which had been the major force in most schools of architecture across the country in the postwar decades, was coming under attack from younger architects who saw the aging leaders of the movement as excessively narrow and puritanical in their ideas. The change in architectural climate was clearly evident at two architectural exhibitions held in Chicago in 1976. One of these, called "100 Years of Architecture in Chicago," followed what had become, through the works of historians like Sigfried Giedion and Carl Condit, the canonical history of Chicago architecture. It traced a straight line from architects like Burnham & Root and Louis Sullivan of the so-called Chicago School to European avant-garde architects like Mies van der Rohe, and from there to his Chicago followers, notably Bruce Graham and Myron Goldsmith of Skidmore, Owings & Merrill and Jacques Brownson of C. F. Murphy. In fact, these Chicago followers of Mies were often collectively grouped together under the label "Second Chicago School." The catalog suggested that the main theme in Chicago architecture was the creation of a structurally rational, gridlike architecture stripped of all historical references or romantic illusions. This show included three buildings by the Weese firm, not surprisingly with the Miesian Time-Life Building most prominent.

The other exhibition, called simply "Chicago Architects," was organized by Laurence Booth, Stuart Cohen, Stanley Tigerman, and Ben Weese and presented a different view of the history of Chicago architecture. It traced a much more complex story, one that included, in the late nineteenth and early twentieth centuries, not just supposed precursors to mid-twentieth-century modernism like Louis Sullivan but also more conservative architects such as Howard Van Doren Shaw. It also focused on American-born pioneers of modernism such as Dwight Perkins, Barry Byrne, and the Keck brothers. The show juxtaposed these earlier architects with contemporary designers, such as Bertrand Goldberg, Walter Netsch, and Harry Weese, who were clearly somewhat peripheral to the mainstream of Chicago history as seen in the "canonical" show. In the catalog for "Chicago Architects," Weese's First Baptist Church of Columbus was given a full-page photograph opposite a steeply gabled brick and shingled early house by Frank Lloyd Wright in Oak Park, suggesting a tradition of architecture that was as much an integral part of the Chicago legacy as the gridlike steel and glass structures of the buildings by Skidmore, Owings & Merrill.

In fact, this show tapped into a much wider movement in the world of architecture away from the orthodox core of modernism, with its emphasis on function and structure as the prime generators of architectural form and toward a renewed interest in history and the symbolic content of architecture. In many ways it would have been logical for Harry Weese to welcome and join this movement. He could have seen it as an indication that the world of architecture was finally catching up with ideas that he had long been espousing. However, as it happened, many of the most zealous promoters of the new movement, which they called "postmodernism," pushed their ideas much farther than modern architects like Harry Weese were willing to go. In its most strident form, advocates of postmodernism turned their back on modernism altogether, denouncing many of the most revered modernist works as boring and inattentive to their surroundings. In their eagerness to recover what they considered to be the larger expressive and symbolic role of architecture in society, the more strident members of the group even renounced the notion that program, structure, and problem-solving lay at the heart of architectural practice.

In retrospect, it is hard to imagine why someone like Harry Weese would have reacted so negatively since he agreed with many of the goals of the postmodernists, and he himself was rarely the object of attacks. Nevertheless, as the years went on, his bemused reaction at the beginning turned to real anger. In part, his reaction reflected a generational split. In many ways, what younger architects were doing was simply a continuation of the spirit of revolt that the modernists had initiated when they were doing battle with the elder statesmen of the Beaux-Arts system before them. But the modernists never expected to find themselves the target of attack, and when it happened many of them were outraged. Another factor in Weese's reaction was personality. Because of their courting of the media and propensity toward the cutting quip, prominent spokesmen for the new trends, such as Philip Johnson in New York and Stanley Tigerman in Chicago, tended to inspire extreme reactions.

There were also more basic reasons for the negative reactions of Weese and other modernists. As personal and whimsical as Weese ever got, he still believed deeply in the modernist project, that architecture was about solving human problems and that it had to be based on rational analysis. He objected violently to decisions that he felt were purely arbitrary. For Weese, as for many modernist architects, the postmodernists were making a mockery of his most deeply held beliefs. The alienation Weese felt from much of what was happening around him contributed to a sense that, despite the great critical success of many of his projects and the enormous triumph of the Washington subway, he had not had the opportunity to create personal masterpieces that could be measured against the most important buildings of men like Frank Lloyd Wright and Le Corbusier and his great mentor, Alvar Aalto. "I'm not terribly optimistic about the future," Weese admitted in *Inland Architect* in 1980, and despite the smile and self-deprecating comments he would continue to make, his writings took on an increasingly strident tone.

One thing that Weese did in the 1980s that garnered almost universal praise was his rescue of *Inland Architect*. That magazine had been the publication of record for Chicago architecture from 1883 to 1908, providing splendid coverage of the city's great architects at the turn of the twentieth century. It was revived by the Chicago chapter of the AIA in 1957 when the newsletter it was publishing under Weese's leadership became so substantial that the organization decided to expand it and rename it *Inland Architect*. For many years the magazine played a major role in Chicago, but it was constantly in a perilous existence, always in need of cash.

Weese had been involved more or less continuously, but over the years his role escalated as the magazine faced crisis after crisis. He became a board member, and then in 1973 took over from William E. Dunlap of Skidmore, Owings & Merrill as president of the Inland Architecture Corporation. In this capacity he helped to pull the magazine back from extinction by working with journalists Nory Miller and M. W. Newman on a new business plan, one that relied heavily on the loan of key personnel from his own office and from the firm of Holabird & Root. By the end of 1977, when Miller left to take over a national magazine, it became clear that the magazine was in deep financial trouble. At that point Weese stepped in once again, this time forming a new nonprofit organization, Inland Architect Press, and becoming publisher of the magazine. From that date until 1990 he subsidized it to the tune of $40,000 to $50,000 a year. At first Judith Kiriazis from his own office served as editor. After about two years her place was taken briefly by William Marlin. Finally, in 1983, Weese hired Cynthia Davidson, who would run the magazine through most of the 1980s. At the same time, Weese's daughter Shirley came aboard to redesign the magazine and work on laying out the issues. During this period *Inland* was produced in the Weese offices, in the back room of the fifth floor.

One of the major features added during the 1980s was a column called "Publisher's Notebook." This was Davidson's way of giving Weese a voice but preserving her own editorial authority over the rest of the magazine. Through much of the 1980s Weese used his "Publisher's Notebook" as a bully pulpit to criticize and praise and propose one major civic scheme after another. However, at the same time he agreed, at least in principle, to let the editor publish whatever she thought was most important, including buildings by quite a few architects whose work he thoroughly disliked. During the eight years of Davidson's leadership the magazine became one of the country's most vital architectural publications. Finally, however, as Weese's health declined, his participation in the magazine lessened. His writing stopped in 1989; in 1990 he stopped supporting the magazine financially and his name disappeared from the masthead; in 1994 the magazine was sold and its key role in the Chicago architectural world effectively ended. According to Davidson, speaking at the Weese memorial service in 1998, "Harry was not the sole individual responsible for Inland Architect and its survival, but he was its primary watchdog, its primary benefactor and its primary believer."

One event of the early 1980s that proved to be highly satisfying personally to Weese was his role in the jury that selected Maya Lin as the winner of the Vietnam Veterans Memorial competition. After this competition was announced in 1980, over a thousand entries poured in. The jury was a distinguished group including, in addition to Weese, architect Pietro Belluschi, landscape architects Hideo Sasaki and Garrett Eckbo, sculptors Richard Hunt, James Rosati, and Constantino Nivola, and journalist Grady Clay. Each time the jury debated, it would eliminate some entries. As it did this, the professional staff would gather the schemes that were rejected and put them behind a new line on the floor of the airline hangar at Andrews Air Force Base, where the jury was meeting. This made it clear which entries were still being actively considered and indicated graphically how far each rejected entry was from serious contention. Characteristically, Weese was never quite satisfied with the consensus that had been reached and would frequently go back to look at the rejected entries. One day after lunch, when he reached number 1026, far in the back of the room, he stopped and decided that the imprecise but highly evocative renderings of the proposal made it the most intriguing and poetic entry of the entire lot. He exercised his right to bring it back for consideration, and after considerable debate and persuasion by Weese, the jury unanimously chose it as the winner of the competition. When the drawings were made public and the creator turned out to be a Chinese-American student at Yale, there was some consternation about the choice, and a major battle broke out when some Vietnam veterans reacted negatively to the design. Throughout the debate that followed, Weese was a staunch supporter of Maya Lin. The controversies have since receded and most people have accepted the Vietnam Veterans Memorial as one of the most successful pieces of public art in our time.

In the early 1980s Weese again turned his attention to real estate, this time to a very conspicuous tract called Wolf Point, just west of the place where the main branch of the Chicago River splits into the North and South branches. For this land he proposed Wolf Point Landings, a highly ambitious mixed-use project (see entry). He probably imagined this as the capstone to his real estate career. However, it did not work out that way. Although the land was in a prime location, and although the plan was ingenious, a combination of bad timing and bad judgment eventually turned the project into a financial disaster. Only two parts were actually built. One was Harbor House, a renovated cold-storage warehouse. The other, perhaps the last project on which Weese did most of the actual design work, was a set of four "River Cottages," elaborate multilevel residences with boat docks attached. He reserved one of these for himself. Given his decades-long crusade for elegant living in the city center and his passion for boats, it would have been a dream house. But by this time the entire project had become a financial albatross; his health was failing; and Kitty was adamantly opposed. Weese never occupied the house.

After the high expectations of the 1950s and 1960s, the triumphs and optimism of the 1970s, the 1980s brought only a few major achievements and many reversals. Certainly business in the office was good, fueled by the dependable and highly lucrative government contracts for transportation projects. In fact, at least during the 1980s, it seemed that the less involved Weese became with the office, the more profitable it became. By the mid-1980s it had reached its maximum geographic reach and complexity, with some forty people in the Chicago office and another eighty-five in branches located in Washington, Miami, Los Angeles, Dallas, and Singapore. However, coordinating work in the offices presented difficulties. Weese had always been reluctant to have such a large office and branches, and he largely left management of them to other people, notably to Stanley Allan. This was a problem because Weese was the major factor in getting new work. After projects in these offices were finished, and new work did not appear on the horizon, they were all eventually closed.

In the meantime, the Washington office was the scene of a major blow-up in what had once been a close-knit Weese organization. This event, often described by former employees as a "mutiny," resulted in part from the long-simmering discontent between Weese and Jerry Karn, the head of the Washington office, over the Federal Triangle project. The trouble finally boiled over in March 1983 with disagreements over designs for the renovation of the Evening Star Building on Pennsylvania Avenue. Karn announced that he was not going to follow a directive from Weese and change a design largely worked up in the Washington office and approved by the client. Instead he announced he was going on vacation. When Weese fired Karn, an entire group of Weese employees defected and founded their own firm, Karn Charuhas Chapman & Twohey (KCCT), and they took with them some Weese projects. At one point when the Washington Metro contract was up for renewal, the newly created firm even came close to taking over that very lucrative commission.

By the middle of the 1980s, mounting health problems meant that Weese was less and less able to play the key role in the office that he had in previous decades. The family became concerned enough with his drinking that it staged a series of interventions. Weese would spend some time in a facility, but once out he would inevitably start drinking again. In addition to the drinking, he started to experience small strokes. At client meetings he would sometimes stop short in the middle of a sentence and become disoriented. He was no longer able to draw as he had in the past. He continued to go to work, and he still played some role in the life of the firm, but he became increasingly isolated in his office on the fifth floor while the staff worked on the floors below.

For a while he also continued to play an active role in civic affairs. In fact, the number of articles and letters grew steadily during the early part of the 1980s. A list prepared by his office noted one letter to the editor in the 1960s, sixteen in the 1970s, and twenty-eight in the first half of the 1980s. There were two kinds of letters. The first was in spirit of the earlier Weese, full of optimism and brimming with plans for the future, particularly for the world's fair of 1992. The second could be characterized as a letter of complaint. His tone became increasingly vitriolic in discussing fellow architects, particularly those like Helmut Jahn, or "Genghis Jahn" as Weese liked to dub him, who embraced the new postmodern style. Weese believed that the world had changed but he had not. "It is only natural that, being with the class of 1938, with all my colleagues retiring, . . . I'm beginning to feel halfway between a lost cause and a defender of the ark," he stated. What made it worse was that he recognized that his complaints weren't having a positive effect. "Sometimes I'm my own worst enemy," he admitted.

Worse was yet to come. Although in the early 1980s the fair moved decisively from the realm of mere proposal toward definite possibility when the Reagan administration approved Chicago's proposal and submitted it to the International Expositions body, Weese was soon disillusioned as the commission for planning the fair was given to Skidmore, Owings & Merrill, and few people in any position of power seemed willing to listen to him. Given his long interest and involvement in the fair, he almost certainly took this as a personal insult. Thomas Ayers, one of the civic leaders of the fair, made a public comment that Weese was too arrogant and inflexible, a comment that would have been almost unthinkable even a few years before. A former employee was quoted in the press as saying that Weese was an unrealistic dreamer. As far as the fair was concerned, none of this infighting made any difference in the long run because by 1985 the dream of fair was essentially dead. Its demise was devastating for Weese.

By the end of the 1980s Weese had ceased to be an active participant in the life of the city or the affairs of his own firm. This withdrawal was confirmed in 1992 when he officially retired and was bought out by a group of senior employees, including David Munson, George Vrechek, James Torvik, Norm Zimmerman, and John Corley. They changed the name from "Harry Weese & Associates" to "Harry Weese Associates." This move only made public what everyone with any firsthand knowledge about the firm already knew—that decision making and day-to-day operations had long since passed on to others.

Even without Harry Weese, the firm was still substantial with a highly skilled staff, and it continued getting work through the 1990s—for example, projects connected with transit and schools, especially new Catholic schools and renovations for the Chicago Public Schools. During the decade, the firm was also involved, either as architect or as associated architect, in a number of large-scale restoration projects, notably Buckingham Fountain in Chicago; Grand Central Station in New York; Union Station in Washington, D.C., which was restored for use as a train station and shopping mall after a disastrous previous redesign in the 1970s had turned it into a national visitors center; and a series of Mormon temples, including the temple in Salt Lake City, Utah. The firm won many awards for these restorations. It designed some new buildings as well—for example, a student union and student residence hall for Chicago State University and the Park Evanston Building in Evanston. However, without the charismatic Weese, it became increasingly difficult for the firm to obtain the kind of commissions that had contributed to its reputation in previous decades. Finally, in 2000 the curtain came down on Harry Weese Associates when the firm was absorbed by Gensler, a San Francisco–based design firm.

Perhaps not surprisingly, given how long the firm had been in operation, during the decade of the 1990s there was a noticeable rise in interest in the earlier history of the firm. The Chicago chapter of the AIA awarded the Seventeenth Church of Christ, Scientists its twenty-five-year award in 1996, and the First Baptist Church of Columbus became a National Historic Landmark in 2000. In 1992 the Chicago Architecture Foundation did an exhibition of Weese drawings, and in 1997 the Chicago Historical Society mounted an even larger exhibition to celebrate the fiftieth anniversary of the firm and to mark the donation of a large collection of office records and materials to the society in 1992.

None of this activity had much effect on Harry Weese himself. During these years he moved out of the family home into a hotel, then a series of nursing homes, before ending up in a Veterans Administration hospital in Manteno, in downstate Illinois. According to Lee Bey of the *Sun Times*, in his last years Weese no longer spoke very much and his memory had faded badly. On October 29, 1998, Harry Weese passed away. He was followed by his wife, Kitty, in 2005.

SOME CONCLUSIONS

Most critics and historians consider the work of Harry Weese and his office as part of an alternative to the "mainstream" of Chicago architecture in the postwar decades. This mainstream is usually described as the minimal modernism developed in Europe in the early twentieth century, brought to Chicago by Mies van der Rohe and elaborated and extended in the work of some of Chicago's largest architectural firms, notably Skidmore, Owings & Merrill and C. F. Murphy Associates. There is some truth to this characterization. Certainly Weese, along with Bertrand Goldberg, Walter Netsch, Edward Dart, and several others, represented a different architectural approach, one that was deeply rooted in a long Chicago tradition and inflected by other modernist traditions, for example, the modernism of Scandinavia.

However, it is possible that the very idea of a mainstream does more to obscure our understanding of figures like Harry Weese than it does to clarify. It is based on a particular notion of history in which one stylistic advance follows another in a logical progression as one age makes way for the next. From the classical mode of Greece and Rome to the Romanesque and Gothic of the Middle Ages to the Baroque and Rococo of the Early Modern period, each style makes its appearance in traditional architectural histories as the representation of its age.

Advocates of avant-garde European architecture in the 1920s tried to use this same idea to identify their own branch of modernism as the logical successor to the great styles of the past. Historians obligingly designated the work of the great modernists Walter Gropius, Le Corbusier, and Mies van der Rohe as the primary exemplars of this representative style. Off to the side, presumably flowing in minor peripheral channels or small eddies along the bank, were the other architects of the time, the ones who weren't part of the inevitable drive toward history's appointed destination. In this scheme of things, Harry Weese, like many of the men who most inspired him—

such as Gunnar Asplund and Alvar Aalto—and many of his most important friends and colleagues—notably Eero Saarinen, Ralph Rapson, Edward Larrabee Barnes, and I. M. Pei—have received only a fraction of the attention paid to the architects who supposedly defined the principal current of architectural modernism.

From a larger perspective, however, the entire mainstream notion is suspect. This view of history has rested on a narrowly conceived vision of architecture as a progression of the tendencies that were in favor among a small elite, including the richest, most powerful, or best-connected individuals of the era. If we look at the built environment as a whole, it becomes clear that although these elite movements had a place, they were rarely dominant. In most cases what they actually represented was a small part of the total architectural production of their day. The vast majority of what was built was instead the work of thousands of other designers, each bringing a different background and vision to his or her task and only occasionally working in what was supposed to be the dominant mode.

The work of Harry Weese was something relatively rare in the late twentieth century—an architecture that had wide appeal both to the architectural elite and to ordinary citizens. It probably had this appeal because it was experimental and innovative on the one hand, and intensely pragmatic and attentive to psychological and physical human comfort on the other. Weese had a profound suspicion of any great overarching theory of architecture. That made him willing to draw inspiration from a wide range of sources. Certainly one of these sources was a key modernist belief that the goal of the architect is to make a better society. However, Weese, unlike many of his contemporaries, never allowed himself to think that he, as an architect, could exactly define how that better society should work or look. He no more believed in a completely egalitarian and collectivist socialist utopia than he did in the notion that a single type of building would fit every citizen. To him the architect's role was more modest and at the same time more ambitious—to use his architectural expertise to help create a built environment where most citizens would be able to find buildings that suited them. He also, from the first, had a vision of buildings as part of a larger fabric set into a landscape. For that reason, he always considered himself as much a planner as an architect and, once the word came into common use, an environmentalist.

In many ways Harry Weese was profoundly conservative. He believed that most of the really important things in architecture had been discovered centuries ago. He had a profound respect for the classical tradition, for example. This showed up in the most obvious way in his designs for the Metro system, but it formed a foundation for much of his work. He also had a great interest in traditional building types. Unlike some of the modernists who wanted to start afresh and remake every building program, Weese was interested in all types of traditional building, from the theaters and opera houses of Baroque Europe to the grand vaults of Moscow's classical subway system. He rarely reproduced these prototypes directly. Nevertheless, his designs almost always derived from a long building tradition.

He was, moreover, partial to traditional building materials. Although he was quite willing to use new materials when they seemed appropriate, he was most at home with a relatively limited palette, which heavily favored the stuff out of which cities had been traditionally made. It is not surprising that brick showed up more often in his work than any other material. An ancient and elemental material, born of the earth itself, relatively inexpensive and durable, it had been used in cities for centuries and eased the task of inserting new construction into an older fabric. He also favored concrete for some of the same reasons. Like stone, concrete derives fairly directly from the earth and has a weight and solidity that convey strength and permanence. Sometimes in his work concrete was paired with brick to express a structural frame and an infill. Sometimes it was used alone, as at the Metropolitan Correctional Center and the Washington Metro, to achieve the kind of monumentality that in previous centuries had been possible using finely cut stone.

On the other hand, despite his interest in the millennial traditions of architecture, Weese also appreciated the work of the great modernist pioneers. With his Time-Life Building he came close to the aesthetic of Mies van der Rohe. But, as the architectural critic M. W. Newman observed in a perceptive review in the Chicago Sun-Times in November 1992, Weese tried to lighten and brighten the rigid geometries of Mies and his followers with gold-tinted windows and a greater interest in three-dimensional spatial play. Newman quoted an anonymous wit as saying, "Mies plus yeast equals Weese." In the church in Neenah, Wisconsin, and in many of the larger buildings of the 1970s—for example, the municipal building in Middletown, Ohio, and the South Lower Campus building at the University of Wisconsin at Madison—he was probably, at least in part, reacting to the grand sculptural compositions of Le Corbusier in his work after World War II. Another attitude he shared with Corbusier was his interest in the design of objects from the scale of the chair or lamp to the scale of the city as a whole. Although he didn't do much furniture design after his first years, and he was thwarted in most of his grand urban schemes, he never lost the desire to design at all scales.

Certainly the most important influence on Weese from the pioneers of European modernism was the tradition of the humanly scaled and naturally textured buildings of Nordic architects such as Alvar Aalto and Gunnar Asplund. From his first visit to Sweden in 1937 through the end of his career, this influence was always potent. It shows up most literally in many of the houses he designed and the Oak Park Village Hall, but the tendency toward simple natural materials and creature comfort appears throughout his work.

Then there was the way he responded to the great tradition of architecture in Chicago. Weese was profoundly impressed by the masters of Chicago architecture, particularly figures like Louis Sullivan. In some designs, this influence resulted in literal borrowings—for example, the three-part Chicago bay windows at 227 East Walton and the Fewkes Tower on Chestnut Street. In others, it was more the straightforward deployment of materials or deep respect for program and budget. In this attitude, despite the differences in their approaches, Weese's work has a great deal in common with the work of his contemporary native Chicagoans Bertrand Goldberg, Edward Dart, and Walter Netsch.

More than most architects of his day, Weese was profoundly affected by vernacular structures that many of his contemporaries didn't consider architecture at all. This was obvious in buildings like the "Studio" that he designed for himself and his family in Barrington, with its nod toward traditional southern rural houses, and Northside Junior High School in Columbus, with its obvious connection to simple industrial loft buildings. There was usually a fair amount of invention and tinkering with these prototypes, however—for example, in the way the actual structure of his Barrington house seemed to contradict the logic of the gable roofs. The economy and restraint that he learned from shipbuilding and his firsthand experience with naval vessels also had an effect, perhaps most noticeably in the compulsive attempts to reduce kitchens and other service spaces to the bare minimum.

One of the reasons why the work was so eclectic was Weese's refusal to specialize. He constantly searched for new kinds of commissions so he could try out new design strategies. Although his work didn't display some of the startling discontinuities found in the projects by his friend Eero Saarinen, it did show a rich diversity. The diverse output of his office also resulted from his ability to tap the talent of a great many other people. Nowhere was this more apparent than in the work of his brother Ben.

Buildings such as the tower at Lake Village East and the Sawyer Library at Williams College have a kind of elemental simplicity and sobriety that is quite distinctive in the work of the firm.

In the end, what can we say of Harry Weese's place in history? As with almost any important architect, there were numerous and contradictory reactions to the work while the architect was still practicing, and then a long period of intense revision of these views. A substantial number of Weese's buildings have always been held in high regard. It is perhaps not surprising that this is true of some of the smaller and simpler buildings, like the First Baptist Church of Columbus and the city hall complex in Oak Park. What is considerably more surprising is that this should be true with the great Metro subway stations in Washington, D.C. Buildings of this scale and prominence almost always provoke controversy in their early years. Indeed the Metro had a few detractors. But within a few years the Metro stations settled into the landscape of the nation's capital as timeless landmarks, designs that transcend the period and command respect from ordinary citizens and architectural critics alike.

Indeed, the Metro takes its place alongside a very small group of national monuments in and around the nation's capital, for example, the great memorials to Lincoln, Washington, and Jefferson, the National Gallery, and a few pieces of more recent vintage, notably Eero Saarinen's Dulles Airport and Maya Lin's Vietnam Veterans Memorial. It is telling, though, that many people associate the Vietnam memorial with Lin and Dulles with Saarinen. Not many, even in architectural circles, think of the Washington Metro as a piece of architecture, let alone know who designed it. This very anonymity is perhaps its most outstanding virtue as a democratic monument. However, it has meant that Weese's name is far less well known than it should be.

In many ways the Metro's opening in 1976 marked the high point in Weese's career. It was the closest he got to large-scale urban planning and urban design, which was probably what Weese considered his real métier. In his audacious proposals for Chicago from the early 1950s through the 1980s, he believed his ideas could serve as the basis for fundamentally reshaping the old, battered industrial city, rejuvenating it, and making it attractive for new generations of middle-class urban dwellers. However, he rarely got the chance to carry out his ideas. Even when he had an opening—for example, for the urban renewal projects in Hyde Park and Southwest Washington—his was never the dominant voice. He felt that his time had finally come with the planning of the 1992 world's fair.

However, even before the fair died during the political squabbles of the 1980s, that task had been snatched from him.

Despite the huge popular and critical success of the Metro and a few other buildings—most notably the First Baptist Church of Columbus—Weese's critical reputation has waxed and waned like that of most other major architects. There was never any doubt about his raw talent. There were doubts about whether he always used this talent in the best way. As Jack Hartray put it, "He was the most exasperating person I ever met. Also, the most gifted person I have ever met, without exception." He was one of the most heavily publicized and acclaimed young architects in the country in the 1950s and 1960s, but his reputation suffered in the 1970s and 1980s from the rise of postmodernism and an attack on what were thought to be the problems of orthodox modernism. Despite the fact that Weese's work was rarely a specific target for these attacks, the assault on modernism in general meant that his work came to be eclipsed in the architectural and popular press.

For some projects there has even been a strong negative reaction, most dramatically with the Humanities Building of the South Lower Campus at the University of Wisconsin in 1970. A vocal contingent at the university decided that it didn't like Weese's building and hated the fact that it occupied such a prominent site at the very heart of the largely classical campus. As I write, the building still stands but the university is committed to demolition. A new science building at Beloit College is under construction adjacent to Weese's science building of 1968, and when the new building is finished, the Weese structure will meet the wrecking ball. The Sawyer Library at Williams College will be replaced by structures rising on either side of it.

There are certainly some grounds for criticizing the design of these buildings, but much of the criticism is misplaced. At the South Lower Campus, for example, the university administrators wanted to put a very large program into a single building. It is hard to imagine how anyone could have done a better job squeezing that much square footage onto one site. The more important problem is that it is it very difficult for most people today to understand or admire buildings of this type from this period. This is true not just of designs by the Weese firm but of those by many of the most important architects of the period. Whether designed by Weese or Paul Rudolph or Gordon Bunshaft or many others, these bold and assertive buildings were going up when the country was reeling from the effects of social unrest at home, a war in Vietnam, and, in architecture as in other fields, a retreat from the bold, optimistic promise of technology and change and a widespread desire to make everything smaller, simpler, and less aggressive. When that happened, buildings such as the South Lower Campus naturally became targets for attack and remain so for some people today.

But within the world of architecture, after the pendulum of opinion swings one way for a while, it inevitably swings back. By the 1990s there was a very noticeable rise in appreciation of modernist buildings of the postwar decades. Critical opinion of the work of the Weese office in those years, particularly the modest houses and other relatively small and simple buildings, rose appreciably. It is almost certain that there will be an equivalent rise in esteem for the larger buildings of the late 1960s and the 1970s. If the Humanities Building can survive for only a few more years, for example, it is almost certain that the University of Wisconsin will realize that it has at the very least a great period piece representing one of the most inventive and exciting eras of American architecture.

In the end, it is likely that after some of the dust settles on the debates currently underway in architectural culture, the work of Harry Weese will be considered a major contribution, one of the most successful attempts by any postwar American architect to extend, enrich, and humanize the modernist ideas and vocabulary of the first generation of European modernists. In this regard the majority of work from Weese's office may well seem somewhat less weighty than that of some of his contemporaries, especially Eero Saarinen. Weese rarely had the occasion to design buildings and complexes as monumental as the General Motors Technical Center or Dulles Airport. Instead, a great deal of the work from the Weese office, while often clever and amiable, never quite attained the level of sustained exploration that was possible in some of the larger commissions that came to Saarinen, Paul Rudolph, and I. M. Pei.

However the one really large complex that Weese was able to achieve, the Washington Metro system, seems likely to hold its own with any design produced in twentieth-century America. Paradoxically, the stunning success of this great project may be due precisely to the fact that it was so atypical in Weese's oeuvre. Unlike so many of the other designs, which he was able to imagine and sketch in all their particulars within a few hours and then delegate to members of his office to develop, with the Metro system the entire process was much slower, and he had to accommodate the views of many more players. Weese, like many architects, frequently complained that too much involvement by clients, contractors, and the general public will inevitably end up compromising the best plans. However, in this project, perhaps this interference—by the engineers, by the strong-willed personalities on the Commission of Fine Arts, and by the conservative weight of the federal client—provided the discipline for an architect who ordinarily had a surplus of inspiration and not always enough patience to see the entire process of design and construction through to conclusion. None of this reduces Weese's role. Without his original intuitive jump to the great vaulted profile of the station and his ability to maintain his vision through years of negotiation and design development, we would not have today the great monument that we have, one of the wonders of the modern world.

As important as Harry Weese was as a designer, even his greatest triumphs in design would not have been possible if he had not been first and foremost a social and civic critic. For decades he used every vehicle of public opinion at his disposal to address the widest possible audience on issues involving the urban built environment. Many people, even the ones who agreed with him, read this as a local effort and a kind of scattershot one at that. After all, most of his publications dealt with Chicago, and they were issued on dozens of topics through lectures, newspaper articles, and magazine essays.

For this ceaseless activity, Weese was widely recognized as a gadfly and the "Conscience" of Chicago. In truth, however, the real lesson of his urban thinking was much larger than this. It was a vision of a good life for all citizens of cities that he knew needed to be healthier and more attractive than the decaying nineteenth-century industrial centers that he saw around him in the early postwar decades. He had a vision of a low-rise, leafy city, preserving much of what was good from previous eras but adapted to new circumstances, to a new affluence, and to a new taste for green space and amenity. In this way he was perhaps more conservative in the largest sense of the word than any of his peers. He was willing to see the nobility of older architecture whether it was the Auditorium Building by Louis Sullivan and Dankmar Adler or the anonymous loft building on a derelict South Loop street, but he was not at all afraid to remove or dramatically edit this existing fabric when needed. He imagined reusing all of these buildings, bringing their systems up-to-date, and making them attractive for to a rising urban middle class.

As Jack Hartray put it so well, "What Harry wanted to be, was a citizen in a great society. And that vision of that society was sort of like Lyndon Johnson's except that it was full of luxuries as well. And it was totally inclusive. He wanted it for everybody." In that vision, architecture, as important as it was, was never the end. It was the means to a better urban life for everyone.

BUILDING ENTRIES

Harry Weese was an extremely prolific architect. During his more than forty years of practice, Weese and the firms that bore his name received more than a thousand commissions, ranging from minor remodeling jobs to entire new cities (see list of major commissions). Understandably, choosing a small group of projects from this immense body of work was not easy. The selection made for this book provides a sample of the type of projects—churches, schools, single- and multi-family residences, commercial buildings, civic buildings, urban projects, transportation systems—completed during Weese's active career. The entries begin with the early Glen Lake Houses he designed for his father in the 1930s and end with the Miami Dade County Transit System, which opened in 1984. Arranged chronologically by the date of completion, they range in scope from mod-est homes such as the Johnson House to comprehensive designs like the Washington Metro, and in size and complexity from the one-room Shadowcliff studio to the thirty-nine-story office tower at 200 South Wacker. They vary in style, form, and materials as well. As Weese told a reporter for the *Chicago Reader* in 1976, "I hope we never become predictable." The buildings shown on the pages that follow attest to the fact that he never did.

The principal source of information for the entries that follow was the set of job files in the Harry Weese archives at the Chicago History Museum. Interviews with Weese family members, colleagues, business associates, clients, and current owners of Weese-designed buildings and published descriptions of these projects provided additional information. The name of the project is generally the name that was used at the time of its completion. In most cases the first date given is the date the commission was received, and the second is the date when construction was finished. The job number is the designation assigned to each project by the Weese office, and it helps to identify all papers and drawings related to a specific commission. The names of the designers and other professionals involved in each commission are included whenever known.

GLEN LAKE HOUSES

Glen Lake, Michigan

SHACK TAMARACK, 1936
COTTAGE TWO, 1939
PRITCHARD HOUSE, 1939

View to the north, Shack Tamarack, the first house designed by Harry Weese. Photographer unknown, but probably Harry Weese, 1937. Courtesy of Ben Weese.

Harry Ernest Weese, Harry's father, first became intrigued with Glen Lake, a rustic retreat set amid the sand dunes of Lake Michigan, in the early 1920s when his position as a corresponding banker for the Harris Trust Bank in Chicago took him to nearby Empire. Harry Ernest proposed the idea of a summer colony at Glen Lake to a group of friends from Huntington, Indiana, his childhood home. The enthusiasm of the others for the project ultimately waned, possibly because of the long distance between Huntington and Glen Lake, but Harry Ernest acquired ten 100-foot lots on the south side of Glen Lake. He reserved three parcels for his own use, sold an adjacent

lot to Harris bank vice president Richard Pritchard, and kept the others for investment purposes.

Glen Lake soon became one of the destinations for the Weese family's two- to three-week summer vacations. For a time, the family alternated between Glen Lake and various destinations in Wisconsin, but in 1935, as Harry Ernest later wrote in his memoirs, the children pleaded to "go to Glen Lake and no place else!" During early visits to Glen Lake, the Weeses stayed at Ocker's Resort, rented houses on the lake, or camped out, but once Glen Lake became the preferred summer vacation spot, Harry Ernest asked his son to design a traditional log cottage for the property.

Young Harry and his father learned from the Forest Products Laboratory in Madison, Wisconsin, that cedar and tamarack logs were the best choices for constructing a house of this type. Cedar was more permanent, but tamarack logs were long and straight and relatively resistant to rot. Joe Gersh, the local contractor selected for the project, owned a tamarack swamp and felled the logs for the house in the winter of 1935. In the spring of 1936, while completing his third year at MIT, Harry drew up plans for a simple, rustic

log cabin with an open, flexible floor plan and plenty of room for the large Weese family and their many relatives. A local team of Polish-American craftsmen assisted by Harry and his brother John began constructing the house in June of 1936, and the cottage was ready for occupancy by late July. The family christened it "Shack Tamarack."

Shack Tamarack became the summer home of Marjorie Weese and the Weese children. On Friday evenings, Harry Ernest drove from Kenilworth to Manitowoc, caught the nine o'clock ferry to Frankfort, Michigan, where he met the family car, and joined the family at the cottage in time for breakfast. On Sunday nights he reversed the journey. In later years, Harry Ernest and Marjorie's children and their families would vacation at Glen Lake.

The first level of Shack Tamarack had a two-story living room with an adjoining screen porch, a dining area, and a kitchen with a pass-through. The living room had a large stone fireplace constructed from local boulders that warmed the entire cottage. A bedroom and a built-in

bench alongside the fireplace provided ground-floor sleeping accommodations.

The second level of the cottage contained five bedrooms, three with bunk beds, bringing the total sleeping capacity to eighteen. Stairs in the living room led to an upper-level hallway that opened onto a covered balcony extending along the south side of the cottage. The balcony provided access to the bunk rooms and one of the other bedrooms. The walls separating the bunk rooms from the rest of the house did not extend all the way to the ceiling, and Harry and Kitty Weese's daughter Marcia recalled standing on the upper bunks to spy on the grownups in the living room below.

In 1939 Harry Weese, having experienced European modernist buildings firsthand during a 1937 trip abroad, turned to the modernist aesthetic for Cottage Two, the second house that he designed for his father on Glen Lake. Weese elevated the cottage on masonry piers to provide space for the storage of boats, and covered the balloon frame with

Exterior of Pritchard
House, which Harry Weese
designed in 1939 for a
Harris Bank vice president.
Robert Bruegmann photograph,
2008.

tongue-and-groove black cherry vertical paneling, originally
stained brown and now painted blue. The glazed north wall
of the living room overlooked the lake, and steps from the
sliding door on the west wall of the living room led down to
a screened porch with an interior garden.

That same year Weese designed a house on Glen Lake
for the Pritchards. This simple modernist cottage had a
shed roof, sliding glass doors in the living, dining, and
kitchen areas, and a dining table that pivoted out from
underneath the kitchen counter. Weese's sister Sue Weese
Drucker and her husband acquired the Pritchard House in
the late 1970s.

Since 1971 Shack Tamarack and Cottage Two have
been held in trust for the fourteen surviving grand-

John Weese in the Pritchard House, probably during the war years. Compared to the cave-like interior of Shack Tamarack, the Pritchard House was extraordinarily open. In fact, it is difficult to imagine at first glance how the structure stands with so little structural support. Photographer unknown, possibly Harry Weese. Courtesy of Ben Weese.

children, twenty-eight great grandchildren, and three great-great grandchildren of Harry Ernest and Marjorie Weese. Sue Weese Drucker continues to manage and preserve all three of the Weese-designed Glen Lake properties. Marcia Weese describes Shack Tamarack today as "the old family homestead," with original furnishings, old quilts on the bed, and watercolors by Harry and John Weese hanging on the walls.

SELECTED BIBLIOGRAPHY

"Vacation Homes on a Michigan Lake," *Arts and Architecture* 62 (July 1945).

Barbara Siepker and Dietrich Floeter. *Historic Cottages of Glen Lake*. Glen Arbor, Michigan: Leelanau Press, 2008.

TEA WAGON

WITH BENJAMIN BALDWIN

1940

Tea wagon. Digital image copyright, the Museum of Modern Art/licensed by SCALA/Art Resource, New York.

Harry Weese met Benjamin Baldwin in 1938 at the Cranbrook Academy of Art in Bloomfield Hills, Michigan, where both had received fellowships in city planning. Cranbrook had no formal classes but instead offered an open, creative environment that encouraged students to explore areas beyond their fields of specialization and to work together on joint projects or competition entries. While there, Weese studied ceramics, sculpture, and weaving and joined other Cranbrook fellows in turning Harry Bertoia's metalworking shop into a furniture workshop.

In 1940, Weese and Baldwin formed an architectural partnership and, along with a number of their former Cranbrook colleagues, submitted several furniture and lighting designs to "Organic Design in Home Furnishings," a contemporary furniture competition sponsored by the Museum of Modern Art (MoMA) in New York. The team of Weese and Baldwin placed first in the category for outdoor furniture and won honorable mentions in the categories for bedroom furniture and for living room furniture other than seating. Among their winning designs was a tea wagon for informal outdoor entertaining.

The tea wagon had a tubular steel frame, removable solid and perforated steel trays, and a wicker basket for transporting items such as tall bottles and dirty dishes. Pneumatic tires allowed it to roll smoothly over grass and pavement.

Weese and Baldwin traveled to New York to attend events held at MoMA and Bloomingdale's department store, which featured prototypes of some of the winning designs. The original idea of the competition was that winners would be given contracts with manufacturers who would put their designs into production. Weese and Baldwin did do some work developing their designs with the Lloyd Manufacturing Company, but U.S. involvement in World War II halted plans for mass production of most of the competition furniture, especially the designs made of metal. The war also ended the architectural partnership of Weese and Baldwin, who both entered the Navy.

SELECTED BIBLIOGRAPHY

Benjamin Baldwin. *An Autobiography in Design.* New York:: W. W. Norton, 1995.

Eliot F. Noyes. *Organic Design.* New York: Museum of Modern Art, 1941.

Robert Judson Clark, et al. *Design in America: The Cranbrook Vision, 1925–1950.* New York: Harry N. Abrams, 1983.

227 EAST WALTON

Chicago, Illinois, 1956

"The best in city living" was how a marketing brochure described 227 East Walton, a multi-family residence developed jointly in the mid-1950s by Harry Weese and John Baird, then a vice president at his family's real estate brokerage firm, Baird & Warner. The project's location on a fifty-foot-wide parcel of land on East Walton Street purchased for $40,000 was just two blocks east of Chicago's prestigious Michigan Avenue and only steps away from galleries, quality shopping, and gourmet dining. In addition to its choice in-town location, the building offered privacy, a quiet environment, and attractive vistas to the east and west.

Weese planned the thirteen-story, twenty-four-unit building, his first tall residential building, for maximum privacy. A central core contained an elevator accessible from either the eighteen-car basement garage or the main lobby. The elevator opened onto small lobbies on the twelve upper floors, each containing only two apartments. The core area also included a service lobby with a trash chute and a second elevator. Private entrances into the service lobby from each apartment allowed residents to accept deliveries and retrieve packages. Because of the location of the central core between the two apartments on each floor, the units shared only a sixteen-foot sound-proofed common wall.

The reinforced concrete frame of 227 East Walton was clad in red brick with limestone sills. What Weese described as "conservative fenestration" limited the building's glazing to one-half of the exterior perimeter, maximizing privacy, preventing excessive glare, and simplifying the arrangement of furniture. The stacked floor-to-ceiling bay or oriel windows of the north façade recalled the traditional fenestration of early Chicago office buildings such as the 1893 Monadnock Building designed by Burnham & Root. These bays reappeared later in Weese's designs for Pierce Dormitory on the University of Chicago campus in Hyde Park, completed in 1959, and the John Fewkes Tower, an apartment building on the southwest corner of Dearborn and Chestnut streets in Chicago, completed in 1967. These traditional bays were actually not Weese's first choice. He initially considered windows that angled toward the Lake Michigan view but revised the fenestration on the advice of I. M. Pei, who suggested that Weese substitute a more traditional bay window design.

The entrance foyer of each apartment led past a modern kitchen, with custom-designed cabinets and Formica

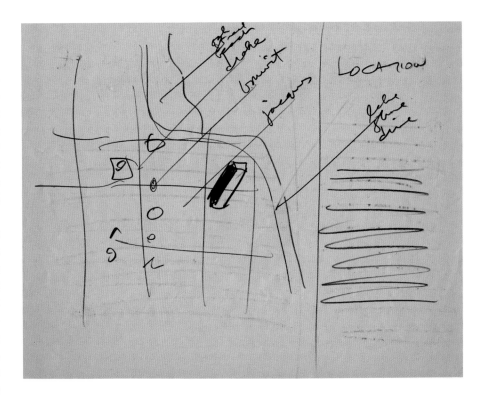

countertops, into a spacious living room illuminated by one bay window and a smaller floor-to-ceiling window. A dining alcove, also with a floor-to-ceiling window, adjoined the living room. A four-foot-wide pass-through with a convenient drop-leaf buffet/bar separated the dining room from the kitchen, and a storage cabinet above the pass-through opened into both rooms.

Weese's flexible plan allowed variations in the size of the units from one to three bedrooms, with each floor containing either two two-bedroom units or one one-bedroom and one three-bedroom unit. Bedroom windows also extended from floor to ceiling, and one wall of each bedroom consisted entirely of wardrobes with upper storage compartments. All units included two bathrooms. As Baird recalled, he and Weese were "neophytes" at the time of the development of 227 East Walton and "tried every new technique in the industry." Among these innovations was a unique radiant heating and cooling system, designed by mechanical engineer Samuel R. Lewis and said to be the first of its kind in a Chicago multistory building. Coils in the plaster ceiling carried warm water in the winter months and cool water in the summer. Radiant cooling may have

Harry Weese's sketch for sales brochure showing the proximity of 227 East Walton to Oak Street Beach, the Drake Hotel, the Bonwit Teller department store, Jacques French restaurant, and Lake Shore Drive. i51996, Chicago History Museum.

worked well in a dry climate but was not readily adaptable to the high humidity in Chicago and was particularly problematic in the building's kitchens. Ceiling condensation promoted the growth of mold, leading later owners to abandon the system and retrofit the building for window air-conditioners.

Efforts by Weese and Baird to market the units in 227 East Walton as cooperative apartments proved unsuccessful. They initially attributed the lack of sales to the modern interior décor of the model apartment and public areas, which were designed by Kitty Weese using furniture from Baldwin Kingrey and may not have been appealing to older buyers. But even after the modern interiors were replaced with more conventional designs, the units failed to sell, perhaps because potential buyers did not find them spacious enough or because the Streeterville area was not yet considered an especially desirable location. With no buyers. Weese and Baird offered 227 East Walton as a rental property managed by Baird & Warner.

Condominium conversions began to boom in Chicago in the 1960s, but the many "innovations" that Weese and Baird had included in 227 East Walton made them reluctant to market the units as condominiums because of concern over possible lawsuits, and they decided to sell the building instead. The new owners converted 227 East Walton to condominiums in 1969.

Reviews of the work of Harry Weese in the architectural press frequently cited 227 East Walton as an early example of his humanistic and functional approach to modern design. Today, the building remains a condominium and is known for its intimacy and now desirable Streeterville location. "If I wanted to live downtown, I would buy there," John Baird says today.

Job 274

SELECTED BIBLIOGRAPHY

"Plan Radiant Cooling for New Building." *Chicago Daily Tribune*, July 2, 1955.

View to the southwest of 227 East Walton, Harry Weese's first tall residential building. Hedrich Blessing photograph, HB20073F, ca. 1956. Chicago History Museum.

Floor plan of apartments. The blue area could be incorporated into either unit, resulting in two two-bedroom apartments or one one-bedroom and one three-bedroom apartment on each floor. From firm brochure.

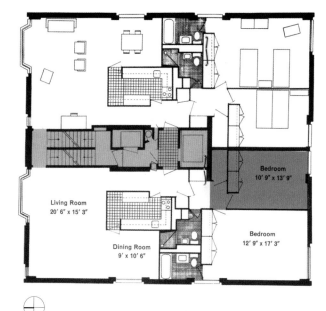

Living Room
20' 6" x 15' 3"

Dining Room
9' x 10' 6"

Bedroom
10' 9" x 13' 9"

Bedroom
12' 9" x 17' 3"

LILLIAN C. SCHMITT ELEMENTARY SCHOOL

1057 Twenty-seventh Street
Columbus, Indiana, 1957

In the early 1950s, the expanding population of the small midwestern town of Columbus, Indiana, was placing a strain on existing educational facilities, and planning was underway for several new schools. Early prefabricated designs for these schools disappointed J. Irwin Miller, board chairman of Cummins Engine Company, the Columbus-based diesel engine manufacturer established by Miller's great-uncle in 1919. Miller believed that well-designed educational facilities would benefit current residents and also attract talented young executives and engineers to Columbus.

In 1954 Miller established the Cummins Engine Foundation for "religious, educational, and charitable purposes" and approached the school board with an enticing proposition. The foundation would pay the professional design fees for the next new school, provided the board selected the architect from a list drawn up by an impartial panel of professionals in the field. The school board accepted his proposal, and Miller appointed Eero Saarinen and Pietro Belluschi, an Italian-born modernist and dean of the School of Architecture at the Massachusetts Institute of Technology, to compile a list of five architectural firms for consideration by board members. That list included the name of Harry Weese. The school board interviewed Weese in 1955 and subsequently awarded him the commission for an elementary school for three hundred students from kindergarten to grade six to be named for Lillian C. Schmitt, an elementary teacher in the Columbus system for forty-three years.

The core of the design developed by Weese and Brewster (Bruce) Adams was an auditorium or Great Hall located just beyond the main entrance on the building's south side and expressed on the exterior by a raised cupola. Removal of the folding doors that formed the walls of this multipurpose room transformed the auditorium, surrounding corridors,

Great Hall with removable folding doors, Lillian C. Schmitt Elementary School. Hedrich Blessing photograph, HB20950G, ca. 1957, Chicago History Museum.

Classroom, with an exterior
glass wall that admitted
natural light. Hedrich Blessing
photograph, HB20950C,
ca. 1957, Chicago History
Museum.

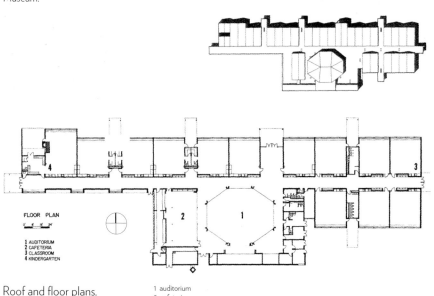

Roof and floor plans.
From firm brochure.

1 auditorium
2 cafeteria
3 classroom
4 kindergarden

and adjacent cafeteria into a large open space for school assemblies.

The designers arranged the school's thirteen classrooms along a skylit east-west corridor with built-in coat storage. They separated the students by age, locating classrooms for kindergarten and primary-grade students to the west adjacent to covered play areas and upper-grade classrooms to the east. The classrooms were identical squares that could be adapted for various seating arrangements.

Glass exterior walls in each classroom admitted natural light, which was supplemented by light entering through clerestory windows on the opposite wall adjoining the corridor. Individual gabled roofs articulated the classrooms on the exterior.

Weese intended the school to give students "a sense of well-being, and an at-home feeling," and adjusted the scale of the interior to the young occupants. The design placed benches and coat closets at child height and limited the height of corridors to no more than eight feet and the height of doors to six feet, six inches. This child-size scale, along with the discrete, age-zoned classrooms, adjacent play areas, central core space, and hallways illuminated by skylights, recalled features of the highly influential 1942 Crow Island School in Winnetka, Illinois, designed by Eliel and Eero Saarinen and Perkins, Wheeler & Will.

The materials selected for the Schmitt school were durable, economical, and easy to maintain. The building had a heavy-timber frame and load-bearing walls of brick and concrete block clad in Chicago common brick with painted wood trim. Interior walls were brick, white-brushed concrete, or glazed structural tile, and floors were concrete, asphalt, ceramic tile, or end-grain wood blocks.

When the favorable response to Weese's Schmitt school led the Columbus school board to ask the Cummins Engine Foundation to underwrite the architect's fees for the next new school being planned, Miller formally established the Cummins Foundation Architecture Program. The program initially paid design fees for Columbus schools and later expanded support to other public buildings.

In the later decades of the twentieth century, a decline in Columbus's school-age population left the town with a surplus of schools. In 1988, the school board made the decision to combine the Jefferson Elementary School with the Lillian C. Schmitt Elementary School, increasing enrollment at Schmitt to 650 and necessitating additional space. The Cummins Foundation Architecture Program guidelines stated that, whenever possible, building additions were to be designed by the original architect, and Harry Weese & Associates had been slated to design the Schmitt addition. Weese lost the commission for

reasons that remain unclear. His failing health may have been a contributing factor, but former Weese employees have speculated that he may have alienated Miller. Instead of Weese, the school board selected the Boston firm of Leers Weinzapfel Associates to design the addition, a structure that many, including members of Weese's staff, found unsympathetic in scale, materials, and color to the original building.

Job 294
Structural Engineer: Frank J. Kornacker
Mechanical Engineer: Samuel R. Lewis & Associates
Contractor: Dunlop Construction

SELECTED BIBLIOGRAPHY

"Lillian C. Schmitt Elementary School, Columbus, Indiana." *Architectural Record* 124 (November 1958):223–225.

View to the south, showing the gabled roofs over each classroom. Hedrich Blessing photograph, HB20950E, ca. 1957, Chicago History Museum.

JOHNSON HOUSE

5617 Kenwood Avenue
Hyde Park, Chicago, Illinois, 1957

"Hyde Park contemporary" was how Harry Weese described the urban townhouse he designed for Dr. and Mrs. D. Gale Johnson in the historic Chicago neighborhood best known as the home of the University of Chicago. Johnson was a University of Chicago economics professor and associate dean of the Social Sciences Division

at the time of the design and construction of the house. He purchased a 50 × 180 foot vacant lot on Kenwood Avenue, one of the few parcels of land available in the Hyde Park community, from the Midway Properties Trust of the University of Chicago with the understanding that the trustees would have the right to review and approve plans for the property.

The Johnsons were especially concerned that their house harmonize architecturally with neighboring buildings, many of which had been built in the early twentieth century. Weese responded to their concern by integrating the home into its surroundings through his choice of building materials—warm red brick, Indiana limestone, and black wrought iron—and through his elegant, unobtrusive contemporary design.

Glazing on the west façade fronting on Kenwood Avenue was limited to a large floor-to-ceiling panel to the right of the recessed entry, the balcony opening of the family room above the garage, and the narrow vertical bathroom and bedroom windows concealed by a limestone grille at the second level. In contrast, the house opened up on the garden façade with spacious picture windows that bathed the interior with light. The terrace off the living room looked out to a deep urban garden.

The plan for the house borrowed from a house Weese designed for his uncle, Robert P. Weese, in Barrington in the early 1940s, although the contemporary exterior of the Johnson home differed markedly from the more traditional Robert P. Weese house. The front entrance opened into a large hall that led on one side to the L-shaped living/dining area and on the other to the kitchen. The living room had a flush fireplace constructed of the same brick as used on the exterior, and pecan-finished birchwood cabinets lined one entire wall of the dining area. Louvered doors separated the kitchen from the dining space.

A family room where their eleven-year-old daughter and fourteen-year-old son could gather with their friends was a necessity for the Johnsons. By placing the garage one-half level below grade, as in the Robert P. Weese house, Weese was able to create a separate level for the family room above the garage between the first and second floors. A nine-foot-wide glass door gave access to a balcony overlooking the garden and supplemented the light entering the family room through the east balcony over the garage. The upper level of the house contained three bedrooms and a bathroom.

The Johnsons moved into their house in August 1957 and found it "an extremely pleasant, comfortable and restful place to be." In December 1957, the *Chicago Daily Tribune* named the Johnson residence "The Home of the Week." As *Tribune* writer Louise Hutchinson stated, "It has warmth and dignity. It has light. It is a friend to its neighbors." The house received a Citation of Merit from the Chicago chapter of the American Institute of Architects, which called it a "significant essay in urban row housing" and commended its "interesting plan" and "bold effort to compose irregular openings."

In 1967 the Johnsons commissioned an addition from Weese to serve as a separate dining room. Weese responded to their request with a long, narrow eight-sided structure that extended from the former dining area into the back-yard and offered views of the garden through extensive floor-to-ceiling glazing.

The Johnson House with its stone cornice and grille, recessed entrance, and balconies served as a prototype for more than 250 subsequent townhouses designed by Weese and I. M. Pei that were constructed between 1958 and 1960 as part of the Hyde Park redevelopment project. The current owners, who purchased the property from Johnson in 1997, have altered the ground-level interior to create a more open, free-flowing plan, but the upper floors and the exterior remain essentially unchanged.

Job 298
Contractor: Zisook Construction

SELECTED BIBLIOGRAPHY

Louise Hutchinson. "The Home of the Week. Tailored to the Neighborhood." *Chicago Daily Tribune*, December 14,1957.

"Tribune Names H.P. House 'Home of the Week.'" *Hyde Park Herald*, December 18, 1957.

"Citation of Merit for Residential Building." *Inland Architect* 2 (May 1959): 2.

Plans. Note family room on a separate level above the garage. Hedrich Blessing photograph, HB22351, Chicago History Museum.

GROUND FLOOR   SECOND FLOOR

View to the north, Weese "Studio," showing the roof suspended from the two timber walls rising to the peak of the gables of the two wings. Hedrich Blessing photograph, HB22311C, ca. 1959, Chicago History Museum.

WEESE "STUDIO"

Hawthorne Road
Barrington, Illinois, 1957

Barrington, Illinois, forty miles northwest of Chicago, had been a country retreat for the Weese family since the 1920s, when Harry Ernest Weese acquired sixteen

acres of property there. After World War II, Barrington also became a haven for Harry and Kitty Weese and their daughters. From the 1950s until the three girls left for college, the Harry Mohr Weese family visited Barrington almost every weekend during the school year and spent the summer there, with Harry commuting daily to his office in Chicago via train.

Weese's first project on his Barrington property was a tennis court he installed to entice Kitty to the coun-

try. He and Kitty then began planning a home for use in the summer and on weekends. After considering as many as thirty different concepts, the couple decided on a simple yet innovative and experimental design filled with whimsical touches and inspired by the houses of the rice farmers of Alabama, Kitty's home state. These dwellings opened out from the main space at the center with attached porches and open loggias appropriate for a mild southern climate.

Weese adapted the design of the "Studio," as the family called the house, to the harsher winters of the Midwest by replacing the open spaces flanking the central area with two wings topped with asymmetrical gables, or "cat ears," reminiscent of the roofline of Illinois farmhouses. The principal structural element was a pair of walls constructed by nailing together four-inch-thick double tongue-and-groove Western red cedar planks to form prefabricated panels that rose to the

View to the east. Kate Weese poses under the arbor leading to the main entrance. Hedrich Blessing photograph, HB22311K, ca. 1959, Chicago History Museum.

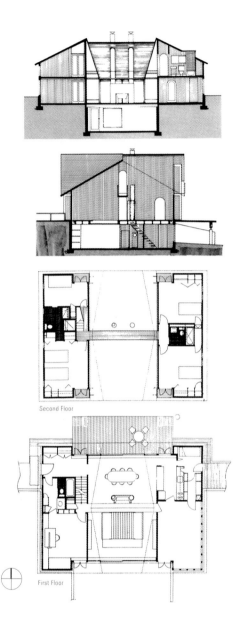

From top: sections, second- and ground level plans. From Kitty Baldwin Weese, *Harry Weese Houses*, 1987.

Second Floor

First Floor

peak of the gables of the two wings. Weese daringly suspended the roof of the wings and the main central space from these walls. He painted the exterior of the house and the ceilings but left the cedar walls of the interior in their natural state.

In an effort to economize, Weese designed the studio with a basement that extended only under the central portion, not under the two wings. Over time differences in the rate of contraction between the center of the house and the sides caused the tall structural walls to lean slightly outward, pulling the roof up over the central portion of

the house and creating gaps between the windows and the roof. A restoration expert called in by Weese at the recommendation of Chicago contractor Sumner Sollitt was able to stabilize the structure.

An arbor covered with Concord grape vines guided visitors to the low round-headed door of the main entrance, which was located in the west wing. The house was rather modest—only 1,600 square feet—but its open design made it appear and feel more spacious. A narrow entrance corridor led to an open central space where a double-sided fireplace separated the two-story living and dining area. The dining room faced north and opened onto a deck sheltering the entrance to the basement level, while the living room, with its conversation pit for informal seating, overlooked the swimming pool to the south. A guest room/study occupied the lower level of the west wing, and the east wing contained a screened porch off the kitchen, which could be enclosed in glass and used as a conservatory in the winter. Green Vermont slate covered most of the floors on the first level.

Weese tucked two bedrooms under the eaves on the upper level of each wing and suspended a seventeen-foot bridge or gangway above the living room to connect the two wings and eliminate the need for two staircases. Harry and Kitty had only to climb the stairs in the west wing to reach their bedroom, which was located directly off the small landing at the top, but Kate, the youngest, also had to navigate a narrow catwalk, and Shirley and Marcia had to cross the gangway. When wearing wet bathing suits, the Weese girls could reach their bedrooms via balconies connected to steel ladders accessible from the pool terrace or deck.

The Weese family and the staff of Harry Weese & Associates enjoyed many memorable times at the Barrington house. Marcia Weese described it as a "fantastic, wondrous house to grow up in." After their daughters left home, Harry and Kitty continued to spend time in Barrington, although they were also busy sailing on Lake Michigan and traveling, so their visits to their country home were more sporadic. However, by the late 1980s Weese's health problems limited his visits there, and after her daughters married and left Chicago in the early 1990s, Kitty sold the house. The new owner was more interested in a speculative investment than a country home and never actually moved into the house. She sold it in the spring of 2000 to a couple who understood and appreciated the home's history and architectural significance. Although they are updating the interior, the exterior remains essentially intact.

Job 335

SELECTED BIBLIOGRAPHY

"Modern Roof Looks Medieval—or Vice Versa?" *Architectural Record 126* (November 1959): 198–200.

A House Full of Practical Whimsy." *Architectural Record, Record Houses of 1960*, 88–92.

Cynthia Kellogg. "Modern House with a Past." *New York Times*, January 24, 1960.

"Barrington Studio." *Time*, September 17, 1962.

"Barrington Studio." In Sherban Cantacuzino, *Modern Houses of the World*. New York, E.P. Dutton, 1964.

"Sommerhaus in Barrington." *Deutsche Bauzeitung* (January 1970): 79–80.

ABOVE LEFT
View into the living room, with Kitty, Marcia, Harry, Shirley, and Kate (on floor) and the gangway above. Photograph by Francis Miller for *Life* magazine, September 1, 1958, Time & Life Pictures/Getty Images.

Stairs to the second level, with the narrow catwalk visible to the right of the stairs. Hedrich Blessing photograph, HB22311I, 1959, Chicago History Museum.

View of the United
States Embassy in Accra.
Photographer unknown. i52150,
Chicago History Museum.

UNITED STATES EMBASSY

Kindu & Liberia Road
Accra, Ghana, 1955–58

The second half of the 1950s was a time of remarkable creativity and innovation in the design of U.S. government facilities abroad. After the end of World War II, the United States embarked on an ambitious foreign building program necessitated by increasing involvement in international affairs. The elegant modernist designs of several of the early postwar embassies won praise in architectural journals, but some observers claimed that the new embassies were too conspicuous, projected an inappropriate image, and failed to acknowledge the uniqueness of the foreign capitals where they were located.

In 1954, the U.S. State Department's Office of Foreign Buildings Operations (FBO), the agency responsible for overseeing embassy design and construction, established an architectural advisory board consisting of three architects and a former Foreign Service officer to encourage a more sensitive approach to architectural projects abroad. Responsibilities of this working committee included formulating guidelines for international government commissions, recommending architects for each project, and reviewing proposed designs.

In 1955, the panel awarded Harry Weese the commission for the U.S. consulate for the British colony of Gold Coast. On March 6, 1957, prior to the start of construction, Ghana became an independent sovereign state, and the U.S. consulate general in Accra was raised to the status of an embassy.

Weese began the design process with a visit to the Ghanaian capital city of Accra to study the site and the local architectural traditions. Most of the recent buildings he found there were Mediterranean-style concrete boxes, with flat roofs and picture windows ill-suited to the hot African climate. Weese also saw buildings with timber frames, adobe plastered walls, and corrugated iron roofs constructed by the natives, and some Victorian-era frame structures with steep roofs and continuous verandas raised on cast-iron columns to prevent damage by Ghana's voracious white ants or termites. Weese received his most vivid impression of traditional sub-Saharan architecture, however, from a postcard of the Wa Na, the traditional chieftain's house located in Ghana's Northern Territories, that he found in the gift shop of his hotel. With its tapered buttresses supporting a long, horizontal mud-brick structure, the Wa Na reminded Weese of native wooden spears and the ubiquitous red-earth anthill towers of Ghana. His concept for the United States Embassy at Accra, which he sketched on the plane back to the states, was the Wa Na turned upside down.

Weese designed the 8,000-square-foot embassy at Accra as a hollow square raised above a concrete platform, which was surrounded by a shallow moat-like depression with a red earth floor. Two sets of square, tapered, reinforced-concrete columns—one set ringing the exterior and the other surrounding the central court—supported the main raised floor. Setting the columns on two-inch steel pins permitted movement in the event of high winds or earthquakes, an important component of the embassy program. Weese tapered the columns from sixteen inches at their midpoint, where they supported the main floor, to six inches at the ground and roof, and rotated them forty-five degrees, giving the columns a profile reminiscent of the buttresses of the Wa Na and, more importantly, enhancing the resistance of the structure to earthquakes. Staggering the columns surrounding the interior court and the exterior perimeter allowed the diagonal placement of the concrete beams supporting the embassy offices, eliminating the need to alter the structural system at the corners and also creating a decorative diamond pattern on the underside of the main floor.

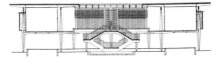

SECTION

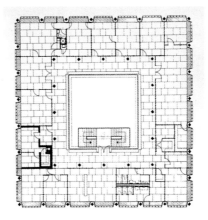

MAIN FLOOR

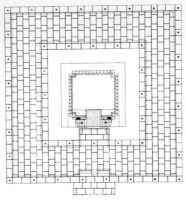

GROUND FLOOR

Section and plans. The embassy offices on the upper level of the building were accessible via a gallery that overlooked the courtyard. i59290, Chicago History Museum. Section from firm brochure.

Weese selected heartwood mahogany, a native, relatively termite-resistant wood, for the embassy's louvered walls and parasol roof and stained it a rich red-brown to contrast with the white-painted concrete frame. Treatment of the wood with preservatives further protected against termite invasion. The roof beams were made from odum or iroko, a durable, native wood with a high calcium oxalate content that deterred destructive insects.

The adjustable screened louvers of the projecting bays allowed through-ventilation while protecting the interior from the intense African sun and tropical downpours. The broad ten-foot overhang of the roof further sheltered the building from sun and rain, and a space between the roof

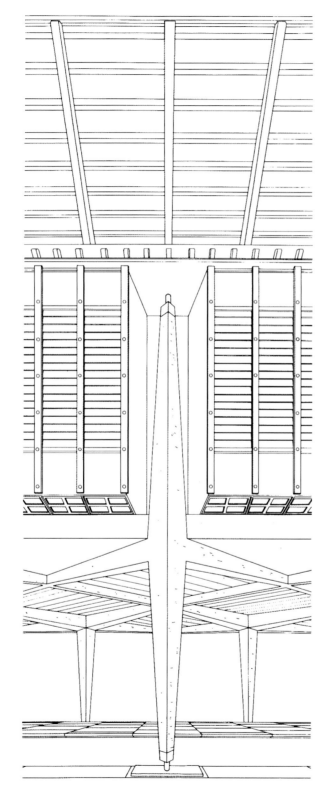

Perspective drawing of structural system, showing the reinforced-concrete columns that are tapered from sixteen inches at their midpoints to six inches at their ends. From firm brochure.

and the ceiling allowed breezes to enter under the parasol and circulate above the offices. The louvers were also intended to conceal standard window air-conditioning units. These units were used in place of a central system, which would have been difficult to maintain.

An open double staircase led from the central court to the elevated main floor of the embassy. The offices of embassy personnel opened onto a sun-screened gallery or veranda overlooking the interior court with its central pool.

True to the modernist aesthetic, applied ornament was minimal. As Weese explained, the decorative effect of the embassy derived "from the structural form and the proliferation of structural members that attempt to characterize architectural aspirations and possibilities for Africa." The structural components not only were functional but also conveyed "the richness of imagery and decoration in the African psyche." The only applied decorations were four reproductions of the Great Seal of the United States carved from native mahogany by Ghanaian craftsmen and placed at the upper center of each of the outside walls. Dedication of the new Weese-designed embassy at Accra took place on February 12, 1959, the 150th anniversary of the birth of Abraham Lincoln.

In 1960, the Fine Hardwoods Association recognized the creative use of native mahogany in the framework and trim of the embassy at Accra by awarding the architects an Honor Award for Architectural Installations. The building also won praise from Attaché Angus MacLean Thuermer, who told Weese how much he enjoyed working in the building in a 1962 letter he wrote while sitting in his "beautiful paneled office, looking out through the slats, enjoying it madly, and muttering to any foreign buildings officer who will listen, 'Let's have another Weese embassy.'"

In the years that followed the dedication of the embassy at Accra, acts of violence against U.S. installations abroad prompted the FBO to institute guidelines to ensure the security of its buildings overseas, including a ban on stilts, which were viewed as targets for terrorists. In the 1970s, the FBO asked Weese to revisit the embassy at Accra to determine if the building could be altered to comply with these guidelines, but he could find no solution. The embassy offices moved to another location, although the State Department continued to use the building for other purposes until the 1990s, when it was abandoned. The former embassy was left to deteriorate until it was acquired by the government of Ghana, which repaired the damage, replaced the roof, and converted it to the Ghanaian Ministry of Women and Children's Affairs.

The changes in attitudes about architecture and colonialism that occurred in the decades following the construction of the embassy at Accra are reflected in later reactions to Weese's design. Writing in the early 1990s, historian Ron Robin claimed that Weese's design "trivialized African culture and tribal lore while dismissing the unique political aspirations of individual nations." Although architectural historian Jane C. Loeffler, author of the 1998 *Architecture of Diplomacy: Building America's Embassies*, questioned the sources of Weese's inspiration and admitted that the building was "functionally flawed," she described the design as "handsome and widely admired" as well as "imaginative" and a break from colonial traditions. As she stated, "While his words may have trivialized African culture, his architecture did not."

Job 293
Project Manager: Ezra Gordon
Structural Engineer: Frank J. Kornacker
Mechanical Engineer: Kravolec & Best
Construction: George Watson & Co.
Construction Supervisor: Dwen Younger, U.S. State Department, Foreign Buildings Operations

SELECTED BIBLIOGRAPHY

"Second Group of American Embassy Buildings." *Architectural Record* 119 (June 1956): 161ff.

"Starting a Tradition." *Time* (March 4, 1957): 74.

"U.S. Embassy, Accra, Ghana." *Architectural Record* 121 (June 1957): 197–202.

"USA Abroad." *Architectural Forum* 107 (December 1957): 114–123.

"Astute Plan for New Embassies." *Life* (December 23, 1957): 111–112.

"Ambassade des Etats-Unis, Accra, Ghana." *L'Architecture d'aujourd'hui* 29 (April 1958): 61.

"Eyeful in Africa." *Architectural Forum* 111 (September 1959): 134–135.

"American Embassy in Accra, Ghana." *Architectural Design* 30 (February 1960): 69.

"Wood Wins Honors." *Inland Architect* 3 (May 1960): 8.

"New Face for America Abroad." *Time* (July 11, 1960): 26.

Ron Robin. *Enclaves of America: The Rhetoric of American Political Architecture Abroad, 1900–1965*. Princeton: Princeton University Press, 1992.

Jane C. Loeffler. *Architecture of Diplomacy: Building America's Embassies*. New York: Princeton Architectural Press, 1998.

View of central court, staircases, and offices. Photographer unknown. i52151, Chicago History Museum.

Perspective drawing of gallery and central courtyard. From firm brochure.

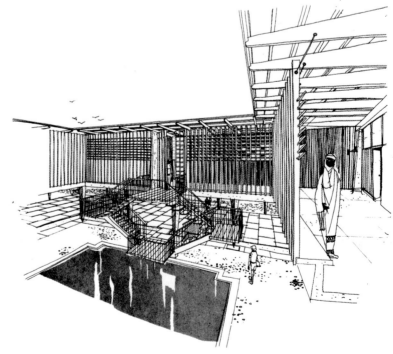

NORTHSIDE JUNIOR HIGH SCHOOL

2700 Maple Street
Columbus, Indiana, 1960–1961

American schools of the late 1950s and early 1960s tended to be sprawling one-story "ranch" structures with light metal frames and brightly colored curtain walls, but Ben Weese's compact masonry bearing-wall design for the Northside Junior High School, now the Northside Middle School, deviated from that trend. The small

site one block east of the Lillian C. Schmitt Elementary School, also designed by Harry Weese & Associates and completed in 1957 (see entry), accounted in part for Weese's approach. Another contributing factor, according to materials prepared by the firm at the time, was the hope that a two- or three-story structure would permit a more dignified appearance and give the architects more options for the architectural treatment.

Using a technique pioneered by Chicago structural engineer Kolbjorn Saether, Weese selected the "ancient and overlooked system of brick bearing piers and arches" for the school's structural system. The one-foot-thick brick piers had hollow cores into which steel reinforcing bars were inserted. The cores were then filled with mortar, creating a strong monolithic structural system.

Economic considerations were among the factors that influenced the choice of brick. Although the Cummins Foundation Architecture Program paid the architect's fee for the design, the school board remained responsible for construction costs, and control of these costs was a critical component of the program. Based on a cost analysis of various wall systems, Weese concluded that masonry construction was the most economical choice, costing an estimated $3.05 per square foot, compared with $3.85 for precast concrete and $4.27 to $5.25 for a metal curtain wall.

Weese elevated the upper two stories of the school above grade level on an earth terrace or platform, allowing him to insert a lower floor one-half level below grade. The school facilities wrapped around an enclosed landscaped courtyard that brought natural light into the interior and provided a pleasant outdoor gathering spot for students and faculty. The simple rhythmic pattern of brick piers and glazed arches constituted the only decoration on the exterior of the building. The same brick piers lined the inner corridor looking onto the courtyard, and student lockers occupied the spaces between the piers. Glazed arches filled the area above the lockers.

The nearly 110,000-square-foot building accommodated approximately 1,000 students and contained twenty-eight regular classrooms and seventeen special classrooms for home economics, science, art, industrial arts, music, foreign languages, and reading. Other facilities included a library, cafeteria, bookstore, a regulation-size swimming pool, and a multipurpose room that was used for physical education classes and community gatherings. Weese located facilities likely to generate noise, such as the cafeteria and shop, on the lower level, which had additional space for future classrooms. The first level contained the bookstore and administrative offices, which were placed near the school's main entrance to the east. Other facilities on this floor included classrooms to the north and south, the swimming pool and multipurpose room to the west, and rooms for science and art instruction along the courtyard to the north and south, respectively. Classrooms and the library occupied the top floor.

One year after the school opened, Superintendent Clarence E. Robbins reported that the teachers and administrators were very pleased, adding that "the architectural design and arrangement have resulted in a climate most conducive to a high-level academic effort with a minimum of discipline."

In the late 1980s, Leers Weinzapfel Associates, the Boston-based architectural firm that designed the addition to the Lillian C. Schmitt Elementary School, also designed an addition to the Northside Junior High School. The school now has a new main entrance to the south marked by a precast concrete portico.

Job 409
Structural Engineer: Kolbjorn Saether & Associates
Mechanical Engineer: Samuel R. Lewis & Associates
General Contractor: Repp & Mundt
Electrical Contractor: Hatfield Electric
Heating, Plumbing, and Ventilating: Dunlap & Company
Landscape Architect: Harry Weese & Associates

SELECTED BIBLIOGRAPHY

"Columbus' Try for Architecture." *Architectural Forum 113* (November 1960): 102-104.
"Year-Long Planning Produces New Junior High School." *Educational Executives Overview* (November 1962): 58–60.
Nesmith, Lynn. "Educating Columbus." *Architecture* 81 (November 1992): 84–91.

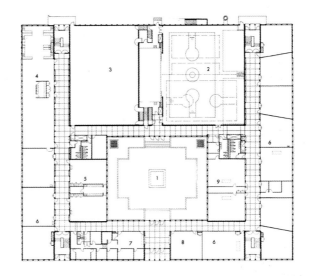

Plan, first level.
From firm brochure.

1 courtyard
2 multipurpose room
3 swimming pool
4 home economics
5 art
6 classrooms
7 administration
8 book store
9 science

Enclosed courtyard.
Balthazar Korab photograph,
probably late 1960s or 1970s.

ARENA STAGE

1101 Sixth Street, S.W.
Washington, D.C.

ARENA STAGE (FICHANDLER STAGE), 1960–62

KREEGER THEATER, 1968–72

Harry Weese had never designed a theater before Zelda Fichandler awarded him the commission for a permanent home for Arena Stage, a resident professional repertory company in Washington, D.C. Fichandler was seeking an architect who had no preconceived ideas of what a theater should be and who would be sensitive and responsive to her dedication to the arena or theater-in-the-round, an intimate theater form dating back to ancient times that focuses the audience's attention on the stage and the performers rather than on settings and mechanics. "I

did not want to waste time arguing with an architect about the respective values of the proscenium versus the arena stage," she later explained. Despite his lack of experience in theater design, Weese had no reservations about accepting the commission and viewed the assignment as an "opportunity for a major breakthrough."

The history of the Arena Stage goes back to the late 1940s when cofounders Fichandler and Edward Mangum, a professor in the drama department at George Washington University, where Fichandler was a graduate student, conceived the idea for a national repertory company. The company's first home was a dilapidated former movie house in Northwest Washington called the Hippodrome, which Fichandler transformed into a 247-seat performance space with an arena configuration. Arena Stage gave its first performance there on August 16, 1950. Six years later the company moved to larger quarters in the former "Hospitality Hall" of the Christian Heurich Brewery in Washington's Foggy Bottom district, but the scheduled demolition of the "Old Vat" in the early 1960s

Entrance and view into the double-story glazed vestibule. Balthazar Korab photograph, ca. 1961.

prompted Fichandler to secure a permanent home for the company.

After acquiring a triangular waterfront site in the Southwest Redevelopment Area, Fichandler began interviewing architects for the Arena Stage. Weese, who was collaborating with I.M. Pei on the master plan for the Southwest Washington urban renewal project at that time, was among the candidates. Fichandler announced her choice of Weese as the architect for the new theater in October 1959, explaining that she selected Weese precisely because of his lack of experience in theater design and his genius "at expressing in terms of architecture the nature of the activity going on inside."

After receiving the commission, Weese began educating himself about theater production and design by frequenting Arena Stage performances, attending Broadway plays with Fichandler, and listening to hours of tape-recorded input from Arena Stage administrators, actors, directors, designers, and technicians. Using this knowledge, he tailored the new building to the practical needs of the company. The

outcome was, according to Weese, "an expression in architecture of the principles of arena staging."

Weese's design placed the performance space and the support facilities in two distinct elements: a polygonal structure that housed the auditorium and a long rectangular wing that contained offices, workshops, dressing rooms, costume and prop rooms, and a green room. The two were connected by a narrow link. The double-story glazed entrance projected from a narrow end of the rectangular support wing. After entering the building, theatergoers passed through an outer lobby to the first-level foyer and ascended a wide staircase one-half level to a lounge, which had floor-to-ceiling windows that opened onto a smoking balcony.

One of the most innovative aspects of Weese's design was the dual means of access to the auditorium. The audience entered on the upper level through a low narrow passageway leading from the lounge to a circulation aisle located along the upper perimeter of the auditorium between the last row of seats and an outer ring of boxes. Actors entered at the stage level through tunnel-like

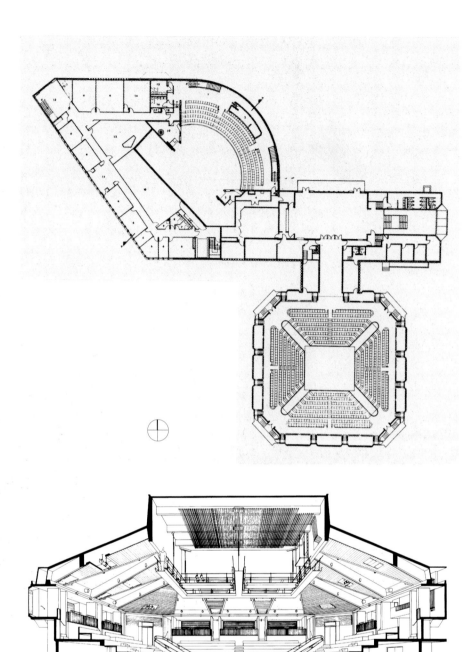

Plan, second level, Arena
Stage (lower right), and
Kreeger Theater (upper
left), and perspectival
section of Arena Stage.
Plan, i59274, Chicago History
Museum. Section from firm
brochure.

Auditorium, Arena Stage.
Balthazar Korab photograph,
ca. 1961.

corridors surrounded by concrete curbs. The separate
entrances for performers and spectators eliminated circulation conflicts between the audience and the actors and
facilitated seating of latecomers.

The focus of the auditorium was the 30 × 36-foot rectangular stage, which was trapped and divided into 3 × 6-
foot sections that could be raised or lowered independently
or in combination. An adjustable catwalk suspended over
the stage supported lighting instruments, and a steel grid
above the lighting bridge allowed scenery to be flown into
and out of the performance area.

Four steeply raked tiers, each with eight rows of seats,
surrounded the stage. One of the tiers could be removed
if a staging configuration other than the arena form was
desired, although because of the cost of disassembly, the
company rarely used this feature. Weese raised the first row
of seats nine inches above the stage and installed a low iron
railing to subtly separate the seating area from the performance space. Eleven private boxes, each containing eight
front-row seats, encircled the outer wall, bringing the total
capacity of the theater to 811.

As Fichandler had hoped, Weese's exterior design corresponded to the theater's interior activities. The performance wing was approximately square with canted corners
and expressed the shape of the stage and the auditorium
inside. The corners opened onto outdoor smoking balconies and fire exits. The rectangular cap rising from the roof

enclosed the lighting and staging grids, and blind, projecting brick bays marked the location of the boxes.

The materials and palette selected by Weese for the exterior of the theater complex harmonized with the neighboring
multistory apartment buildings of the Southwest Washington renewal program. Both the theater and the administrative wing had a concrete frame with infill of gray-brown
Roman brick and exposed concrete with a bush-hammered
finish that gave it a highly textured appearance. A ribbed,
dark gray terne, or sheet metal, roof covered the theater.

The subdued, almost neutral interior designed by
Dolores Miller, an interior designer who frequently collaborated with Weese, reflected Weese's vision of the auditorium as a background for art. Orange and dark gray seats
and carpeting provided contrasts to the muted beige walls.
Exposed sections of the light gray concrete ceiling alternated with sections sheathed in wood to conceal lighting
ports, a crawl space, fly lines, and ducts.

Groundbreaking for Arena Stage took place in October 1960, and on October 31, 1961, the new theater
opened with a production of Bertolt Brecht's *The Cauca-
sian Chalk Circle*. In 1966, Arena Stage received an Honor
Award for Design Excellence from the U.S. Department
of Housing and Urban Development. The jury noted the
excellent use of materials and described the theater as "an
outstanding building both in functioning of the plan and
external architectural quality."

In the late 1960s, Fichandler again turned to Weese for an addition to the Arena Stage complex. Named the Kreeger Theater for Washington philanthropist David Lloyd Kreeger, who contributed substantially to its construction, the addition adjoined the administrative wing of the original building but had a separate entrance.

The new theater was a small but structurally complex building. Structural engineer Frank Kornacker worked closely with Weese and project architect Ezra Gordon to design the concrete roof, which was built like a classical dome with a perimeter tension ring. The intimate, flexible performance space of the Kreeger Theater offered an alternative to arena staging. The auditorium had a modified ninety-degree thrust stage with a back wall and wings but no permanent proscenium.

Panels on either side of the stage allowed the performance space to vary in width from thirty to forty-two feet. A full grid and fly space extended over the entire stage, and exposed lighting accessible by catwalks hovered over the audience. The fan-shaped house contained 514 seats distributed between the main floor and a second-level balcony. Like the tiers of the Arena Stage, the seats of the Kreeger Theater were steeply raked. The colorful interior included brown velour walls, purple seats, and a burnished gold carpet.

The ground-floor level of the Kreeger Theater also contained workshops and a rehearsal room of the same size and configuration as the Arena Stage, which allowed complete sets to be used during rehearsals of plays planned for that space. When one performance closed in the Arena Stage, the sets for the new performance could be moved overnight from the rehearsal space. The rehearsal room, which could accommodate 125 folding chairs, also provided a space for experimental theater, works-in-progress, dramatic readings, and panel discussions.

The lower level of the Kreeger Theater contained dressing rooms, storage areas, a kitchen, and an informal, multiuse 200-seat restaurant and lounge called the "Old Vat Room," a name from the earlier days when the company resided in the Heurich Brewery. The second level housed administrative offices and a library/conference room.

The exterior materials used in the Kreeger addition were similar to those of the Arena Stage—brick and exposed concrete walls and painted sheet metal covering the roof. And, as in the Arena space, the exterior mirrored the interior configuration. A square cap rising from the flat roof corresponded to the stage house, and the sweeping curve extending from the Kreeger entrance to the junction with the existing support wing reflected the long curved back wall of the auditorium. Dedication of the Kreeger Theater took place on November 29, 1970.

After guiding Arena Stage for forty years, Zelda Fichandler left the company after the 1990–91 season. In 1992 the main arena was renamed the Fichandler Stage in honor of Zelda and her husband, Thomas.

The Vancouver-based architectural firm Bing Thom has now designed a new experimental theater for the Arena Stage. This third space, called the Cradle, will offer an intimate venue for new plays and serve as an incubator for emerging American playwrights. As part of this project, the Fichandler Stage and the Kreeger Theater will be refurbished and acoustically enhanced, and both will be united with the Cradle in a transparent glass envelope with a cantilevered roof. The complex is scheduled for completion in 2010.

ARENA STAGE
Job 427
Project Designer: Ezra Gordon
Structural Engineer: Frank Kornacker
Mechanical Engineer: Samuel R. Lewis & Associates
Consultant Acoustic Engineers: Bolt, Beranek & Newman
Contractor: John Tester & Son
Interior Design: Dolores Miller

KREEGER THEATER
Job 549
Structural Engineer: Engineers Collaborative
Mechanical Engineer: Samuel R. Lewis & Associates
Electrical Engineer: Kerekes & Kerekes

SELECTED BIBLIOGRAPHY

Gardner, R. H. "Arena Stage in D.C. Puts the Actors Back Where They Belong." *Baltimore Sun*, November 12, 1961

"Washington Builds a True Theatre-in-the-Round." *Times* (London), December 27, 1961.

"New Image, Old Plan for Arena Stage Theater in Washington, D.C." *Architectural Record* 131 (February 1962): 121–124.

"Arena for a Resident Company." *Progressive Architecture 43* (February 1962): 125–130.

Gutheim, Frederick. "Arena Is Bold Step in Design." *Evening Star*, May 19, 1962.

Collins, Peter. "Total Theatre." *Manchester Guardian*, November 15, 1962.

"Scrutiny and Excitement on Viewing Arena Stage." *Potomac Valley Architect* (October 1963): 5–8.

"Kreeger Theater Complex Makes Debut in Capital." *New York Times*, November 30, 1970.

"New Thrust for Arena Stage." *Progressive Architecture* 51 (December 1970): 52–54.

Von Eckardt, Wolf. "Two Architects' Dramatic Art." *Washington Post*, December 12, 1970.

"Kreeger Stars at Its Own Premiere." *Washington Post*, January 11, 1971.

Maslon, Laurence. *The Arena Adventure: The First 40 Years.* Washington, D.C.: Arena Stage, 1990.

TANGEMAN HOUSE

Muskoka Lakes, Ontario, Canada, 1961–66

Kitty Weese likened the multifaceted, copper-clad roof of the Tangeman House to a fanciful work of folded origami. Harry Weese's clients for the project were Clementine Miller Tangeman and her husband, Robert Tangeman, professor of musicology at Union Theological Seminary. The Tangemans were the sister and brother-in-law of J. Irwin Miller, chairman of the Cummins Engine Company and a longstanding client of the Weese firm. Since 1886, the Miller family had summered in the Muskoka Lakes district of Ontario, Canada, 150 miles north of Toronto. Several relatives of Clementine and Robert Tangeman had summer houses on a nearby mainland peninsula, but the couple chose to build their vacation home on a rocky, wooded, three-acre island located three hundred yards offshore. The island was connected to the mainland by underwater power and telephone cables and was accessible only by boat.

With the encouragement of the Tangemans, Weese consciously borrowed features from a summer cottage on the mainland designed by Eero Saarinen for Irwin and Xenia Miller. As Saarinen had done, Weese carefully insinuated the house into the topography, taking advantage of the unique natural setting and preserving the many pine, hemlock, and birch trees covering the island. The undulating roofline expressed both the complex floor plan and the changes in elevation dictated by the unusual site. As Weese explained in descriptive data submitted to the 1971 American Institute of Architects Honor Awards program,

Granite terrace with fireplace off the living room. *Balthazar Korab photograph, ca. 1966.*

Model, Tangeman House. *Balthazar Korab photograph, ca. 1966.*

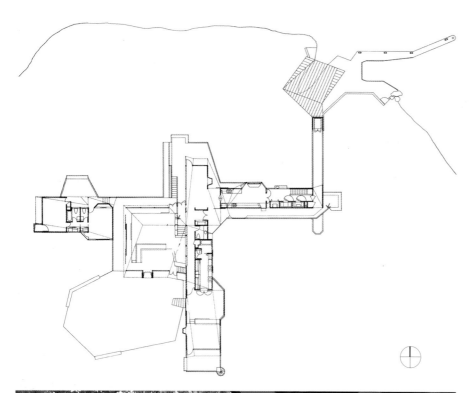

Plan. Radiating from the living room at the center of the house were the master bedroom and sitting room to the south, guest quarters to the west, dining room to the north, and kitchen and utility area to the east, all connected by a catwalk to the boathouse tower and elevator. i59319, Chicago History Museum.

ABOVE
Covered walkway to principal entrance. Balthazar Korab photograph, ca. 1966.

"The roof planes rise to capture a view, accent a space, and descend when the space requires intimacy" and "always return to a horizontal at the edges of the ridge."

The roof framing system combined folded planes with discontinuous supporting joists and could not be analyzed by conventional means. To determine the feasibility of the design, Weese and Martin Price conferred with Don Anderson, a structural engineer and partner with the Engineers Collaborative who had previously worked with Skidmore, Owings & Merrill on the Air Force Academy in Boulder, Colorado. Using a large-scale model, they were able to predict that when completely assembled, the structure would be rigid. The contractor framed the house using a system of temporary shoring. If any movement occurred when the shoring was removed, the contractor was to notify the Weese firm so that diagonal bracing could be added before the roof collapsed. The structure required only two such braces.

The Tangemans commissioned Weese to design not only the family's living quarters but also an electric ferry that shuttled the owners, their guests, and, at the beginning and end of the season, their grand piano to and from the mainland. The ferry, a double-ended vessel powered by a golf cart motor, docked at a boathouse tower equipped with an elevator, which lifted the family and their visitors thirty-five feet to the main level of the house. The elevator opened onto a catwalk that connected to a covered walkway leading past the kitchen and service wing to the principal entrance. A wildflower-lined footpath to the house offered an alternative for the more adventuresome. A separate bridge from the elevator tower provided access to the servants' quarters on the lower level.

The focal point of the plan was the grand piano in the 30 × 30 foot living room, the largest space in the house. Spanning the living room posed a particular challenge. Weese placed the high point of the ceiling off center and arranged the 24-foot-long, 2 × 12 inch joists of the upper portion of the roof horizontally. The joists of the lower roof cascaded in a diagonal pattern and acted as struts to support the upper roof. The glass wall forming the south side of the living room contained a fireplace jutting out onto an expansive terrace paved in local granite, creating a large "outdoor room" similar to one that Saarinen had incorporated into the cottage he designed for the Millers. Living room windows to the north offered views of the natural wooded landscape.

Glass walls wrapped around three sides of the pavilion-like dining room, which was surrounded by broad outside decks, and bay windows extended from the kitchen and master bedroom into the outside environment. Decks also opened off both the master suite at the south end and

Living room. Balthazar Korab
photograph, ca. 1966.

the guest quarters, which Weese located to the west, apart from the more central areas. Protected outdoor walkways connected the wings of the 4,000-square-foot structure, and irregularly shaped glass panes fitted into the walls of the interior passageways framed dramatic views.

Weese made extensive use of native materials and traditional construction techniques, both on the interior and on the exterior of the house. He exposed the wood joists, as Saarinen had done in the Miller cottage, and strengthened the wood frame with knee bracing typical of Pennsylvania Dutch architecture. Vertical redwood siding with tongue-and-groove joints covered the frame on the exterior. The lichen-green stain applied to the siding allowed the house to blend with the surrounding landscape. Interior walls, like those in Saarinen's design, were unfinished basswood. The furnishings, selected by Kitty Weese's Design Unit, included lamps with conical shades, built-in seating, and Alvar Aalto–

designed furniture, which, as Kitty explained in *Harry Weese Houses*, complemented the natural finishes and echoed the shapes and textures found throughout the house.

The house proved to be a source of constant delight for the owners. As Clementine Tangeman wrote, "Each time we return we feel a new sense of joy and discovery. It is a house to renew one's spirit."

Job 464
Construction Drawings: Martin Price
Associate Architect: George Buchan, Toronto
Landscape Architect: Harry Weese & Associates
Interior Design: Design Unit (Kitty Weese)
Contractor: Milton Goltz

SELECTED BIBLIOGRAPHY

Architectural Record Houses of 1970 (mid-May 1970): 50–53.

HYDE PARK
A & B URBAN RENEWAL
PROJECT

Parcels between Fifty-third and Fifty-seventh streets,
Kimbark Avenue and Lake Park Avenue
Chicago, Illinois, 1956–63

This entry was written by Leslie Coburn.

The Chicago neighborhood of Hyde Park, a community famous, among other things, as the home of the University of Chicago, was established in the mid-nineteenth century as an affluent railroad suburb. Although it remained a largely middle-class community into the early twentieth century, by the 1940s the neighborhood, like much of the South Side, was experiencing racial changes, overcrowding, and physical deterioration. In the late 1940s and early 1950s, many Hyde Park residents, clergymen, and businesspeople decided to take action, and two influential groups—the Hyde Park-Kenwood Community Conference and the South East Chicago Commission (SECC)—were formed to address these perceived problems. Their efforts culminated in a forty-five-acre urban renewal project known

Site plan of the Hyde Park A & B redevelopment project designed by I. M. Pei and Harry Weese, as built, including a new shopping center located at East Fifty-fifth Street and East Lake Park Avenue (large open boxes to right in drawing), a pair of ten-story apartment buildings on an island in East Fifty-fifth Street, and two- and three-story townhouse groupings scattered in nearby blocks north and south of East Fifty-fifth Street. *From Oscar Newman, Defensible Space & Crime Prevention through Urban Design,* 1973.

as "Hyde Park A & B," which dramatically transformed the heart of old Hyde Park through a program of clearance and redevelopment and became one of the most conspicuous and well studied of the major American urban renewal efforts of the postwar years.

The groundwork for Hyde Park A & B was laid around 1953, when the SECC initiated a study to identify Hyde Park's most "blighted" sections and to propose a plan for redevelopment. This project followed on the heels of one that had been carried out by students and faculty from Harvard (including Walter Gropius, Hideo Sasaki, and Reginald Isaacs), the Illinois Institute of Technology (led by Ludwig Mies van der Rohe and Ludwig Hilberseimer), and the Sociology Department of the University of Chicago. This study had examined Hyde Park in the context of a much larger area of the South Side, and had produced several alternative redevelopment proposals. For its own, more focused study, the SECC hired Harry Weese as architect and engineering consultant, and Jack Meltzer, a veteran of earlier Chicago redevelopment projects, as planning director. Weese used building inspection data to identify a potential clearance area that contained the neighborhood's most deteriorated commercial and residential blocks, areas that might qualify for "slum area" designation and thus be eligible for federal redevelopment assistance. The irregularly shaped area he mapped out was composed of two sections—an area centered along East 55th Street and Lake Park Avenue to the south, later called "Hyde Park A," and a smaller (4.6 acres) area, located along East 54th Street to the north, which became "Hyde Park B."

In 1954, the SECC included Weese's suggestions in its published proposal, *South East Chicago Renewal Project No. 1*. SECC executive director Julian Levi called it a plan for "carving out the infected tissue of our neighborhood and replacing it with good tissue." The report included, in addition to Weese's clearance maps, a site plan for the area and sketches by Weese for an arcaded shopping center and several new types of residential buildings. Near the Illinois Central Railroad tracks and major arterial streets, Weese suggested a series of elevator apartment buildings. On the quieter streets he recommended townhouses, for their "economy of ground use, private garden space, inherent privacy, sharing of walls, and homogeneity." He also proposed building "double maisonettes," four-story structures that he described as "one row house on top of another," for rental and cooperative housing.

In its October 1954 issue, *Architectural Forum* reported favorably on the SECC proposal, commenting that it might well become a "prototype of the attack on city slums, envisaged in the Housing Act of 1954."

Stemming the flight to suburbia was a driving force behind Hyde Park's renewal project, as it was for other urban renewal efforts of the period, and many of the project's goals seemed focused on making Hyde Park more like its suburban competitors. These goals included reducing the neighborhood's density, creating more light and space, introducing modern shopping facilities, providing off-street parking, offering affordable modern homes with open flowing living spaces and space for outdoor living, and creating safe places for children to play.

By the summer of 1956, with federal funding secured and demolition underway, private developers were invited to submit proposals for the redevelopment of Hyde Park A & B with the stipulation that the plans follow the boundaries and spirit of the SECC's 1954 proposal. Five proposals were submitted, including one from the successful Chicago developer Herbert Greenwald. Greenwald's plans were the work of Mies van der Rohe and Hilberseimer, the same team that had recently designed Greenwald's Lafayette Park redevelopment project in downtown Detroit. New York–based Webb & Knapp, run by the flamboyant William Zeckendorf, also submitted a proposal and was ultimately selected as developer for the project. Webb & Knapp's proposal was designed by its chief architect, I. M. Pei, and generally followed Weese's 1954 plan, although it deviated strikingly in its inclusion of a scheme to split the eastbound and westbound lanes of Fifty-fifth Street to create an island on which two ten-story apartment buildings would be erected. This arrangement was intended to transform what was perceived as a busy, rundown commercial thoroughfare into a quiet residential street.

Once Webb & Knapp was selected as project developer, Pei invited his old friend Harry Weese to serve as the local associate architect. In this capacity Weese would be expected to obtain zoning variances and building permits and work with Pei and the Webb & Knapp staff on the final site plan. Because both Pei and Weese were involved with all aspects of the design work and shared credit for the commission, it is not always obvious who actually designed the various parts of the project. It is clear that both offices worked together to arrive at the final site plan and traffic layouts. The record indicates that Pei was responsible for the design of the ten-story University Apartments on Fifty-fifth Street and the two-story housing units immediately north of that complex. Harry Weese & Associates was primarily responsible for the first two-story townhouses in Hyde Park B, a larger courtyard complex of townhouses in Hyde Park A, and the shopping center. The two offices together produced designs for the majority of the three-story townhouses.

Webb & Knapp used the term "townhouse" to avoid the negative connotations of "row house." The first residences completed in the renewal project were a row of fifteen Weese-designed townhouses on East Fifty-fourth Street in Hyde Park B. These houses were intended for Hyde Park Cooperative Homes, Inc. (HPCH), an organization formed in the mid-1950s by a group of Hyde Park residents to ensure that at least some of the homes built in the new redevelopment project would be modestly priced and cooperatively owned. However, because of delays in obtaining financing, the townhouses were sold outright (in fee simple) in early 1959. Weese's two-story townhouse design featured an open floor plan on the first level, a modern kitchen, and efficiently used space—for example, many units had four bedrooms on the second floor. The materials and exterior details, which included a limestone screen framing the façade's narrow vertical windows, a limestone cornice, and a decorative iron balcony, resembled features of the Weese-designed single-family home built for the Gale Johnson family on nearby Kenwood Avenue in 1957 (see entry).

After some alterations in the original design, thirty-four townhouses with three different floor plans were completed in August 1962 for HPCH on a nearby block in

"View Looking North Up Harper," sketch by Harry Weese published in 1954 in the SECC's publication *South East Chicago "Renewal Project No. 1."* This view, looking toward East Fifty-fifth Street, shows the three housing types Weese suggested in the initial proposal: the townhouse (at left), elevator apartment building (in distance), and double maisonette (at right). From *South East Chicago Renewal Project No. 1.*

Hyde Park A, between South Blackstone and Dorchester avenues, and East Fifty-fourth Place and Rochdale Place. Each unit had a small front and back yard, and the rows of townhouses formed a square that enclosed a shared central courtyard.

The two- and three-story townhouses that Pei and Weese worked on together were built in Hyde Park A, slightly nearer the University of Chicago, and were planned for somewhat more affluent residents. Although many designs were proposed, only a few were used—two slightly different two-story designs, probably designed by Pei, and two three-story designs. The three-story models—the "E-1" and "E-2" townhouses—bear some resemblance to Pei's Society Hill townhouses, which were built in Philadelphia for another Webb & Knapp redevelopment project from this same period, suggesting that Pei may have played a larger role than Weese, at least in the final exterior appearance.

Inspired by earlier European precedents, such as the terraces, squares, and green spaces of Bath and London, and American examples, such as the residences of Beacon Hill and the South End of Boston, as well as nearby Madison Park, laid out in Kenwood in the late nineteenth century, Weese and Pei arranged many of the townhouses in Hyde Park A and B around open spaces like the HPCH's courtyard. In a project brochure, the architects explained

that their courtyard concept was a way to avoid monotony, give unity to the project, and at the same time create sheltered inward-looking private spaces. These shared common areas were also partly intended to compensate for the small size of the individual gardens. The three-story townhouses of "Harper Square" along South Harper Avenue between East Fifty-sixth and Fifty-seventh streets faced a central oval green that was formed by splitting South Harper Avenue to form one-way lanes on either side.

As part of an effort to design "residential squares in a variety of shapes," the architects also initially planned a circular townhouse group directly north of Harper Square aligned with the axis of South Harper Avenue and just north of East Fifty-sixth Street. Called "The Circle," this proposal again suggests the influence of earlier urban models, such as The Circus, built in Bath, England, in the eighteenth century. The Circle scheme and its unusual townhouses—the "F" model—were eventually replaced with straight rows of townhouses.

All of the townhouses were constructed of a similar palette of materials, including a buff-colored brick, which set the new buildings apart from the mostly red brick structures seen elsewhere in the neighborhood, and limestone trim. The horizontal bands of clerestory windows and recessed entrances unified the townhouse units, creating a clean and seamless aesthetic, and the use of durable exterior materials ensured that this uniformity would be preserved over time, even with changes in ownership. Because the architects felt that maintaining this uniformity would be essential for the long-term success of the project, they presented homeowners with a set of guidelines covering issues such as the position of television antennas and appropriate landscaping choices and recommended that these guidelines be adopted and enforced by the homeowners' groups for each of the non-cooperatively owned segments of the project.

Design of the Hyde Park shopping center was largely handled by the Weese office. Its most striking features were a floating concrete arcade roof and the center's central courtyard, which opened to East Fifty-fifth Street. The courtyard area, planned to serve as a community gathering space, was an instant success, and although much of the shopping center was altered in the 1990s, the courtyard space remains and its benches and tables are in constant use. The courtyard also continues to host annual neighborhood events, such as the spring and fall garden fairs and a used-book sale. Until 2008, the center's major tenant was the Hyde Park Co-op Grocery, which, on its opening, was said to be the largest supermarket in the Midwest. There were also many smaller shops, many of them designed in

Cover of sales brochure for the Hyde Park Cooperative Homes. The promised "Fall 1961 Occupancy" was off by one year. Harry Weese papers, box 327 A&B, i59317, Chicago History Museum.

View to the northeast of the three-story Harper Square townhouses designed by I. M. Pei and Harry Weese. Iron fencing was later added around the central oval park and individual gardens. Hedrich Blessing photograph, HB24243, 1961, Chicago History Museum.

the Weese office by Jack Levin for tenants like Fannie May Candies, Neumode Hosiery, and Wimpy's Hamburgers.

As one of the first urban renewal projects in the country to receive federal funding, and one of Chicago's earliest neighborhood redevelopment projects, Hyde Park A & B attracted a great deal of attention and was widely debated. One of the most prominent critics was Jane Jacobs, who in her classic book *Death and Life of Great American Cities* claimed that Hyde Park's renewal plan "designates and removes . . . chunks of blight and replaces them with chunks of Radiant Garden City designed, as usual, to minimize use of the streets. The plan also adds still more empty spaces here and there, [and] blurs even further the district's already poor distinctions between private and public space." She continued, "so far as security is concerned, nothing will have changed except that the opportunity for street crime will be a little easier, if anything, because of the added emptiness."

This was a curious verdict. Although it could have easily applied to most other urban renewal projects of the era, it appears to miss the mark in the case of Hyde Park A & B. Oscar Newman, writing in *Defensible Space: Crime Prevention through Urban Design,* saw things quite differently: "The [townhouse] units are disposed on their site in a manner similar to the patterns of an older neighboring single-family residential development. They have been provided with a formal entry area, immediately off the sidewalk, defined by low walls, a paved walk, and a set of stairs which leads a half flight up to the ground-floor level. These devices serve to designate very clearly the ten feet in front of the dwelling, and to put this area under the zone of influence of its occupants. Activities on the street are easily monitored from the dwelling units proper and from passing vehicles." According to Newman, the common interior courtyards expanded this zone of influence. Similarly, *Architectural Record* commented that the "fenestration of

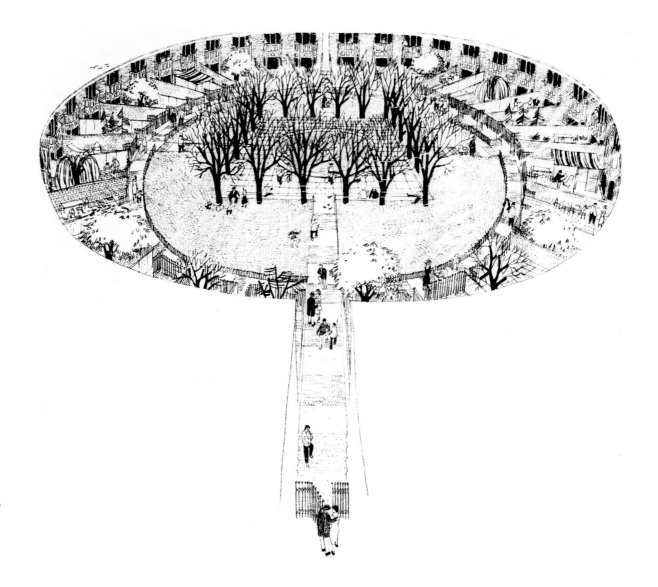

"Hyde Park A: Interior of Circle." This sketch by Harry Weese, dated December 17, 1957, shows the townhouse group originally planned for Hyde Park A just north of East Fifty-sixth Street. HB22376, Chicago History Museum.

the town houses is such that many pairs of 'eyes on the street' are possible—if residents wish."

The most serious objection to the project was its displacement of businesses and residents. Demolition, particularly along Fifty-fifth Street, was responsible for destroying a large number of neighborhood businesses, many of them cherished local institutions. Although the new shopping center did accommodate some of these businesses, the project as a whole did not replace a great deal of local retail. Even more serious was the project's impact on the community's lower-income residents, who had occupied apartment buildings and rooming houses that were slated for clearance, and were effectively cleared away along with the buildings.

Nevertheless, the project was counted a success on many levels. It was unusual for the remarkable degree of involvement it received from the community. It was also notable for its site plan—especially for its common areas and courtyards. The successful revival of the townhouse inspired later renewal and infill projects throughout Chicago and elsewhere in the nation. Most importantly, because Weese was attentive to matching the character and scale of the existing neighborhood, both in his initial SECC work and later in his work with Pei, and because Hyde Park's clearance, unlike earlier Chicago projects, had been selective rather than wholesale, Hyde Park A & B has been widely hailed as one of the most sensitive and successful of the early renewal projects.

SELECTED BIBLIOGRAPHY

"Hyde Park A & B Redevelopment" (Project brochure). Hyde Park Historical Society, Special Collections Research Center, University of Chicago Library, n.d.

I. M. Pei & Associates. *Community Appraisal Study: A Summary of Current Proposals.* Chicago: South Side Planning Board, 1952.

South East Chicago Commission, (Lawrence A. Kimpton, et al.). *South East Chicago Renewal Project No. 1.* South East Chicago Commission, 1954.

"News: Chicago Will Add Touch of Country to City." *Architectural Forum,* (October 1954): 126–127.

"5 Submit Bids to Redevelop Hyde Park Site." *Chicago Tribune,* October 2, 1956.

Jane Jacobs. *Death and Life of Great American Cities.* Vintage Books: New York, 1992 [1961], pp. 44–45.

"High-Rise Low-Rise and Shopping for Chicago Redevelopment." *Architectural Record,* 131 (April 1962): 163—170.

Oscar Newman. *Defensible Space: Crime Prevention through Urban Design.* Revised Edition. New York: Collier Books, [1973].

View of central courtyard, looking north, Hyde Park Shopping Center. Hedrich Blessing photograph, HB24758A, 1961, Chicago History Museum.

IBM BUILDING

611 East Wisconsin Avenue
Milwaukee, Wisconsin, 1961–66

The "Poor Man's Rational Office Building" was how Harry Weese described the prototype he developed in the early 1960s for an economical speculative office tower. In a 1962 *Architectural Forum* article describing his proposal, Weese identified the probable client as the developer "for whom an office building is a money-making, not a prestige, proposition" and the probable tenants as "humble corporations." The prototype's multifunctional precast concrete construction system provided a structural framework, accommodated mechanical elements, and created a deeply modeled sculptural façade. A compact central service core of cast-in-place concrete braced the structure, and precast concrete wall units and floor slabs hooked together around this core. In the early 1960s when Weese developed his prototype, the cost of a prestigious office building could reach as high as $40 to $50 per square foot. He projected the cost of his design at $17.50 to $18.00 per square foot, and the estimated time for construction for a thirty-story tower at a seemingly impossible sixty days.

Weese soon had the opportunity to apply and expand the principles illustrated in his "Poor Man's" building in a Milwaukee project that, ironically, involved two large and highly profitable corporations. The building's owner was the Milwaukee-based Northwestern Mutual Life Insurance Company and the intended occupant was the Milwaukee branch office of International Business Machines Corporation (IBM).

The design developed by Weese for this project was a long, narrow, seven-story structure resting on a cast-in-place concrete podium. Cast-in-place concrete columns and girders at the lobby level supported the walls of the upper floors. As in Weese's prototype, precast concrete panels formed the building's load-bearing walls. The panels measured nine feet wide by eleven feet (or one story) high, and each panel contained two windows separated by narrow concrete mullions.

The vertical edges of the wall panels had semicircular indentations so that when two panels were placed next to one another, the edges fit together to form a hollow tube that could accommodate an air supply duct. Behind the semicircular edges were two vertical six-inch holes surrounded by spiral reinforcing bars. Once a panel was in place, these holes aligned with those of the panels above and below to form a continuous channel. Threading ver-

View to southwest, IBM Building, Milwaukee. Balthazar Korab photograph, ca. 1966.

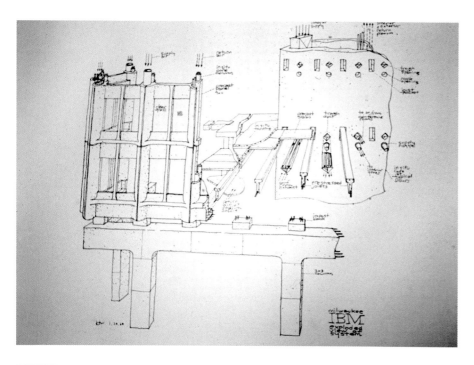

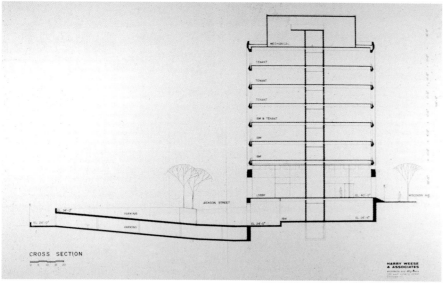

Diagram of the precast concrete construction system. *Chicago History Museum, i59255.*

Section, showing the narrow cast-in-place concrete core. *Chicago History Museum, i59254.*

tical reinforcements through these channels and then filling the cavity with concrete produced a slender but sturdy monolithic column that united the panels.

Like the prototype, the IBM Building had a narrow cast-in-place concrete core that contained the washrooms, elevators, and stairwells. T-section concrete floor joists spanned the space between the central core and the exterior wall panels, and lightweight concrete planks filled the spaces between the joists. Rather than a dropped ceiling, Weese used the underside of the floor slab as the ceiling for the floor below. The troughs between the joists provided space for triangular light fixtures with fluorescent lamps.

The air supply and return ducts hidden in the channels of the exterior walls fed induction units located below the windows to supply air to the building's perimeter. Cone-shaped nozzles, first used by Weese in his renovation of Chicago's Newberry Library, directed air to the interior zone. The troughs between the floor joists doubled as air supply and return ducts for enclosed spaces, such as private offices and conference rooms.

The space between the recessed lobby and the outer edge of the building formed an arcade. A basement garage and a structure at the rear of the building housed parking facilities.

Engineering News-Record described the building as "elegant simplicity," and James Bailey's review in *Architectural Forum* characterized it as "an impeccably ordered, logical, handsome and articulate structure" that "was cheap, too." As Weese predicted, the cost of the nearly 200,000-square-foot building was a modest $17.52 per square foot, with a $2.00 per square foot allowance for tenant partitions.

Job 497
Structural Engineer: Engineers Collaborative
Mechanical and Electrical Engineer: Samuel R. Lewis & Associates

Lighting Consultant: William Lam
General Contractor: Selzer-Ornst.
Landscape Architect: Office of Dan Kiley

SELECTED BIBLIOGRAPHY

Harry Weese. "'Poor Man's' Precast Office Building." *Architectural Forum* 116 (January 1962): 106–111.
"The Price of Graceful Simplicity: Meticulous Attention to Detail." *Engineering News-Record* (March 25, 1965): 46–48.
James Bailey. "Making Precast Concrete Do More for Less." *Architectural Forum* 123 (November 1965): 52–55.

Lobby, with the surrounding exterior street level arcade. Balthazar Korab photograph, ca. 1966.

View of fourth level,
office of Harry Weese &
Associates, prior to the
1974 fire, showing atrium
with ficus trees. Joe Karr
photograph, May 1971.

OFFICES OF HARRY WEESE & ASSOCIATES

10 West Hubbard Street
Chicago, Illinois, 1965; remodeled, 1976

In 1947, after his service in World War II and a brief return to the Chicago office of Skidmore, Owings & Merrill, Harry Weese established his own architectural practice. His first office was located in the Michigan Square (Diana Court) Building at 105 East Ohio Street in a room behind the sales floor of Baldwin Kingrey, the furniture store founded that same year by Weese, wife Kitty, and Jody Kingrey. As the practice expanded, Weese required larger quarters, and between 1951 and 1965, the firm occupied various spaces along the Michigan Avenue corridor.

By the mid-1960s, Weese was again searching for more space. Rather than designing a new building or leasing expensive rental space, he decided to purchase and renovate an abandoned nineteenth-century loft building at 10 West Hubbard Street that had once housed the H. T. Thompson & Company Wool Commission. The fruit packer that owned the building sold the 100 × 100 foot, five-story structure to the 10 Hubbard Corporation, the entity created by Weese to purchase the structure. Although the brick walls were in disrepair, the heavy-timber beams were splintering, the roof had gaping holes, and the interior was littered with whiskey bottles and pigeon droppings, Weese recognized the building's potential. He began making plans to install his offices on the upper two floors and lease the lower three and turned over his preliminary sketches to Bob E. Bell to develop.

In the remodeled structure an elevator in the building's vestibule with doors opening to the east and west rose to the firm's offices on the fourth and fifth levels. The clear plastic roof of the elevator cab and the skylight that topped the shaft brought in sunlight and exposed the mechanical equipment overhead. Chicago building inspectors questioned the legality of the design but were never able to locate a city code specifically prohibiting it.

Weese preserved the historic character of the old warehouse by exposing the brick walls and heavy-timber columns and ceiling joists. To increase the amount of natural light entering the space, he cut a two-story skylit atrium into the center of the building. Circular and trapezoidal cutouts in the walls ringing the atrium allowed light from the angled skylight to enter into the offices on the fifth floor. Because the skylight sloped toward the south, it was necessary to provide shades that could be drawn over the glass in sunny weather.

Fourth-floor offices surrounded a central courtyard with travertine paving and potted trees, originally acacia trees and later ficus trees when the acacias proved too challenging to maintain. Staff members had the option of entering the offices either from the courtyard or from a corridor along the outer perimeter of the space. The walls on the courtyard side were not vertical but slanted outward. Consequently, when staff members entered or exited their offices through the courtyard, the doors automatically slammed shut, generating considerable noise heard throughout the space. Weese located drafting rooms at the north and south ends of the fourth floor to take advantage of natural light entering through the windows in the front and rear façades of the building. The windowless areas adjacent to the common walls to the east and west contained stairways, storage spaces, support areas, and bathroom facilities.

Weese originally occupied an open office facing the fourth-floor courtyard but soon found that he wanted more privacy. He first enclosed his space in Plexiglas panels but eventually retreated to a private office on the fifth floor. A green room at the fifth level adjacent to Weese's office served as a conference facility as well as a waiting area for clients and other visitors. A gallery on the south side of the fifth floor provided display space for models and drawings. The hanging display panels were on pulleys that could be raised to transform the gallery into what one former Weese staff member described as "a fine party room." Other spaces on the upper level housed Kitty Weese's interior design firm and the office of landscape architect Joe Karr.

The new offices provided a stimulating and creative work environment for Weese and his staff for nearly ten years. Then on New Year's Eve of 1974, fire broke out at 10 West Hubbard Street while Weese was vacationing in Aspen. Although the fire caused the floor of the fourth level to collapse, the slow-burning heavy-timber structure saved the building from total destruction. And because the firemen took care to cover the drafting tables, very few drawings were lost, and the firm was able to continue to use the space during subsequent clean-up and renovation. Staff members with current projects moved to the fifth floor while the others helped to clean up.

The most significant design modification that Weese made in his post-fire renovation was the expansion of the office to include a portion of the building's third floor. He used the hole in the fourth floor caused by the fire to extend the atrium down into the central portion of the third level, which became a display space for models

View of the redesigned fourth level after the 1974 fire, showing the offices surrounding the atrium, which overlooked the third floor display area. Hedrich Blessing photograph, HB41319G, ca. 1974, Chicago History Museum.

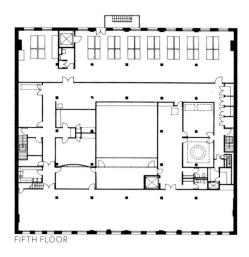

FIFTH FLOOR

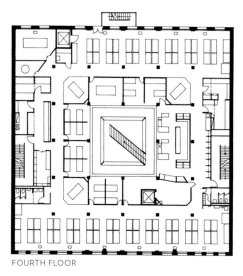

FOURTH FLOOR

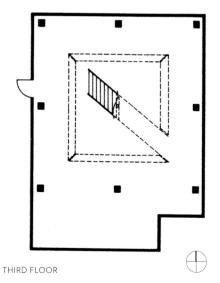

Plans after the 1974 fire.
From firm brochure.

THIRD FLOOR

and photographs. The fourth floor contained partitioned offices open on the side facing the atrium and a reception area. A dramatic diagonal staircase slashing through the atrium connected the fourth floor to the lower level. As was the case before the fire, drafting stations lined the perimeter at the north and south ends of the fourth floor, and the executive offices, including Weese's own, occupied the fifth floor. During the 1980s, after Weese became the publisher of *Inland Architect*, he moved the journal's offices to the fifth floor of 10 West Hubbard.

In his post-fire design, Weese replaced the angled skylight that had topped the atrium prior to the fire with a 30 × 30 foot sawtoothed skylit roof that illuminated all three levels. According to Weese employee Kim Clawson, the atrium acted as a "heat chimney," collecting hot air that could be vented by opening the skylight.

Harry Weese remained at 10 West Hubbard until his retirement in 1992. The staff members who subsequently purchased the firm, renaming it "Harry Weese Associates," continued to occupy the space, which they initially rented from Weese's wife, Kitty, and then from the new owners when Kitty sold the building in 1994. In November 2000, Gensler, an architecture, design, planning, and consulting firm with home offices in San Francisco, purchased Harry Weese Associates, and staff members who remained moved from 10 West Hubbard to the Gensler offices.

Today Ross Barney Architects occupies much of the space that once housed Harry Weese & Associates and its successor firm. The space retains much of the character of the Weese era, although offices no longer surround the atrium and a second staircase now connects the fourth and fifth levels.

Jobs 564, 864

SELECTED BIBLIOGRAPHY

Nory Miller. "Four Architects Who Set Up Shop on the Offbeat Side of the Street." *Inland Architect* (June 1972): 12-13.

"Architects' Offices. Harry Weese & Associates." *Architectural Review* 162 (October 1977): 242.

View of drafting stations, after the 1974 fire. Hedrich Blessing photograph, HB41319E, ca. 1974, Chicago History Museum.

FIRST BAPTIST CHURCH OF COLUMBUS

3300 Fairlawn Drive
Columbus, Indiana, 1962–65

By the early 1960s, Harry Weese's reputation in Columbus, Indiana, was well established. Weese's firm had designed an apartment complex, a youth center, an ice skating rink, a home for the aged, schools, banks, and office and manufacturing facilities for the Cummins Engine Company. In late 1961, Gene Paul, a Cummins vice president and member of the church's board of trustees, contacted Weese to ask for his input on possible architects for the new home of the First Baptist Church of Columbus. The architect ultimately selected by church leaders for the commission was not one of the candidates mentioned in Paul's letter to Weese, but rather Weese himself.

The First Baptist Church of Columbus had been worshipping in an 1854 building near the town center that had been remodeled and reconstructed several times. By 1956, the growing congregation needed more space and

purchased a flat eight-acre tract northeast of downtown. The program for the new complex included not only a main sanctuary but also a chapel, administrative offices, a fellowship hall, Sunday school classrooms, and a nursery.

When Weese received the commission for the First Baptist Church, the North Christian Church, a striking modern church designed by Finnish-born architect Eero Saarinen for a group of former members of the First Christian Church, including Cummins Engine chairman J. Irwin Miller, was under construction. Jack Hartray recalls that Donald E. Tull, president of Cummins and building committee chairman of the First Baptist Church, told Weese that he wanted a church "as good as Irwin's but half the cost."

Formulation of the program for the church began with a series of twenty tape-recorded committee meetings at which church members defined the detailed requirements of the new building. As he analyzed these requirements, Weese realized that the educational portion of the complex would be much larger than the main sanctuary and chapel and that the Sunday school space could potentially dominate the design. His solution was to place the nave and chapel above the school, thereby providing the

Perspective sketch by Harry Weese of an early concept for the First Baptist Church of Columbus. In the final design, despite a change in location, the form and organization of the church remained essentially the same as Weese initially proposed. Columbus Indiana Architectural Archives.

FACING PAGE

View of entrance, showing the bridge over the moat-like space that brought light into the classrooms below. Hedrich Blessing photograph, HB28683Y, ca. 1965, Chicago History Museum.

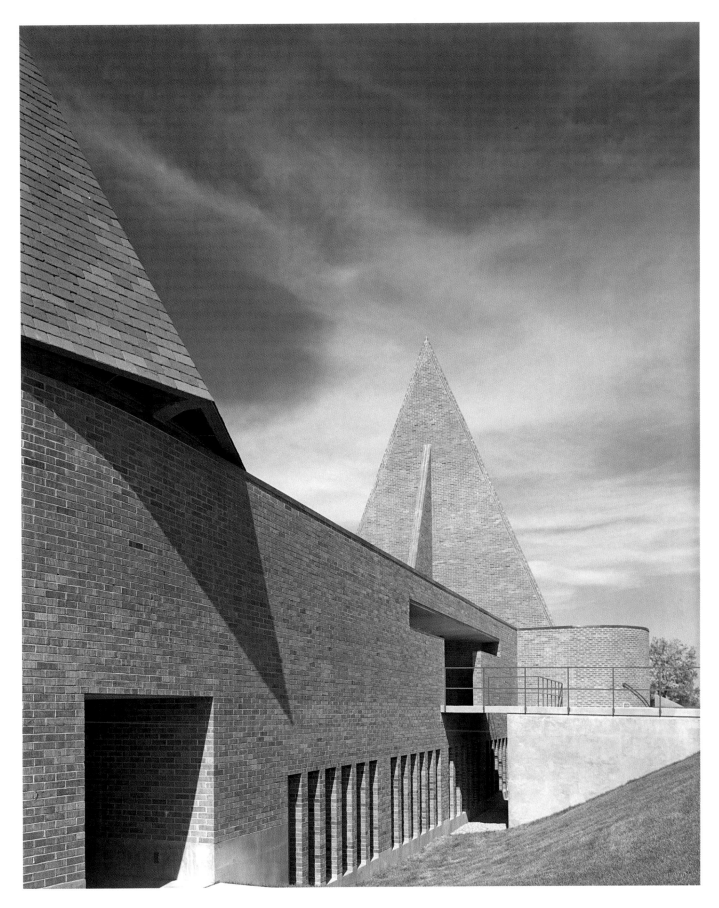

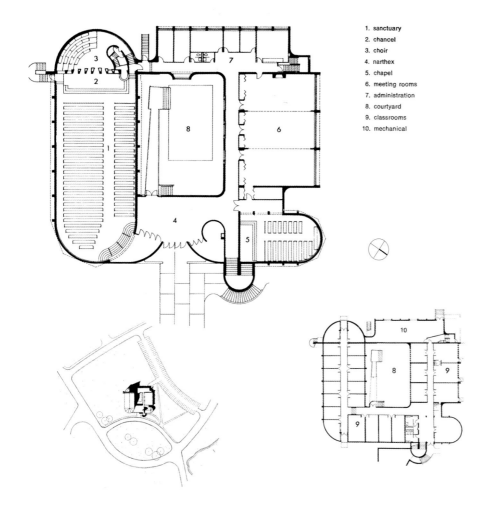

1. sanctuary
2. chancel
3. choir
4. narthex
5. chapel
6. meeting rooms
7. administration
8. courtyard
9. classrooms
10. mechanical

Site plan and plans for lower (bottom right) and main (top) level. i59288, Chicago History Museum.

large amount of space required for the social and educational requirements of the church but permitting the worship spaces to dominate.

Weese unveiled his sketches for the church, a two-level structure surrounding a central courtyard, at a congregational meeting in November 1962. The design blended the abstract and the familiar, merging the simple but bold geometric shapes of the modern movement with the steeply sloped roofs of the medieval era and combining poured concrete walls, painted white, with a contrasting timber and wood shingle roof. A display of the model and renderings in the church sanctuary allowed the congregation to become familiar with the proposed design.

Many members of the congregation reacted unfavorably to Weese's modern approach. There were objections to the unconventional design and materials and the high cost of a building that some members perceived as a "showplace." Others voiced concern over the inadequacy of the school facilities and the lack of room for expansion and suggested that the classrooms be placed in a separate struc-

ture. Still others preferred a scheme that could be built, and paid for, in progressive stages. After considering this input, the church building council rejected Weese's design at a meeting held in early January 1963 and requested that he submit an alternative.

Weese was reluctant to accept the council's verdict. As he explained in a February 1963 letter to Paul, "Subjective statements such as 'showplace' reveal a lack of understanding as to the basic simplicity of the concept, essentially exposed structure in simple spaces, two of them with high ceilings. No frills, no finish." If the dilemma posed by a demand for more space at a lower cost could not be resolved, Weese suggested that the church consider shelving the project. As he advised, it would be unwise to "trade the venerable if inadequate old church for an unvenerable, inadequate new church." But he ended the letter with the hope that "this cause is not lost."

Weese did agree to substitute reinforced brick for concrete for the walls of the building, a change that not only was more appealing to church members but, surprisingly, also lowered contractors' cost estimates owing to the elimination of the expensive formwork that would have been needed to pour the high concrete walls. To solve the problem of future expansion, he advised a separate annex, never built, rather than a piecemeal venture, which, he pointed out, would ultimately prove more costly. In the end, Weese's diplomacy reassured the congregation, and they decided to proceed with the construction of a new church that differed little from Weese's original design. Although materials changed from concrete and shingles to brick and slate, the form and organization remained largely unaltered.

The working drawings for the church had already been completed in September 1963 when access problems and proposed zoning changes caused the congregation to reconsider the location. After evaluating possible options, church members decided to sell the land originally selected for the church and purchase a seven-acre site with a gently sloping knoll in a rapidly developing section even farther northeast of downtown Columbus known as Fairlawn, one of the highest points in Bartholomew County. Today this area is an attractive residential neighborhood, but in the early 1960s it was fairly isolated and sparsely populated. Construction began at the site in the spring of 1964 and was completed in the fall of 1965. The Fairlawn site with its gently sloping knoll was much better suited to Weese's design than the original flat site because it solved the access problems inherent in the two-story structure. Later critiques frequently commended the sensitive fitting of the building to its location. The site also provided the church with a compatible neighbor, the W. D. Richards Elemen-

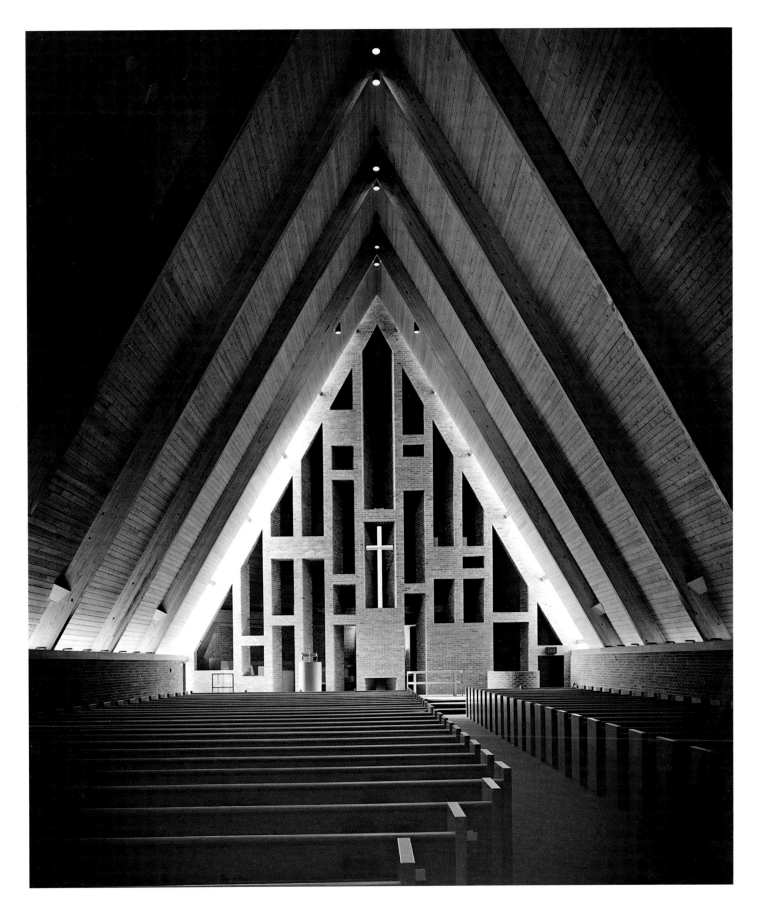

tary School, designed by Edward Larrabee Barnes and completed the same year as the church.

Congregation members arriving for services at the new church entered on the upper level through a low, wide T-shaped opening in the brick masonry walls reached via a bridge constructed over a moat-like space which brought light to the classrooms below. The entrance opened onto the narthex, which served both the sanctuary to the left and the chapel to the right of the entrance. A short flight of stairs led up to the sanctuary, where light-colored wood pews arranged on both sides of a wide off-center aisle accommodated five hundred worshippers. The off-center placement of the pulpit and communion table contributed to this asymmetrical design. A perforated brick wall shielded the organ, choir, and access to the baptistery from the sanctuary and chancel.

The night before the opening of the church, Jack Hartray and the building contractor suddenly realized that they had neglected to include a cross in the chancel and hurriedly fabricated the largest cross they could from cedar boards found in the contractor's woodshop. They hung the simple wooden form, which blended with the interior finishes, at the center of the brick wall at the back of the chancel. Visitors would later interpret the brick lattice on which the cross hangs as a medieval rood screen and the congregation would regard it as symbolic of the rending of the veil of the temple following the crucifixion, but its design by Houng-Lin Swei, a Buddhist, was actually motivated by a more utilitarian concern—the hollow brick columns carried ductwork for a future air-conditioning system.

The great roof structure of the sanctuary rested on low red brick walls. To shut out distractions these walls were left essentially windowless, but narrow glazed openings between the walls and the roof provided indirect natural lighting and a row of glazed panels piercing the sloping roof on either side of the chancel illuminated the cross. The exposed wooden rafters and decking of the timber roof soared almost fifty feet above the floor of the sanctuary and reminded many viewers of the keel of a great ship.

The chapel, located on the other side of the entrance door from the main sanctuary, was a smaller version of the sanctuary, with low brick walls, a high-pitched wooden roof, and glass panels on either side of the roof slope, located in this case near the rear wall rather than in the chancel. The chapel had a capacity to seat one hundred and was used for Sunday evening services, Bible studies, weddings, and small group meetings. The other facilities on the upper level included the fellowship hall, meeting rooms, and a small kitchen on the northwest and offices on the southwest.

Two primary routes led from the main entrance to the lower classroom level of the complex. One was an interior stairway enclosed in a semicylindrical brick element adjoining the chapel. The visitor could also pass through a door from the narthex and walk down a ramp that descended to the floor of the central sunken courtyard, which resembled a medieval cloister. The courtyard contained the cornerstone from the original church and provided space for meditation, fellowship and refreshments after church services, summer evening services and weddings, and Sunday school classes in pleasant weather. A door off the courtyard led to twenty-five classrooms.

Viewed from the east the complex appeared to consist of a low brick basement and two soaring roofs clad in hand-laid green Vermont slate. The silhouette of the sanctuary, with its flat frontispiece pierced by a bell at one end and faceted apse-like arrangement at the other, strongly recalled medieval churches. Viewed from the other sides, particularly the rear, the full expanse of this twentieth-century religious complex became apparent.

The building that Weese designed for the First Baptist Church of Columbus continues to serve its congregation in the early twenty-first century. Although minor changes have been made—the addition of a ramp to make the sanctuary handicapped-accessible, installation of new lighting, a new sound system, air-conditioning, and the relocation of the administrative offices to the lower level—the overall design remains faithful to Weese's original concept. In 2000, the National Park Service designated the First Baptist Church of Columbus a National Historic Landmark, recognizing it as "an outstanding representation of the work of a distinguished American architect, Harry Mohr Weese, and generally thought to be his best work in Columbus." Oddly, though, this building, which has always been one of Weese's most popular designs for both critics and the general public, seems never have to won a major award, possibly because the design was so unlike most of the work by major architects of the 1960s.

Job 487
Project Manager: Jack Hartray
Project Designer: Houng-Lin Swei
Structural Engineer: Engineers Collaborative
Mechanical Engineer: Samuel R. Lewis & Associates
Lighting Consultant: William Lam
Interiors Consultant: Dolores Miller & Associates
Landscape Architect: Dan Kiley and Partners
General Contractor: Repp & Mundt Construction Service

SELECTED BIBLIOGRAPHY

"First Baptist Church. Columbus, Indiana." *Architectural Record* 133 (May 1963): 128–131.

"A Baptist Church by Weese." *Architectural Record* 138 (December 1965): 113–117.

"Eglise Baptiste a Columbus Indiana." *L'Architecture d'Aujourd'hui* 36 (April/May 1966): 72–73.

Nory Miller. "Exploring the Fundamentals in Fundamentalist Columbus, Ind." *Inland Architect* 16 (December 1972): 10–13.

View to the southwest toward the entrance to the church with the main sanctuary to the left and the chapel to the right. Hedrich Blessing photograph, HB 28683P, ca. 1965, Chicago History Museum.

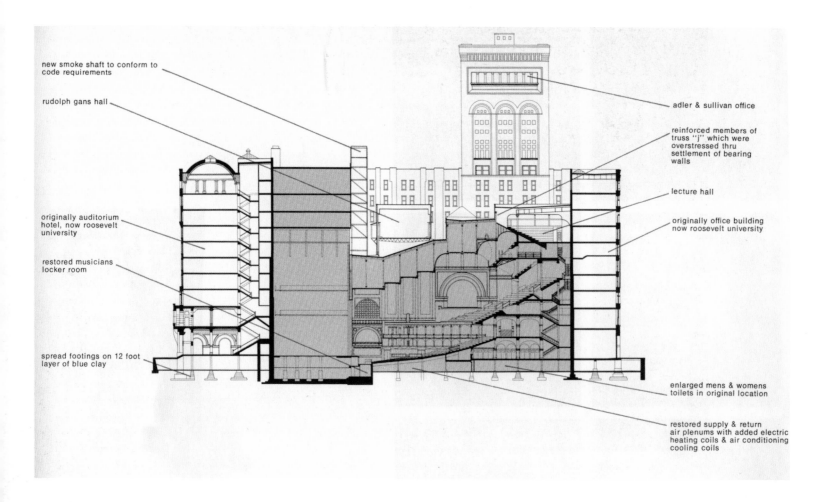

new smoke shaft to conform to code requirements

rudolph gans hall

originally auditorium hotel, now roosevelt university

restored musicians locker room

spread footings on 12 foot layer of blue clay

adler & sullivan office

reinforced members of truss "j" which were overstressed thru settlement of bearing walls

lecture hall

originally office building now roosevelt university

enlarged mens & womens toilets in original location

restored supply & return air plenums with added electric heating coils & air conditioning cooling coils

Section through Auditorium Theater, designed by Adler and Sullivan, with renovation notes by Harry Weese & Associates. From firm brochure.

AUDITORIUM THEATER RESTORATION

70 East Congress Parkway
Chicago, Illinois, 1964–67

Chicago's Auditorium Theater with its renowned acoustics, excellent sightlines, elaborate stage machinery, and exquisite ornamentation was, from the time of its completion in 1889, widely regarded as the masterpiece of Dankmar Adler and Louis Sullivan. In its early years it was also the center of cultural life in Chicago, serving as the setting for performances by Adelina Patti, Mary Garden, Ignace Paderewski, Richard Strauss, Sarah Bernhardt, Eleanora Duse, Anna Pavlova, and John Philip Sousa.

As the twentieth century progressed, however, the hall that Frank Lloyd Wright once called "the greatest room for music and opera in the world, bar none," started to lose its standing as Chicago's premier performance space. The Chicago Symphony Orchestra departed for the newly constructed Orchestra Hall in 1904, and Chicago's resident opera company moved to Samuel Insull's Civic Opera House on North Wacker Drive in 1929. With the onset

of the Depression, revenues from the hotel rooms and office suites in the Auditorium Building complex that were intended to provide support for the theater declined, leading the Chicago Auditorium Association to declare bankruptcy. The landowners who assumed control of the Auditorium Building considered demolition, which was prevented only because the cost of razing the massive structure was higher than the value of the land. The theater closed in 1941 when the City of Chicago seized the Auditorium Building for back taxes. During World War II, the theater became a social center for servicemen, and its once magnificent stage was converted to a bowling alley.

The building received a new life in 1946 when Roosevelt University, a fledgling educational institution dedicated to providing all students with the opportunity for higher education regardless of race or status, purchased the property. The university converted the office suites and hotel rooms into classrooms, faculty offices, and laboratories. Reuse of the theater was a particular challenge, and various options were considered. Architects went so far as to draw up plans for its conversion into a gymnasium, but the university ultimately decided against this course of action. However, Roosevelt lacked resources to restore the theater, which fell into disrepair due to poor maintenance.

View of the auditorium and stage. Hedrich Blessing photograph, HB31105C, ca. 1967, Chicago History Museum.

In 1960, the first step toward resurrecting the Auditorium Theater was taken when the board of trustees of Roosevelt University established the Auditorium Theater Council, a nonprofit body independent of the university that was empowered to restore, operate, and manage the theater. Mrs. John V. Spachner, a Roosevelt University trustee, chaired the council, along with Chicago attorney Harold W. Norman.

In 1961, restoration design consultant Crombie Taylor Associates and Chicago architecture and engineering firm Skidmore, Owings & Merrill initiated a structural study at the request of the Auditorium Theater Council to evaluate the condition of the theater. Chicago contractor Sumner Sollitt assisted in construction cost estimates. The study report identified structural problems, most of which were attributable to the twenty-seven-inch differential settlement of the heavy masonry walls at the sides of the auditorium. Over time these walls had pulled down the relatively lightweight cast-iron and steel floor structure, resulting in curvature of the main floor of the auditorium and distortion of the alignment of the roof trusses over the theater. The report also concluded that areas of the ceiling masonry and plaster were "unsafe and beyond repair"; described virtually all mechanical and electrical facilities as "obsolete, deteriorated, or missing"; and noted that the original exit system did not conform to the current codes. The estimated cost for total restoration exceeded $4 million.

This assessment caused concern for Harry Weese and other admirers of the vanishing designs of Louis Sullivan. Weese, who feared that the theater would be lost, sent a letter voicing his concerns to the Auditorium Theater Council. That letter prompted the council to call a meeting in the summer of 1963. At that meeting the council appointed Weese chairman of the Building Committee.

Weese and Fred N. Severud, a structural engineer with the New York firm of Severud, Elstad, Krueger & Associates who had extensive experience with historic restorations, conducted a series of thorough inspections of the theater's structure. Severud pointed out that although the tension members of the trusses were distorted, the trusses were not fully stressed. These findings convinced Weese that much of the fabric of the original structure could be safely reused. He approached the restoration project with a respect for both the aesthetics and the structure of the historic building and with the goal of preserving as much as possible of the existing fabric and replacing only what could not be repaired.

This strategy was guided by input from leading consultants, architects, engineers, and construction experts,

including, in addition to Severud, George C. Izenour, director of the electro-mechanical laboratory at Yale University School of Drama; Raymond D. Berry of Gallaher & Speck, who handled the stage rigging and machinery; and Sumner Sollitt, the general contractor. Weese's estimate of the total cost of the restoration was $2.75 million. Work on the auditorium began in early 1964 and proceeded in phases over the next four years as funding became available. The first priority was renovation of the stage, including the strengthening of a weakened roof truss, installation of smoke vents, reactivation of the hydraulically operated asbestos fire curtain by installation of a new pump, reconditioning of the stage rigging, and total restoration of the stage, including replacement of the floor.

The cleaning, repair, and decoration of the auditorium constituted the second phase. Much of Sullivan's lush ivory and gold plaster ornamentation required only cleaning or minor repairs. Where the plaster decorations were severely damaged or missing, replacements were cast using latex molds prepared from the existing ornament. Exposed carbon-filament light bulbs similar to the originals were specially manufactured to illuminate the ornamentation on the arches that framed the stage.

Removal of some box seats that had been added in 1910 in a double horseshoe configuration at the rear of the orchestra restored the original continuity between the foyer and the auditorium. Weese and his team had been unable to locate drawings or photographs showing the original configuration of the orchestra, but an 1892 concert program with a seating plan that was discovered behind a wall by a plumber served as a guide. An added bonus of removing the box seats was the discovery of the original paint and well-preserved Sullivan-designed stenciling on the wall behind them.

The third phase of the restoration involved the updating of the heating, electrical, ventilation, and plumbing systems. Weese kept Adler's original duct system intact but added new fans and heating and cooling coils. He also installed equipment for the conversion of alternating current to the direct current originally used for the theater's electrical system.

The fourth phase involved painting the original seats of the auditorium and reupholstering them with a fabric replicating the original design. Missing seats were rebuilt to match the originals. This phase also included recarpeting the aisles and foyers in a red carpet based on the original. The final phase of the restoration was the decoration of the lobbies and the vestibules, including the installation over the main entrance of six stained-glass windows discovered

Detail of plaster arches designed by Louis Sullivan. Hedrich Blessing photograph, HB31105K, ca. 1967, Chicago History Museum.

in storage. The original marble floor of the main lobby was intact and required only cleaning and polishing.

In addition to the funds raised by the Auditorium Theater Council, many professionals, including Weese, donated time, services, and materials to the restoration project. An added and unexpected bonus of Weese's restoration plan was the final cost of $1.7 million, even less than projected at the start of the project.

The Auditorium Theater reopened on October 31, 1967, with a performance of "A Midsummer Night's Dream" by the New York City Ballet. In 1969, Weese's restoration received a National Honor Award from the American Institute of Architects.

Job 534
Consulting Architect: Crombie Taylor
Theater Consultant: George Izenour
Interior Consultant: Dolores Miller & Associates
General Contractor: J. W. Snyder Construction

SELECTED BIBLIOGRAPHY

"The Auditorium: A Restoration." *Architectural & Engineering News* (January 1966): 41–43.

Wilbert R. Hasbrouck. "Chicago's Auditorium Theater." *Prairie School Review* (Third Quarter 1967): 7–17.

Peter P. Jacobi. "The Awakening Auditorium." *Chicago Magazine* (Spring 1967): 33, 37–38.

"Rebirth of Chicago's Auditorium." *AIA Journal* (June 1967): 65–68.

SEVENTEENTH CHURCH OF CHRIST, SCIENTIST

55 East Wacker Drive
Chicago, Illinois, 1965–68

Since 1924 when it was initially organized as the Christian Science Society of Chicago, Seventeenth Church of Christ, Scientist had assembled in rented quarters. In the mid-1950s, the congregation took the first step toward a permanent home by purchasing three pie-shaped parcels of land totaling 11,000 square feet at the busy intersection of Wabash Avenue and East Wacker Drive, just south of the Chicago River. The committee that was established to select the designer of the church for the site compiled a list of more than thirty possible architects, including Frank Lloyd Wright, and subsequently narrowed the choices to three, including Harry Weese & Associates. During the screening process, the committee asked the finalists about their own religious affiliations, to which

Weese, who was raised a Methodist, responded, "My father was Episcopalian, my mother Presbyterian, and I'm an architect." His response apparently satisfied the committee, which awarded the project to the Weese firm.

The small triangular urban lot and the substantial requirements of the congregation, which needed not only an auditorium for church services but also a Sunday school, offices, meeting rooms, a nursery, and off-street parking, governed Weese's design. He overcame the restraints of the small, irregularly shaped site by stacking the various functional elements on seven floors, two below grade and five above. By packing the spaces behind a sweeping semi-circular exterior wall that defined the outer edge of the auditorium seating area, he was even able to add a wide plaza surrounding the church.

Weese elevated the auditorium, which occupied the bulk of the structure, above street level. Staircases at the rear of the lobby led up to the auditorium, and, as in Frank Lloyd Wright's Unity Temple, the congregation entered the room from the front on either side of a raised platform containing the reader's desk. Because Christian Science

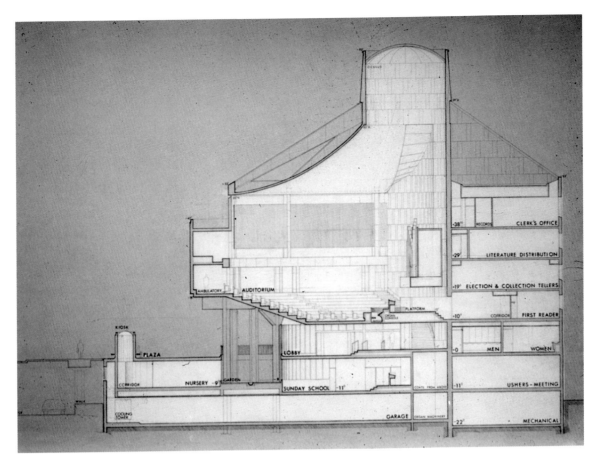

Section and plan of auditorium level, Seventeenth Church of Christ, Scientist. Section: i59256; Plans: i59257 and i59259, Chicago History Museum.

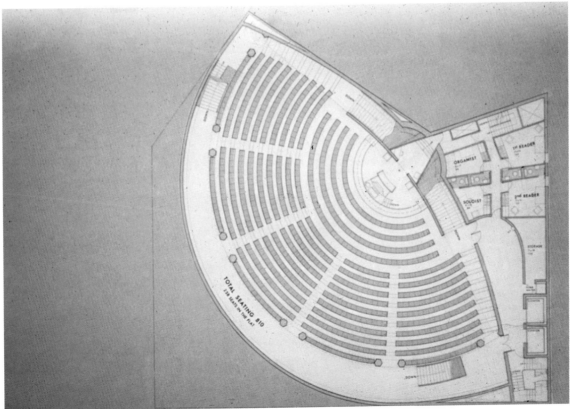

services are based not on ritual or liturgy but on readings and testimonials, sightlines and acoustics were of utmost importance in the auditorium design. To focus attention on the readers leading the service, Weese adopted the form of a Greek theater, arranging the thirteen rows of 764 seats in an ascending semicircular configuration so that all were within fifty-four feet of the reader's desk.

Church members rising from their seats for testimonials activated microphones and loudspeakers incorporated into the backs of every other seat. A bench at the rear of the auditorium and a two-tiered upper-level gallery provided additional seating. Because organ music and singing of hymns were also important components of the Christian Science services, Weese gave the congregation's Aeolian-Skinner pipe organ a prominent place behind the reader's stand.

Italian travertine sheathed the high interior walls of the auditorium, which were left essentially windowless at the request of the church in order to eliminate noise from the street. The sloped tentlike plaster ceiling combined with the semicircular design to enhance the room's acoustics. Natural light filtered into the space through long, rectangular slitlike openings at the top of the curved walls, a

skylight inserted in the oculus of the lantern or cupola that topped the auditorium, clerestory windows at the base of the lantern, and skylights over the reader's platform.

According to project architect Michael Lisec, the building committee and the church membership "eagerly accepted and embraced" Weese's modernist concept for the exterior, which deviated markedly from the more traditional neoclassical designs of earlier Christian Science churches in Chicago. An unbroken, two-hundred-foot curvilinear concrete wall provided a dramatic contrast to the angular profiles of the neighboring high-rise towers and expressed the back of the semicircular auditorium inside. Weese clad this curved façade in the same travertine used on the interior walls of the auditorium. Travertine also camouflaged the steel trusses of the conical roof, which was covered in lead-coated copper.

The overhang of the back portion of the auditorium sheltered two glass-roofed vestibules at either end of the plaza that marked the entrances to the glass-enclosed lobby. Although almost the entire church exterior was clad in travertine, Weese chose to leave the reinforced concrete structure exposed at the entrance and in the lobby and reading room.

A moatlike space with a sunken garden between the plaza and the lobby insulated the lobby from the street and brought natural light down to the Sunday school classrooms and nursery on the lower level. The Sunday school occupied the space to the east of the garden and below the lobby, while the nursery extended to the west underneath the plaza. The floor below the Sunday school and nursery provided space for a garage with parking for thirteen cars that opened onto the lower level of Wacker Drive. A separate multilevel wing east of the auditorium contained church offices and meeting rooms, a board room on the top floor, and the building's mechanical equipment at the lowest level.

In 1969, Seventeenth Church received a Distinguished Building Award from the Chicago chapter of the American Institute of Architects, which described it as an imaginative and handsome building sensitively related to the city site. In 1996, the AIA Chicago chapter again recognized the design with a Twenty-Five Year Award, calling it "a modern solution to a traditional building type" and "a vital landmark in the Chicago Loop today, as well as an important addition to contemporary church design."

In early 2006, the report of a developer's proposal to raze Seventeenth Church, along with the Art Deco Wacker Tower (originally the Chicago Motor Club building) to the east, caused concern among Chicago's preservation community. At that time, a spokesman for the congregation denied any plans for the sale of the site or the demolition of the church.

Auditorium. Orlando Cabanban photograph 142394-12, ca. 1968, Chicago History Museum.

Sketch of lower level, showing how natural light entered the Sunday school classrooms and nursery on the lower level. i5944317, Chicago History Museum.

Job 529
Assistant Designer: Michael Lisec
Structural Engineer: Engineers Collaborative
Mechanical and Electrical Engineer: Samuel R. Lewis & Associates
Acoustical Consultant: Bolt, Beranek & Newman
Interior Consultant: Dolores Miller & Associates
General Contractor: Sumner Sollitt Construction

SELECTED BIBLIOGRAPHY

Richard Philbrick. "Plan to Build New Church in Wacker Drive." *Chicago Tribune*, January 2, 1965.

"Wacker Drive to Boast Unusual Church." *Chicago Tribune*, September 4, 1966.

Richard Philbrick. "Loop Church to Be Opened This Sunday." *Chicago Tribune*, November 7, 1968.

John Morris Dixon. "Church in a Grove of Skyscrapers." *Architectural Forum* 130 (June 1969): 42–45.

FOURTH LEVEL

8 labs
9 art
10 music
11 cafeteria
12 library
13 classrooms

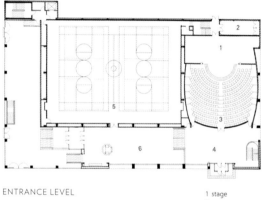

ENTRANCE LEVEL

1 stage
2 green room
3 auditorium
4 lobby
5 gymnasium
6 gallery lobby
7 loggia

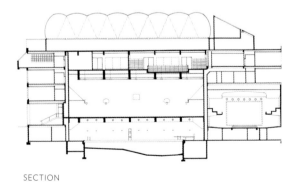

SECTION

LATIN SCHOOL OF CHICAGO

59 West North Boulevard
Chicago, Illinois, 1966–69

The sprawling one-story complex designed by Harry
Weese & Associates in the 1950s for the Lillian C.
Schmitt Elementary School in Columbus, Indiana, was well
suited to its open, parklike setting, but the Latin School of
Chicago demanded a more compact design. In the 1960s,
the Latin School, a private educational institution founded
in 1888, was located on Dearborn Parkway in Chicago's
Northside Gold Coast neighborhood. The need for
additional space prompted the purchase of a nearby site at
the southeast corner of North Boulevard and Clark Street
for a new upper school (grades seven through twelve), to be
designed by Harry Weese & Associates.

Program requirements for the new school, which was
to accommodate 350 students, included small classrooms
allowing a maximum class size of twenty, administrative
and faculty offices, a gymnasium, a theater/auditorium, a
library, a cafeteria, an Olympic-size swimming pool, special rooms for art, music, and physical science classes, and
an outdoor recreation area. Principal designer Ben Weese
packed all of these components into the dense urban site
by stacking those requiring a large unobstructed space—
the pool, gymnasium, library, and cafeteria—above one
another at the building's core and pushing the offices and
classrooms to the perimeter.

A loggia extending along the north and west façades
sheltered the principal entrance at the northwest corner of
the four-story structure. The wide vestibule beyond the
glass entryway flowed into a spacious two-level gallery with
a reception center and space for informal gatherings, display cases, and student activity booths. The first level also
contained a theater/auditorium with a rounded thrust stage
and 450 seats, divided between the main floor and a horse-
shoe-shaped wrap-around balcony. A separate entrance to
the theater permitted its use by the community after nor-
mal school hours while maintaining the security of the rest
of the building. A three-story gymnasium with two col-
legiate-size basketball courts and seating for three hundred
spectators occupied the remainder of the first floor.

Weese placed the swimming pool on the lower or basement level, below the gymnasium. Other facilities located
on this level included lockers, showers, storage for sports
equipment, an exercise room for wrestling and weightlift-
ing, and the manual arts shop. A separate entrance under

Science laboratory.
Balthazar Korab photograph,
21417, ca. 1969.

the loggia facilitated access to the basement by students returning from the athletic fields across the street in Lincoln Park.

The middle level of the gymnasium and the theater balcony occupied much of the second floor, with administrative and faculty offices and student services wrapping around these facilities to the north and west. Classrooms, additional offices, and a faculty lounge surrounded the top level of the gymnasium on three sides of the third floor.

The cafeteria and library occupied the central space on the fourth floor, above the gymnasium. The library featured a sunken informal reading area reminiscent of Alvar Aalto's multilevel design for the Viipuri Library, which was completed in 1935 in what was then part of Finland. The upper level contained the library stacks and carrels for private study. The library and cafeteria shared

an outdoor terrace offering views of Lincoln Park and Lake Michigan.

Cantilevered extensions projecting seven and a half feet beyond the building's north and west façades housed the music and art studios and the science laboratories. These brick bays had sloping glass roofs that brought in natural light and resulted in a gain of an additional 500 square feet for the studios and 750 square feet for the laboratories. A spiral staircase led from the laboratories to a rooftop botanical greenhouse, a "garden in the sky" used for classes and individual horticulture projects.

Harry Weese proposed a rooftop recreation area covered with a translucent, air-supported plastic dome for year-round use. The enclosed area, which would have been large enough to accommodate two tennis courts or two basketball courts, would have compensated for the lack of space for outdoor athletic facilities. Harry Weese & Associates received a $7,500 grant from the Ford Foundation's Educational Facilities Laboratories for design studies related to the dome, but plans for the enclosed play deck disintegrated when the Chicago Building Department rejected the concept. Because the Chicago Building Code contained no provisions for air-supported structures, the building department classified the dome as a permanent roof requiring a degree of fire resistance that could not be met by any materials suitable for the purpose at that time. Students used the uncovered roof for recreational activities until a more conventional structure was built, also designed by Harry Weese & Associates.

Materials selected for the school's exterior were durable, cost-effective, and easy to maintain. Orange-brown iron-spot bricks covered the concrete frame. The use of so-called engineered bricks, 8 inches long and 2 3/4 inches high, ½ inch higher than standard, reduced material costs, and the lead-coated copper cladding of the lintels and sills of the frameless glazing, which fit directly into the walls, lowered maintenance costs by eliminating the need for painting. These features—the use of brick and lead-coated copper and the insertion of fixed glass panels directly into the brick—reflected ongoing practices at the time in the office of Harry Weese & Associates, as seen in other projects such as the Illinois Center for the Visually Handicapped, Kenwood Gardens, and St. Louis Community College (Forest Park Community College).

In 1995, Nagle Hartray, the firm formed in 1966 by Jack Hartray and Jim Nagle after Hartray's departure from the Weese office, formulated a program for the expansion and renovation of the Latin School, which it subsequently implemented. In 2008, an 80,000-square-foot middle-school building designed by the same firm, now known as Nagle Hartray Danker Kagan McKay Penney Architects, opened to the east of the original structure.

Job 583
Structural Engineer: Engineers Collaborative
Mechanical Engineer: Samuel R. Lewis & Associates
Theater Consultant: Lustig & Associates
Interiors: Design Unit
General Contractor: Power Construction

SELECTED BIBLIOGRAPHY

"The Latin School: A Lesson in How to Build beside a Park." *Inland Architect* 14 (February 1970): 15.
"Box Full of School." *Architectural Forum* 132 (May 1970): 58–61.
"Harry Weese's Private School in Tight Urban Setting." *Building Design and Construction* (July 1970).

Aerial perspective showing the building with an inflatable roof structure, a relatively new concept at the time, proposed by Harry Weese & Associates as a light and inexpensive way to cover a rooftop play deck. i52020, Chicago History Museum.

SHADOWCLIFF

Ellison Bay, Wisconsin, 1968–69

The face of a limestone wall rising almost 150 feet vertically above the waters of Green Bay near the town of Ellison Bay, Wisconsin, provided the setting for Shadowcliff, the cliffhanging studio designed by Harry Weese for Northwest Industries president Ben W. Heineman. The unique site of this one-room glass box offered expansive views of the bay and at the same time preserved the vistas from Heineman's main summer house atop the bluff.

Weese and Heineman had been friends for a long time prior to the Shadowcliff commission. Both sailed and skied and spent Christmas vacations with other Chicagoans on the slopes of Aspen, Colorado. Weese and his wife, Kitty, also visited the Heinemans at their summer and weekend retreat in Door County, Wisconsin, a house dating to 1924. Early one morning in the 1950s during one of these visits, Heineman found Weese at the dining room table redesigning the house. Weese proposed opening it up to the view by encasing the dining room and screened porch in sheets of glass, a plan that Heineman subsequently implemented.

During summer visits to his Green Bay home, Heineman often conducted business from a dining table on the porch, but for some time he had wanted to build a separate studio. When he decided in the 1960s to proceed with the project, he asked Weese to design it. As Heineman told Weese, he wanted the roof of the office flush with the top of the cliff so that it would not be visible from the main house. But he also wanted to see the cliff and its wildflowers from the office, so a traditional cantilever with the rear wall attached to the bluff was not an option. The building had to hang. In addition, Heineman wanted a panoramic view, meaning that the office had to be surrounded by floor-to-ceiling windows. When Weese heard Heineman's idea and his specifications for the project, he became, according to Heineman, "wildly excited."

Heineman rejected Weese's initial design for a glass structure supported by cables rising above the cliff, but he accepted his alternative proposal for a double cantilever, meaning a cantilever that cantilevers from itself. The principal supports for the structure were a pair of steel beams inserted into twenty-foot trenches hollowed out of the limestone and fastened to the cliff with rock bolts and high-strength grout. The beams angled inward and extended midway across the roof to connect with a third beam. Two additional beams welded to these main sup-

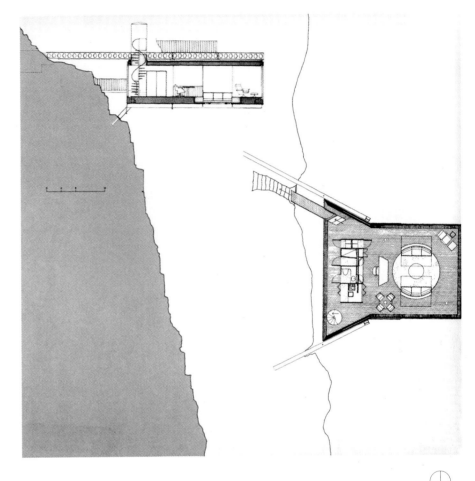

ports extended to the outer corners. The beams above the roof carried the vertical loads and formed a triangulated system that resisted the horizontal loads imposed by the wind. The twenty-four-foot-square steel and glass box hung from six 2-inch-square steel bars suspended from the rooftop grid. Fifteen-foot diagonal steel rods or struts positioned on either side braced the structure.

Weese selected COR-TEN steel, a self-weathering alloy that naturally forms a dark-brown protective rust coating and never needs painting, for the support beams and cladding of the studio. Hexagonal perforations in the beams lightened their visual appearance.

The studio faced west toward the bay, and the main entrance was located on the east side of the structure facing the cliff, which provided the view requested by Heineman. Access to the entrance was via a path that led down

Section and plan.
From firm brochure.

FACING PAGE
View of Shadowcliff.
Orlando Cabanban photograph, 175222-6, ca. 1969, Chicago History Museum.

View from below.
Orlando Cabanban photograph, ca. 1969, Chicago History Museum.

Design Unit, Kitty Weese's interior design firm, selected the furnishings for Shadowcliff. A long, rectangular, white plastic laminate surface edged in teak and supported by polished brass columns served as Heineman's desk. The desk sat on a raised platform in front of the service unit. Electric motors controlled glass panels on the north and south, allowing cross ventilation and giving Heineman unobstructed views of the bay while he worked.

To the north of the workspace was a heavy plate-glass dining table on a fixed, polished brass stanchion that could be adjusted to three positions. The sunken sitting area to the west, overlooking the bay, contained built-in, semi-circular, bronze-colored chamois sofas designed by Harry Weese that converted to full-size beds. A laminated glass porthole in the floor of the sitting area offered a downward view of the treetops, the water, and the cliff, which was illuminated at night. If guests became queasy, the Heinemans could cover the porthole with a circular carpet.

In a nod to the nautical interests of both architect and client, the interior of the studio was fitted out predominantly in teak. Weese also used teak for the treads of the spiral staircase leading to the roof and for the floor of the observation deck.

Weese equipped the studio with electric heat and air-conditioning, which were seldom used because of the high cost of operating these systems. A remote, inconspicuous structure located in the woods atop the cliff housed mechanical equipment. By removing heavy vibrating equipment from the house, this ancillary service shed not only reduced the load on the structure but also simplified acoustical isolation.

Construction of Shadowcliff began in the winter of 1968 and was completed in time for the 1969 Memorial Day Weekend. Shadowcliff received awards from the 1971 Design in Steel Awards Program sponsored by the American Iron and Steel Institute and from the 1973 Homes for Better Living Awards Program sponsored by the American Institute of Architects in cooperation with *House & Home* and *American Home* magazines.

Heineman and his family enjoyed Shadowcliff for more than three decades and "never changed a thing" from Weese's original design. In 1999, the Trust for Public Land purchased approximately one-half of the Green Bay land owned by Heineman and used it to expand the adjacent Ellison Bluff County Park. Heineman subsequently sold the remainder of the land, including the houses and the studio to a private party, which began making plans to construct several new houses on the site. When neighbors proved successful in blocking these plans, the new owner resold the site and both structures. The current owner is renovating the main house and plans to keep the property as it was when Heineman owned it.

a stone stairway cut into the rock and across a four-foot footbridge. A second bridge connected the cliff to a rooftop observation deck, where a bronze-tinted cylinder capped a spiral staircase leading to the space below.

Because the main house did not lend itself to entertaining, Weese equipped the studio with a kitchen and bar, and it became the setting for cocktails and hors d'oeuvres prior to dinners in the main house. A freestanding cabinet of white painted plywood placed near the east wall housed these facilities, along with a bathroom, a shower compartment, bookcases, and storage space.

Job 637
Project Manager: Paul Hansen
Design Team: Andrew Dzienicki, Andre Georgel, Tom Hickey and Doug Tilden
Structural Engineer: Engineers Collaborative
Mechanical and Electrical Engineer: Cosentini Associates
Interiors Consultant: Design Unit
General Contractor: Turner Construction Company, Chicago

SELECTED BIBLIOGRAPHY

"A Real Cliffhanger." *Architectural Forum* 134 (February 1971): 62–64.
"A Cliffhanging Retreat for a Three-Career Man." *Fortune* (March 1971): 105–107.

View of interior.
Orlando Cabanban photograph, 175219-12, ca. 1969, Chicago History Museum.

TIME-LIFE BUILDING

541 North Fairbanks Court
Chicago, Illinois,
1967 design started
1968–70 construction

Since 1946, the Subscription Services department of publishing giant Time Inc. had occupied the Michigan Square (Diana Court) Building on North Michigan Avenue, the same building that housed the Baldwin Kingrey furniture store from 1947 to 1957 and the office of Harry Weese from 1947 to 1951. By the mid-1960s, the expanding division had outgrown this space. Time considered vertical expansion of the Michigan Square Building but rejected this solution because of the high cost and the disruption the construction would cause to Subscription Services operations, and so decided instead to construct a new facility. The service-oriented division did not require a downtown location, and could easily have been moved to the suburbs, but Time wished to retain its loyal workforce. Locating the new building near Michigan Avenue would allow employees to use the same means of public transportation, with the added bonus of convenient lunchtime access to the many shops and restaurants in the area. In May 1966 Time purchased a 40,000-square-foot site in a largely derelict industrial area at Fairbanks Court between Grand Avenue and Ohio Street, only two blocks east of the current site. The plan was to use fifty to sixty percent of the structure for Subscription Services at the outset and lease the remaining space until needed.

The company's Architectural Committee, formed in the summer of 1966, realized that hopes for improving the area chosen for the new structure hinged on a high-quality architectural statement. "Because our site is in the midst of an industrial slum, our building must set the right tone for the future redevelopment of the entire area" and "must be of such architectural excellence that it will command the attention and favor of critics and the public alike," Joseph Hazen, editor of Time-Life Books, publisher of *Architectural Forum*, and a member of the Architectural Committee, told Time editorial chairman Henry R. Luce in a January 1967 memo. Hazen suggested that the "steel and glass stereotype" of most recent Chicago office buildings be avoided in favor of a "distinctive architectural expression" with a "richer, more textured façade, rendered in warmer materials." The building had to be handsome, dignified, and appropriate to the corporate image of Time Inc. At the same time, because it was essentially a service facility rather

than a monumental corporate headquarters, proportions were to be modest and the cost reasonable. Enticing interior appointments that would appeal to both employees and tenants and a comfortable, stimulating, and efficient working environment were other requirements. "The fact that our subscription fulfillment business is largely a routine clerical operation further suggests that the interior of the building must be designed with warm respect for the human being," Hazen told Luce.

Because early Chicago architects had been pioneers in the development of the skyscraper and the city was the site of some of the most significant office buildings under construction in the 1960s, the Architectural Committee made a commitment to award the new project to a Chicago firm. Hazen recommended Weese, who was among nine local architects whose qualifications were reviewed by the committee and among the four selected for interviews. The day after the Weese interview, the Architectural Committee assigned the commission to Harry Weese &

Associates despite the fact that Weese had the smallest staff of any of the architects considered, had never designed a high-rise office building, and had never designed a prominent building of any kind in downtown Chicago. To the firm's surprise, Time even offered a fee of 5 percent rather than the expected standard of 3.5 percent. Although selection of a larger architectural-engineering firm might have been easier, safer, and more convenient, the committee felt that Weese, whom Hazen characterized as "one of the most imaginative, resourceful, creative architects in America," would deliver more thoughtfully researched solutions to design problems and a more distinguished work of architecture. "The decision to select Harry Weese was a decision of the heart as well as the mind," Hazen explained.

The "distinctive architectural expression" provided by Harry Weese & Associates was a thirty-story rectangular tower, three bays wide and seven bays long, rising to a height of four hundred feet, with a gross floor area of approximately 700,000 square feet. The firm developed

Wall panel being lifted into place. ca. 1969. i52312, Chicago History Museum.

FACING PAGE
View to northeast, Time-Life Building. Hedrich Blessing photograph, HB33664B2, ca. 1970, Chicago History Museum.

designs for both a steel-frame and a concrete-frame structure with a curtain wall of either steel or aluminum. When bids for the concrete frame came in $900,000 cheaper than for steel, the architects specified concrete. A combination of historical, structural, practical, and aesthetic considerations led to the choice of COR-TEN steel for the curtain wall. Historically, metal curtain walls had a long tradition in Chicago, beginning with the cast-iron façades of pre- and early post-fire commercial buildings and continuing with the postwar steel-clad Miesian towers. Structurally, the similarity in thermal expansion between steel and concrete essentially eliminated the need for expansion joints. From a practical standpoint, the self-weathering COR-TEN steel never required painting, and aesthetically, it took on a rich texture and an earthy russet patina as it aged.

Harry Weese, brother Ben, and Jack Hartray admired the COR-TEN-clad walls of the Chicago Civic Center, now the Daley Center, a prominent structure in the center of the Loop that had been completed in 1965 and had received an extremely enthusiastic response in the architectural world. The three reacted less favorably to the Civic Center's dark glazing, which Hartray characterized as forbidding and grim. For the Time-Life Building the architects chose a gold mirror glass that complemented the auburn tones of the self-weathering steel. This double-glazed reflective glass with its exceptionally high insulating and heat reflecting properties eliminated the need for window coverings. Dropping window heads to six feet, eight inches above the floor further reduced glare and sunlight, and setting the glass flush with the exterior skin maximized usable area. Low window heads and residential-size door frames gave the offices a comfortable domestic scale, which at the time was thought to appeal to the female workforce.

The 12 × 30 foot prefabricated COR-TEN steel wall panels corresponded to the building's floor height and structural column spacing and were possibly the largest window wall units produced in the United States to that time. The General Bronze Division and Steel Weldments Division of Allied Products Corporation on Chicago's southwest side manufactured the panels at an average rate of four per day. A flatbed trailer hauled three completed panels to the building site via a specially mapped route of streets wide enough to accommodate the oversize load. Limited storage space at the building site precluded stockpiling of panels, so the trailer remained parked on the site until the panels were installed. Lifting a panel from the ground and fastening it temporarily into place required only about fifteen minutes, which was fortunate since city regulations limited the use of the crane for hoisting the panels to two 90-minute periods in the morning and early evening each day. Workers installed insulation and glazing from the interior after the panels were bolted in place.

At the time of the building's completion, Subscription Services was one of the largest mailing operations in the country. Each week, the department processed approximately twelve million pieces of paper, including renewal forms, promotional materials, bills, and mailing labels. An extensive analysis of materials handling and storage culminated in an integrated system of vertical and horizontal conveyers that connected floors and departments and directed materials to coded destinations, warehousing and loading facilities, waste disposal, and mail handling machinery.

Because most Subscription Services employees arrived and departed at the same time, rapid vertical movement of people during morning and evening rush hours was also essential. An initial study suggested that the building would need three banks of six elevators, a total of eighteen, to handle the traffic during peak periods. Weese's facetious suggestion that operating more than one cab in the elevator shafts would reduce the size of the building's core reminded Marvin Mass, president of Cosentini Associates, the mechanical and electrical engineer for the project, of the underslung service cab shown on early patent drawings of elevators. The ensuing discussion led to a tandem or double-deck elevator system, which reduced the number of elevators to twelve. Passengers headed to odd-numbered floors descended a half level to board the bottom cab in the building's lower lobby, while those destined for even-numbered floors climbed a half level and boarded the top cab in the upper lobby. The two cabs simultaneously transported employees to odd- and even-numbered floors during periods of peak use. During other hours, a single cab serviced all floors. The 1932 Cities Service Building in New York had included tandem elevators intended to link the building with the subway, but the system was never used. Thus, the Time-Life Building marked the first time that the concept of double-decker elevator cabs was actually put into operation in the United States.

The upper and lower elevator lobbies, twenty-seven feet high and enclosed with clear plate glass, created a dramatic split-level space described as "spatially spectacular" in a 1970 review in *Architectural Forum* by John Morris Dixon. The same red-brown granite paving of the sidewalk covered the lobby floors and sheathed the lobby and elevator shaft walls, uniting the exterior and the interior. Stamped-metal coffers suspended from the lobby ceiling expressed the concrete waffle slab above, and the area between provided space for ducts and conduits. Outside the glass enclosure of the lobby, exterior arcades offered shelter to persons entering the building or waiting for buses.

Lower lobby. Entrance
doors to the north and
south led to a dramatic
split-level space. The lower
and upper elevator lobbies
are visible at the center.
Balthazar Korab photograph,
22707, ca. 1970.

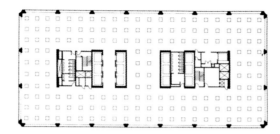

TYPICAL OFFICE FLOOR

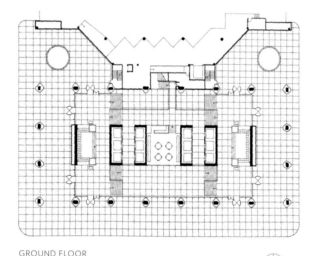

Ground floor and typical office floor plans. The lobby of the tower adjoined the service annex containing the loading dock. From firm brochure.

GROUND FLOOR

Amenities located in the lower-lobby concourse included a restaurant, bar, and convenience shops as well as the Time Gallery for public exhibitions. The Time Library, located on the upper lobby, contained bound volumes of all past issues of Time, Inc. publications and was also open to the public. The upper portion of the adjacent four-story, windowless, COR-TEN–clad service annex connected to the tower at the upper-lobby level and contained an employee cafeteria and a small auditorium. The ground level of the annex housed a drive-through loading and receiving dock.

Above the lobby was a large windowless warehouse space, and above this a mechanical area concealed by vertical louvers. Offices began on the fifth floor, eighty-seven feet above the street. With the exception of the executive floor, the office floors occupied by Subscription Services consisted of large open spaces subdivided by low storage units into working areas for about twenty clerks. Because of the relatively small floor area, all division employees sat within thirty feet of the windows. Angled recesses in the curtain wall extending from the window head of each office floor to the floor above sculpted the façade without diminishing floor space. The mechanical floors at the top of the building also contained Subscription Services electronic data processing and printing equipment.

The "pleasing proportions," "great sophistication in the use of materials, each playing its proper restrained role in the total expression," and interior public space "much more interesting than the ordinary new lobbies seen in recent buildings" earned the Time-Life Building a 1973 American Institute of Architects Honor Award.

Job 600
First Project Manager: Jack Hartray
Second Project Manager: Robert E. Bell
Third Project Manager: Tom Devine
Interior Design Consultant: Dolores Miller & Associates
General Contractor: Turner Construction
Structural Engineer: Office of James Ruderman
Mechanical/Electrical Engineer: Cosentini Associates

SELECTED BIBLIOGRAPHY

John Morris Dixon. "30-Story Slab of Ingenuity." *Architectural Forum* 133 (September 1970): 21–27.
"Time Inc., Chicago, Illinois." *AIA Journal* (May 1973): 52.

GIVEN INSTITUTE
OF PATHOBIOLOGY

100 East Francis Street
Aspen, Colorado, 1970–72

Harry Weese first visited Aspen with his wife, Kitty, during the drive back to Chicago from California, where his naval destroyer had docked after World War II. During subsequent years Harry, Kitty, and their three daughters spent many Christmas holidays at the mountain resort, and in 1968 Kitty purchased a Victorian house with profits from her interior design business. Over the years Weese bought and sold property in Aspen and designed a number of houses and other projects of all types in Aspen, nearby Snowmass, and Vail.

Through their Aspen and Chicago connections Harry and Kitty Weese came to know fellow Chicagoans Walter Paepcke, founder of the Container Corporation of America, and his wife, Elizabeth. Key figures in transforming Aspen into a cultural center as well as a ski resort, they founded not only the Aspen Skiing Company but also the Aspen Institute. Created by Paepcke in 1950, the institute provided a focal point for a wide range of intellectual and artistic endeavors and led to the creation of numerous other activities and organizations, among them a series of summer pathobiology seminars held in Aspen in the 1960s under the auspices of the University of Colorado. Dr. Donald W. King, chairman of the Department of Pathology at the University of Colorado Medical School, organized the seminars, which combined lectures and discussions with recreational and social activities, such as hiking, fishing, and concerts. During the first six years, the conferences took place in the gymnasium of the Aspen Middle School. More than nine hundred participants from the United States and abroad attended, but several thousand more had to be turned away because of space limitations. In addition, expansion of the programs into other scientific fields, such as cell biology, genetics, and virology, created a need for a space for laboratory demonstrations.

To fulfill these needs, King hoped to establish a pathobiology institute where physicians and university and medical school faculty members could gather for courses, seminars, symposia, and postgraduate medical education programs. He envisioned a more centrally located facility equivalent to coastal facilities such as those at Woods Hole in Massachusetts, Bar Harbor in Maine, and Pacific Grove in California. Such a center would help to close the communication gap that he felt existed at that

Harry Weese with Elizabeth Paepcke on the grounds of the Given Institute of Pathobiology. ca. 1972.
Photographer unknown.
i51243, Chicago History Museum.

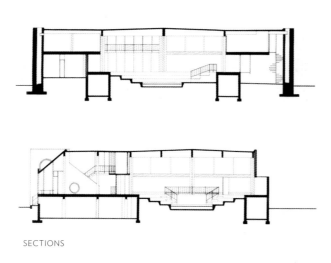

SECTIONS

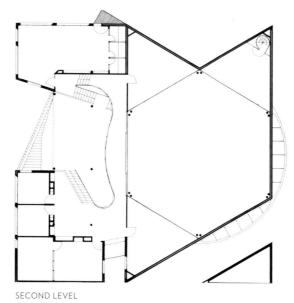

SECOND LEVEL

Section and plans.
151998-152000, Chicago History Museum.

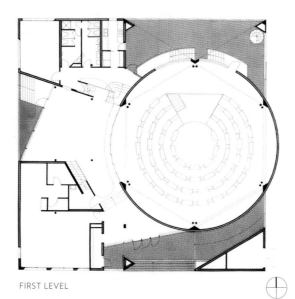

FIRST LEVEL

time between the acquisition of scientific data by research laboratories and its dissemination to the medical community. He also hoped that the institute would promote the integration of knowledge among various disciplines, such as biology, medicine, pathology, microbiology, immunology, and pharmacology.

In 1967 King left Colorado to chair the Pathology Department at Columbia University College of Physicians and Surgeons in New York City, where he met the chairman of the Irene Heinz Given and John LaPorte Given Foundation. The foundation board agreed to commit funds for the construction of the institute, which was named for the Givens. Land for the facility came from Elizabeth Paepcke, who in 1970 agreed to sell a parcel adjacent to her Aspen home to the University of Colorado at a price well below market value. The gift came with the stipulation that Harry Weese serve as architect for the project. In addition to naming Weese as the architect, the agreement with Paepcke stipulated that the grounds, which were covered with fir and spruce trees up to sixty feet high, were to be appropriately landscaped and that paving for parking facilities was to be kept to a minimum.

The university requested a simple design that would harmonize with other buildings on the grounds and relate well to the site, a bluff overlooking Hallam Lake. Program components included a main seminar room, a laboratory, a library, and several smaller conference areas, along with office facilities, a printing/reproduction area, storage space, restrooms, and a kitchen. Other specifications were a seminar space configured to promote free interchange between speakers and audience and interior spaces that were warm, relaxed, and comfortable and conducive to informal, spontaneous discussion.

Weese's design for the Given Institute incorporated many of the geometric motifs that he favored in the late 1960s. The plan of the 12,000-square-foot facility was essentially a 90 × 90 foot square defined by the building's walls and the brick terraces, which bridged the diagonal slices and angular notches that enlivened the façade. An apse-like projection from the square expressed the two-story circular seminar room. Concentric rings of desks arranged around a central working area and dais provided seating for seminar participants. The first floor also contained a conference room, demonstration laboratory, and kitchen. Three small triangular conference rooms, the library, offices, and supply and reproduction rooms occupied the second floor. A separate windowless triangle at the southeast corner of the site housed mechanical equipment.

The circular shape of the seminar room reappeared in porthole windows framing a view of the garden adjacent to

the center and the mountains in the distance. Large rectangular windows in the library and first-floor conference room afforded additional views of the beautiful natural environment surrounding the center.

In keeping with the client's wishes, Weese's design relied on simple materials and finishes. Budgetary restrictions caused him to abandon the painted brick he initially proposed for the exterior and interior walls in favor of concrete block with raked horizontal joints. The building was painted white and accented with black railings and mullions. The columns and roof were

heavy timber. Weese made a special effort to preserve the natural beauty of the site, even notching a wall to accommodate a cottonwood tree. Because of his careful positioning of the building, only one existing fir tree had to be relocated.

The University of Colorado continues to own and operate the Given Institute, now known as the Given Institute of the University of Colorado School of Medicine, but the center has evolved into a year-round conference facility for medical and nonmedical groups and a community resource for Aspen area residents. The Aspen Given

View to west showing the apse-like projection. The vertical slots on the right provided spaces for bicycles. ca. 1972, Photographer unknown. i52144, Chicago History Museum.

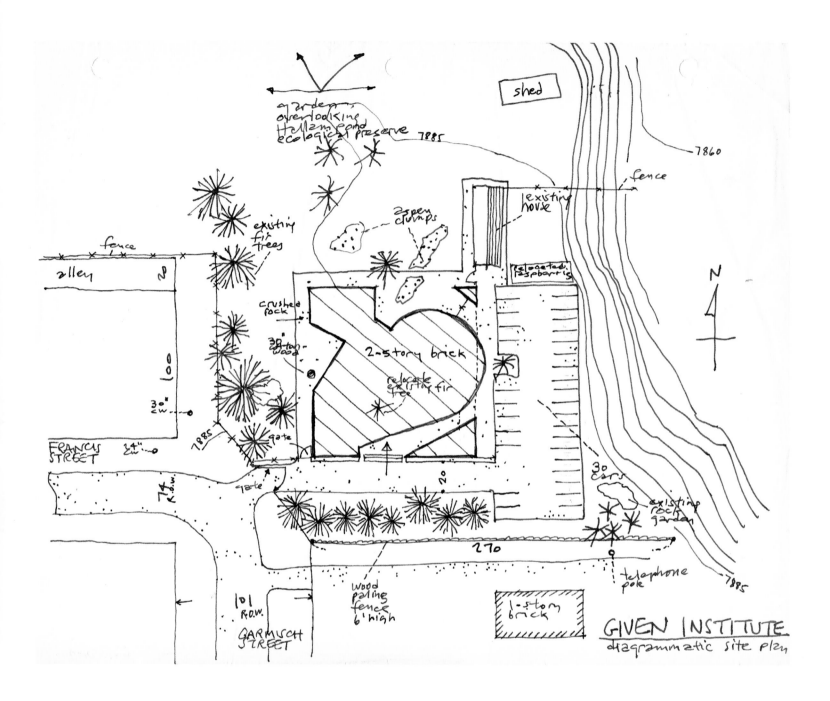

Sketch of the site plan.
i52032a, Chicago History
Museum.

Foundation, founded in 1999, raises funds for the public programs and health events offered at the institute.

Since its completion some alterations have been made to the building. Some of the interior finishes and color schemes have been changed and the open treads of the staircase have been filled in. Plans are now underway to expand the facility and to create an endowment for restoration of the original structure and expansion of the institute's public educational programs.

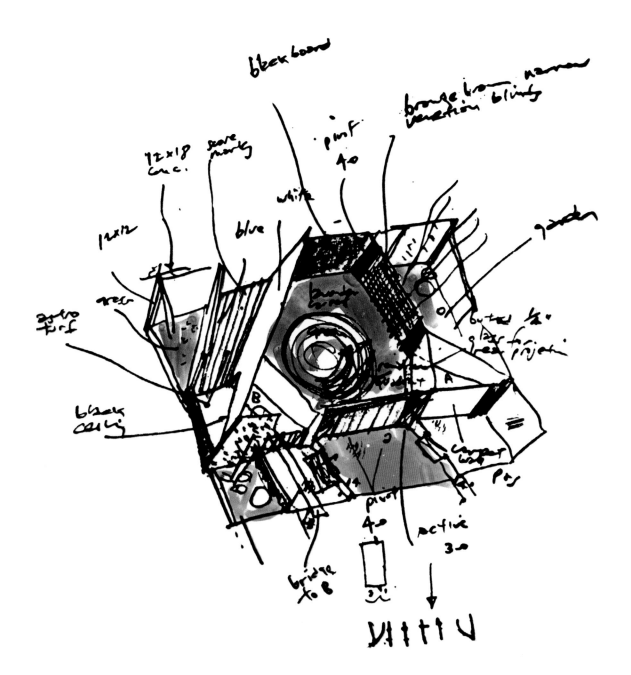

Sketch diagram. Weese put the seminar room at the center of the composition, with lobby, offices, and ancillary spaces around it. Chicago History Museum.

Job 657
Project Manager: William Bauhs
Job Captain: Philip Prince
Structural Engineer: Engineers Collaborative
Mechanical and Electrical Engineer: James Burke & Associates
General Contractor: H. E. Anderson

SELECTED BIBLIOGRAPHY

Janet Bloom. "Playful Rigor." *Architectural Forum* 138 (March 1973): 62–65.

ACTORS THEATRE OF LOUISVILLE

316 West Main Street
Louisville, Kentucky, 1970–72
Renovation, addition, 1990–94

Actors Theatre of Louisville debuted in 1964 in rather modest accommodations—a 100-seat space above the Gypsy Tea Room on Louisville's South Fourth Street. The company, formed by the merger of Actors, Inc. and Theatre Louisville, soon outgrew its quarters in the small loft building and moved to the waiting room of an abandoned Illinois Central Railroad station along the Ohio River with an expanded capacity of 350. But by 1969, plans to demolish the former station to make way for a riverfront expressway meant that Actors Theatre had to find another new home.

Actors Theatre had hoped to occupy space in a large-scale performing arts center for Louisville's riverfront thtat was then being designed by Harry Weese & Associates. Weese obtained the commission for the center through Cyrus MacKinnon, a former Chicagoan and a good friend of both Harry and Kitty Weese. MacKinnon had moved to Louisville to become the general manager of Bingham Enterprises, an important local business organization. MacKinnon recommended Weese to Barry Bingham Sr., editor and publisher of the Louisville *Courier-Journal* and head of a subcommittee formed to identify possible architects for the center. In late 1967, the Committee for the Kentucky Performing Arts Center, the organization established to develop the complex, named Weese as the center's designer. However, the project never materialized.

With relocation to the performing arts center no longer an option, Actors Theatre of Louisville commissioned Weese to evaluate four proposed alternatives for a new theater. One of these alternatives was the adaptive reuse of

Exterior view of the north façade of the Actors Theatre of Louisville. The former Bank of Louisville building is to the right, and the Myers-Thompson Display Building to the left. Actors Theatre photograph, ca. 1972, i59681, Chicago History Museum.

FACING PAGE
View of lobby, with the coffered dome and oval skylight of the former banking hall. Actors Theatre photograph, ca. 1972, i59680 Chicago History Museum.

160

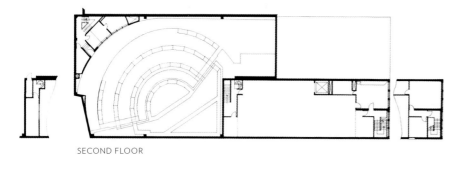

SECOND FLOOR

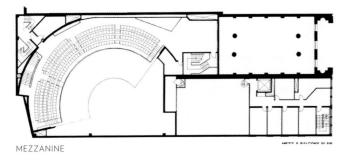

MEZZANINE

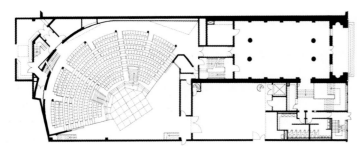

FIRST FLOOR

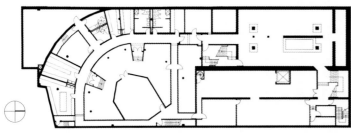

BASEMENT

Floor plans for the Pamela Brown Auditorium, the semicircular performance space to the south (left) and two renovated historic structures to the north. i52007, i52008, Chicago History Museum.

the historic Bank of Louisville building, an 1837 Greek Revival structure reportedly designed by New Orleans architect James H. Dakin, with construction supervised by Gideon Shryock.

Weese advised Actors Theatre of Louisville to acquire not only the Bank of Louisville building but also an adjacent nineteenth-century warehouse, the Myers-Thompson Display Building, and an easement along the east wall of the warehouse. The warehouse building would provide the width needed for the performance space and the easement would facilitate the loading and unloading of scenery and supplies. The company proceeded to obtain an option on the warehouse, but purchasing the bank proved more problematic. The Louisville Credit Men's Association, the building's owner since 1936, was reluctant to negotiate because of potential tax liabilities resulting from the sale of the fully depreciated structure. To circumvent these financial consequences, the two parties agreed to an exchange of property. Actors Theatre of Louisville would build a new credit union building for the association, which would in turn hand over the deed for the former bank to the theater company.

Weese began transforming the two older buildings in early 1972. The elegant Bank of Louisville, which fronted on the city's Main Street, became the principal entrance to the new theater, and the grand rectangular banking hall with its coffered dome and oval skylight became the lobby. The bank's basement, with its exposed brick walls and heavy-timber frame, was reborn as an intimate subscribers lounge. Weese adapted the former warehouse next door to accommodate administrative offices, a workshop, storage space, and a rehearsal room.

Demolition of the rear portion of the bank, which was wider than the banking room and appeared to be a later addition, provided space for the performance hall, which was constructed behind the two existing buildings. The program, formulated by Actors Theatre of Louisville producing director Jon Jory, called for an intimate space on a human scale. Other requirements included a stage, preferably a thrust stage that would accommodate eight to fifteen players, flexible lighting, a trap, and moderate fly space. Desired capacity was approximately 500, with seats arranged in the minimum number of rows necessary to reach this number.

Weese designed a simple, semicircular 637-seat performance hall with a main floor and cantilevered balcony. The eleven rows of seats on the main floor of the auditorium wrapped around a slightly raised trapped thrust stage. Two 72-foot steel trusses supporting the roof eliminated the need for interior columns and provided

View of interior of the
Pamela Brown Auditorium.
Actors Theatre photograph,
ca. 1972, i59677, Chicago History
Museum.

unobstructed views of the stage. Weese responded to the need for flexibility in lighting and stage effects with a system of catwalks that followed the contours of the hall. A pierced brick wall at the rear of the theater performed a dual function by both dampening sound and eliminating reflections.

The restoration project took eight months, at a cost of $1.7 million, approximately one-third the time and half the cost of all-new construction. The main stage, named the Pamela Brown Auditorium in honor of the wife of Actors Theatre president Owsley Brown II, opened in 1972, followed by the opening in 1973 of an intimate Off-Broadway theater, the Victor Jory Theatre, in the rehearsal room on the third floor of the former warehouse.

In 1994, Brown provided funding for the enlargement of the Actors Theatre of Louisville complex. By this time, illness had led Weese to sell his firm, but Norm Zimmerman, the project manager for the original restoration, returned to complete an expansion and renovation project that included a 318-seat arena space named the Bingham Theatre and a nine-level parking structure.

Job 696, 8913
Project Manager: Norm Zimmerman
Structural Engineer: Sendler Campbell
Mechanical and Electrical Engineer: Kaestner-Lunch

SELECTED BIBLIOGRAPHY

Carlton Knight III. "New Life for Old Buildings." *Preservation News Supplement* (April 1973).
"Buildings can be Recycled Too," *Fortune* (May 1975): 197.

CROWN CENTER HOTEL

1 East Pershing Road
Kansas City, Missouri, 1968–73

Kansas City locals called it "Signboard Hill," a shale and limestone bluff two miles south of the city center littered with unsightly billboards. In 1973, the Crown Center Hotel, an elegant hostelry designed by Harry Weese & Associates, replaced the ugly signage, and this rocky outcropping became an indoor tropical garden within the hotel lobby.

The story of the Crown Center Hotel began in 1922 when Kansas City–based Hallmark Cards located its offices and main production facility at Twenty-sixth and Grand streets in Kansas City, two miles south of downtown and near the city's new main railroad station. By the time the company's international headquarters building was completed in the mid-1950s, however, Hallmark was surrounded by old warehouses, used-car lots, abandoned buildings, and rundown residences. It was at this time that Joyce C. Hall, Hallmark founder and chairman, first conceived the idea of a mixed-use development, a city within a city, that he hoped would transform this decaying inner-city area into a pleasant and attractive urban environment.

During the next several years, Hall consulted with designers, developers, planners, and architects; conducted market, feasibility, and land-use studies; and commissioned a preliminary plan from architect Victor Gruen. This scheme, however, failed to move forward. In 1967, Hall's son and successor, Donald J. Hall, announced a new eighty-five-acre, twenty-five-block plan for the Crown Center Redevelopment Project, to be privately financed by Hallmark, with Edward Larrabee Barnes as coordinating architect and master planner. Groundbreaking occurred in 1968, and the initial component of phase one, five interconnected seven-story office buildings designed by Barnes, opened in 1971. Crown Center would eventually include a bank, residences, additional offices, underground parking garages, retail complexes, and cultural and entertainment facilities, but what the *Kansas City Star* called the "most dramatic and commanding structure in the entire development" was Weese's Crown Center Hotel.

The design philosophy adopted for the hotel by the Crown Center Redevelopment Corporation, the wholly owned subsidiary of Hallmark Cards formed to direct the project, meshed closely with Weese's own. The corporation called for "a completely functional facility" characterized by simplicity, honesty of materials, and an awareness of the needs of its users and occupants. It urged restrained elegance over opulence, timeless design over fads and clichés, and harmony of components over monotonous unity.

Weese, a champion of cities and a critic of decentralization, welcomed the chance to assist in the revitalization of central Kansas City and applauded Hallmark's role in spearheading the redevelopment. "The Crown Center effort should be an example across the country of what responsible business leadership can do for its community," he commented.

The site for the hotel was the north slope of Signboard Hill. Weese and Barnes originally envisioned the hotel as a horizontal structure with rambling cabana-type rooms sprawled over the rocky hillside, a concept in keeping with the mid-rise massing of Barnes's master plan and his office complex design. However, the experience of the hotel operator, Western International Hotels, indicated that both hotel guests and staff preferred efficient vertical circulation to circuitous paths through long corridors. Weese accommodated this preference by separating the hotel into two distinct but connected elements: a five-story lobby-func-

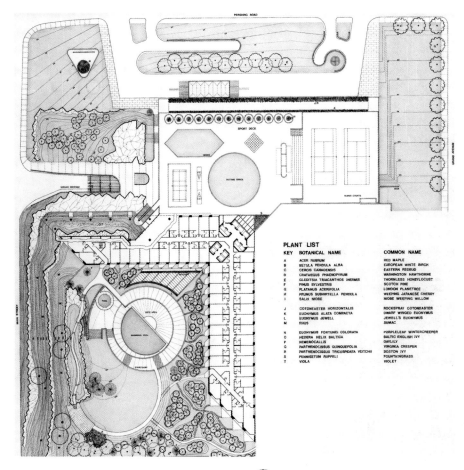

Landscape site plan, showing the lobby-function wing nestled into the hillside to the north, the L-shaped guest wing to the southwest, and the sunken semicircular swimming pool and sunbathing deck occupying the space between the two arms of the guest wing. i52345, Chicago History Museum.

FACING PAGE
View to southwest, Crown Center Hotel, now the Westin Crown Center Hotel. The five-story lobby-function wing is seen in the foreground, and the fifteen-story guest wing atop the hill rises behind it. Hedrich Blessing photograph, HB36958K2, ca. 1973, Chicago History Museum.

tion wing nestled into the hillside and a fifteen-story, 728-room guest wing sited atop the hill. The lower public wing contained the lobby and registration area, restaurants, a sunken cocktail lounge, shops, a ballroom, meeting rooms, executive offices, kitchens, and service areas. An outdoor sports deck with tennis courts and other recreational facilities topped the lobby wing.

The architects selected poured-in-place and precast concrete panels with a sandblasted finish for the exterior of the hotel. The towers of the guest wing had reinforced-concrete walls between each room with a five-inch concrete floor slab. Reinforced-concrete slabs and columns and steel trusses formed the structural system of the public areas.

A retaining wall was initially planned to prevent loose rocks from falling down the slope of Signboard Hill. At one meeting, Weese facetiously proposed omitting the wall and letting the rocks roll through the lobby and, provided the doorman was fast enough to get the door open in time, out onto the lawn in front of the hotel entrance. Weese's offhand remark led landscape architect Dan Kiley, who was also present, to suggest planting a garden and securing the loose rocks with bolts, and Joe Karr prepared an initial design for an interior rock garden at the rear of the lobby carved from the rugged stone of Signboard Hill.

Hallmark commissioned Landscape Associates of Little Rock, Arkansas, to complete the garden based on Karr's

design. The precast concrete selected for the walls and floors in the garden area distinguished this space from the more finished, formal sections of the lobby and enhanced the sense of being outdoors. A waterfall cascaded down the sixty-foot bluff amid trees and tropical plants. Skylights provided natural illumination. Guests could meander along a winding staircase that zigzagged across the hillside garden to a cocktail lounge overlooking the tropical landscape. A double-deck sky bridge provided access to the sports deck or the sunken semicircular outdoor swimming pool and sunbathing deck, which were located between the two arms of the guest wing amid the hotel garden designed by Kiley.

The hilltop location of the guest wing seventy feet above the street maximized privacy while minimizing noise from the traffic below and provided outstanding views from the guest room balconies—to the north to downtown, to the west to Penn Valley Park, to the east to Crown Center, and to the south to the hotel's outdoor gardens. Guests could also enjoy these vistas as they ascended to their rooms in the glass-enclosed elevator located at the junction of the two arms of the guest wing. Topping this wing was a cocktail lounge overlooking the city.

Guest rooms staggered on opposite sides of the hallways increased privacy, and the recessed entrances to the rooms avoided a monotonous, institutional, tunnel-like effect. Most of the guest rooms were rectangular with French balconies, but Weese angled the ends of the two guest wing arms to create unique trapezoidal rooms with triangular balconies.

In 1975 the Chicago chapter of the American Institute of Architects recognized the Crown Center Hotel with a Distinguished Building Award. The AIA jury described the project as "a first-rate hotel integrated into its site and urban context" and commented on the "spectacular garden" generated by the imaginative use of the site. The hotel has undergone two major renovations since its completion in 1973, but the exterior has remained essentially unchanged. A glass-enclosed elevated pedestrian walkway, added in 1988, connected the hotel with Crown Center shops and offices as well as the Hyatt Regency Crown Center, completed in 1980. Another bridge connects the hotel to Union Station. The hotel is currently the Westin Crown Center Hotel.

Job 633
Project Manager: Norm Zimmerman
Project Designer: Norman Johnson
Structural Engineer: J. D. Gillum
Mechanical/Electrical Engineer: Holloway, Perkins, Eisman
Associate Architect: Marshall & Brown
Contractor: Eldridge & Son

View of lobby, showing the central sunken cocktail lounge around which guests circulated to reach the front desk, shops, restaurants, and elevators. Hedrich Blessing photograph, HB36958B2, ca. 1973, Chicago History Museum.

View of indoor rock garden.
Hedrich Blessing photograph,
HB36958W, ca. 1973, Chicago
History Museum.

SELECTED BIBLIOGRAPHY

"Crown Center Hotel." *A + U* (January 1982): 54–61.

"Showplace Hotel Opens Tuesday." *Kansas City Star*, May 6, 1973.

"Crown Center." *Interiors* 82 (July 1973): 48–67.

"Arcade of Life." *Building Design and Construction* 114 (August 1973): 43–46.

"Crown Center." *Architectural Record* 154 (October 1973): 113–126.

SAWYER LIBRARY, WILLIAMS COLLEGE

Williamstown, Massachusetts, 1975

The Williams College catalog of 1922–23 proudly
described Stetson Hall, the new library building, as
having "spacious rooms, the latest devices and equipment
for modern library administration, and a metal stack with
a book capacity of over 200,000 volumes." The Georgian-
inspired fireproof building was more than adequate at
that time to meet the demands of the Williams College
community. But over the next forty years, the number of
students and faculty members more than doubled, library
holdings more than tripled, circulation rose fivefold,
faculty and student involvement in research expanded,
and new technologies came into use, placing a severe strain
on the facility. By the mid-1960s, the college needed a
larger, updated library to serve current and future needs of
students and faculty.

Planning for the new library began in 1966. Over
the next four years, a committee composed of faculty
and student representatives provided input on functional
requirements that became the basis of the library program. Williams College president John Sawyer was actively

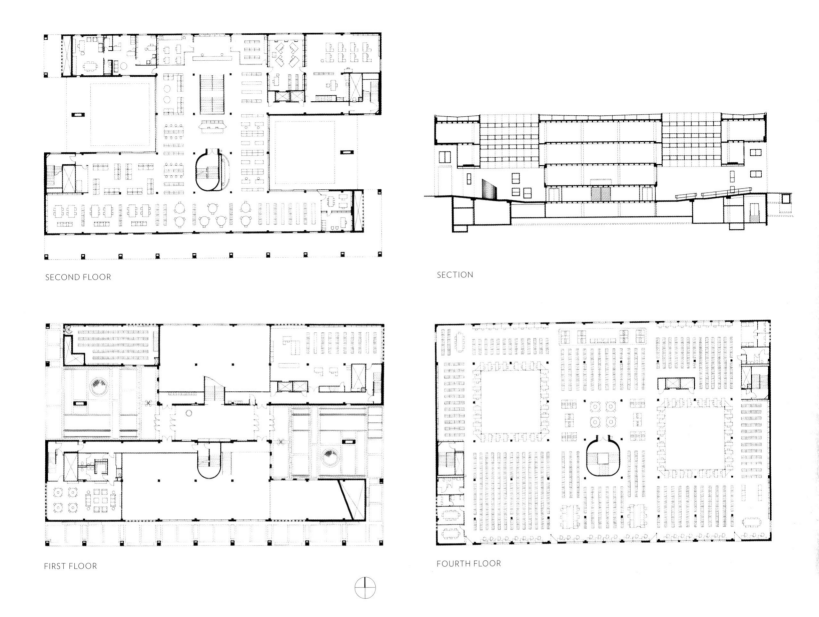

SECOND FLOOR

SECTION

FIRST FLOOR

FOURTH FLOOR

involved in the planning and design process, and it was Sawyer who chose Harry Weese & Associates as the architect for the project.

The program specified that the venerable Stetson Hall remain intact and be connected with the new structure, a provision that required the disassembly and relocation back to Albany of the turn-of-the-century Van Rensselaer mansion, which blocked the only viable site immediately to the west of Stetson Hall. With the removal of the mansion, the library could be centered on the north-south and east-west axes of the Williams campus, making it visible on all four sides and providing space for future expansion to the north. A pedestrian

square on the east separated the new library and Stetson Hall, which were connected via an underground tunnel. The original loading dock at Stetson Hall served the Sawyer Library as well.

The library program stipulated access to the library from the east and the west. To meet this requirement but maintain a single point of entry, Ben Weese, designer of the project, included a ramp that led to a corridor under the building, one-half level below grade.

This ramp formed an east-west concourse that brought library users to a staircase leading to a central control point, the main desk of the library, which was located on the first of the four levels above grade. This main level also contained staff offices, periodicals, the card catalog, and reference areas.

To maximize energy efficiency, Weese directed light and air into the building by organizing the three upper stories around two open light courts to the east and west. Because of the ample natural cross ventilation and the location in the Berkshires, the library had no air-conditioning at the time of its completion. Windows were large and numerous on the north façade and fewer, smaller, and recessed on the sunnier south side. An exposed duct system that could be closed when the windows were open provided natural ventilation, and a double roof equipped with exhaust fans functioned as a traditional attic, pulling off hot air. Equipping the reading stations with flexible "luxo" lamps allowed the general ambient light level to be kept low. A light interior décor featuring white ceilings and ducts, champagne-colored stacks, light gray carpeting, and bleached ash wood trim compensated for the low lighting.

The faculty requested an open, free, and inviting plan for the library with easy access to the collections and varied and interesting study and seating configurations. Weese responded to this request by arranging the open stacks and reading stations on the two upper levels around the open courts. A continuous study shelf with pedestal swivel chairs installed along the operable sash windows of the south wall allowed seated students to enjoy both fresh air and views of the Berkshires. Other innovative seating configurations designed by Ben Weese specifically for the library included over-under interlocking carrels, crow's nest or double-deck study structures with carrels tucked underneath a mezzanine study area reached by ladder, step-down carrels around the light courts, and tandem arrangements of extra-wide sofa-style upholstered lounge chairs. When librarian Larry Wikander wanted proof that these innovative designs would work, Harry Weese & Associates built prototypes that were pretested and graded by the students.

The red brick cladding covering the reinforced-concrete frame of the library harmonized with Stetson Hall and other existing campus buildings, which ranged in style from Neoclassical to Gothic Revival to Richardsonian Romanesque. A catalog accompanying an exhibition of William College architecture described the Sawyer Library as a restrained composition that related to the "highly functional, no-nonsense tradition" of the Chicago school of architecture. Harry Weese regarded the building as "an understatement in a nervous era tending toward architectural one-upmanship" and postulated that its "quiet virtues" would still be appreciated after flashier projects "done as calculated risks or experiments" had become outdated.

In the late 1980s, Weese Langley Weese, the firm formed by Ben Weese, wife Cindy Weese, and Dennis Langley in 1989, added air-conditioning to the library to help preserve the valuable collection. The firm also converted Stetson Hall stacks to faculty offices.

In January 2006, the Williams College Board of Trustees approved funding for a project that includes a new library/information technology complex to be designed by Bohlin Cywinski Jackson. When the new library is completed in 2011, the existing Sawyer Library will be razed and the space it currently occupies will become a new quadrangle.

Job 655
Partner in Charge: Ben Weese
Project Manager: Carl Klimek
Job Captain: Arnie Seegers
Structural Engineer: Severud-Perrone-Sturm-Bandel
Mechanical and Electrical Engineer: Cosentini & Associates
Landscape Architect: Joe Karr & Associates
General Contractor: Dwight Building Company

SELECTED BIBLIOGRAPHY

"Low Voltage Library." *American School & University* (August 1977): 56–57.
"Design for Readers." *Architectural Record* 164 (July 1978): 89–94.

View of reading area, showing Ben Weese's innovative seating configurations, which included over-under interlocking carrels.
Hedrich Blessing photograph, HB39550H, ca. 1975, Chicago History Museum.

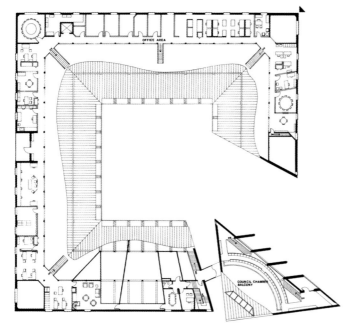

MEZZANINE

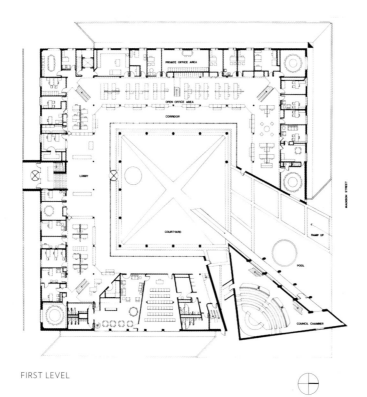

FIRST LEVEL

Plans, Oak Park Village
Hall. Chicago History
Museum, i51997, i51215.

OAK PARK
VILLAGE HALL

123 Madison Street
Oak Park, Illinois
1971 design starts
1973–75 construction

From traditional Queen Anne houses and classical public buildings to the revolutionary early designs of Frank Lloyd Wright, the village of Oak Park, nine miles west of Chicago's downtown, is characterized by a distinguished architectural history. Harry Weese sought to continue these traditions when he received a commission in the 1970s for the community's new Village Hall.

Village offices at that time were scattered among cramped and antiquated facilities throughout the municipality. The program for the new civic complex called for space that would accommodate all of these offices, with the exception of the fire and public works departments, in one structure. The site was the north third of a block containing three and a half acres on Madison Street between Taylor and Lombard avenues in the village's southeast side. Village officials hoped that the civic center would revitalize this neighborhood and encourage investment and development.

The Village Board requested an impressive structure that emphasized its importance as a major public building but did not dominate the neighborhood. Weese responded with a plan that he characterized as "a marriage of both function and monument, expressed modestly in pure forms and human scale." The open courtyard, geometric elements, and brick walls in Weese's design recalled the Säynätsalo Town Hall in Finland designed by Alvar Aalto, the Finnish architect whom Weese considered his most important mentor.

The one-and-one-half-story, 70,000-square-foot complex, finished in 1975, contained a half basement, a main floor, and a partial upper-level mezzanine. To create the impression of a large structure while remaining within the $4 million budget, Weese wrapped the Village Hall around a central elevated courtyard, or "Village Square."

A broad ramp from the sidewalk along Madison Street, the busy commercial street to the north, extended in a southwest direction to the courtyard five feet above street level. The ramp led past a reflecting pool and fountain on the west side of the Council Chamber, which stood at the entrance to the courtyard. The elevated, triangular form of the Council Chamber was the dominant feature of the complex.

View to the southwest, showing the ramp to the courtyard level on the right and the triangular Council Chamber on the left.
Hedrich Blessing photograph, HB39171M, ca. 1975, Chicago History Museum.

View of interior of the Council Chamber. Hedrich Blessing photograph, HB39171l, ca. 1975, Chicago History Museum.

A second ramp paralleling the entrance ramp extended from the courtyard up through an arcade to the chamber's entrance. The two-story Council Chamber contained a semicircular conference table for Village Board members and raised built-in benches that could accommodate up to two hundred citizens. The configuration of the benches placed citizens attending council meetings no more than nineteen feet from the Village Board president.

The Weese firm's design placed the main entrance to the Village Hall at the rear of the courtyard. The open interior plan of the building was intended to reflect the transparency and accessibility of the municipal government. A continuous glass-walled public corridor ringing the courtyard on three sides led to the offices of the various village departments, which were separated from the public only by counter-high modular storage units. Conference spaces and enclosed offices for village officers and department heads were tucked under the mezzanine or arranged around the perimeter of the upper level.

The lower level of the Village Hall, accessible from a separate entrance to the south as well as from the main level, contained the police department, with offices, a communication center, the lockup, and a firing range. An open park created at the south end of the site beyond the parking areas allowed room for expansion.

Harry Weese & Associates originally proposed a structural frame of heavy exposed timbers with stucco-like cement plaster infill and a copper roof for the Village Hall. Maintenance and cost concerns led to the use of heavy-timber framing only for the mezzanine and roof and the substitution of reinforced concrete for the basement and first level. Brick replaced stucco for the walls, and terne metal replaced copper for the roof.

The Oak Park Village Hall continues to serve as the administrative center of the village. Renovations to the building over the thirty years since its completion, some undertaken by Harry Weese & Associates, are for the most part sympathetic to the original design. Mechanical difficulties with the pool in the courtyard led to its removal during a redesign of the plaza.

Job 791
Project Manager: Bill Dring
Project Designer: Bill Bauhs
Landscape Architect: Joe Karr & Associates

SELECTED BIBLIOGRAPHY

"Civic Center Design Unveiled." *Oak Leaves*, April 4, 1973.
"A Visible and Accessible Village Hall." *Inland Architect* (September 1974): 12–13.
"Village Hall Reflects Oak Park Openness and Excellence." *Village Views* (June 1975).

View of interior of open offices and stairs to mezzanine level. Hedrich Blessing photograph, HB39171A2, ca. 1975, Chicago History Museum.

METROPOLITAN CORRECTIONAL CENTER

(WILLIAM J. CAMPBELL U.S. COURTHOUSE ANNEX)

71 West Van Buren Street
Chicago, Illinois, 1971–75

View to the southeast, William J. Campbell U.S. Courthouse Annex. The concrete plugs expressing the openings used by workmen during the post-tensioning process are visible at the second and tenth floors. Hedrich Blessing photograph, HB39636D, ca. 1975, Chicago History Museum.

Harry Weese's skyscraper detention center was a product of a reform initiative undertaken by the Federal Bureau of Prisons in the late 1960s to provide more humanitarian prison conditions. The bureau's ten-year master plan included a new type of institution, the Metropolitan Correctional Center, or MCC, a multipurpose facility for persons awaiting trial or sentencing, serving short sentences, testifying at federal trials, or requiring protective custody. In contrast to traditional detention facilities, which were typically large and overcrowded and located in remote areas, the MCCs were limited to a capacity of 550 and were constructed in or near metropolitan areas with ready access to social and human services.

The Bureau of Prisons selected Chicago as the location of one of five MCC prototypes and Harry Weese & Associates as the center's architect. The MCC was the first federal correctional facility to be built in the Chicago metropolitan area. Previously, local institutions had provided detention and correctional services for federal prisoners through contractual agreements with the Bureau of Prisons.

The bureau decided to locate the Chicago MCC at Clark and Van Buren streets in the south end of the Loop, Chicago's central business district. This downtown location had a number of advantages. It was only a block from the Mies van der Rohe-designed courthouse in the Chicago Federal Center at Dearborn and Jackson streets and was convenient for lawyers and family members of detainees. This location also provided easy access to university and social service programs. However, not all Chicagoans favored this central location. Concern that the jail would lower land values and discourage development of Dearborn Park, a new community planned for the South Loop, led several leading banks and civic organizations to launch an unsuccessful campaign aimed at stopping construction of the MCC.

Bureau of Prisons officials explained the philosophy underlying the MCC to Weese but imposed no rigid design guidelines. The only mandatory feature was a self-contained "functional unit" composed of a common multipurpose area and single rooms for no more than fifty

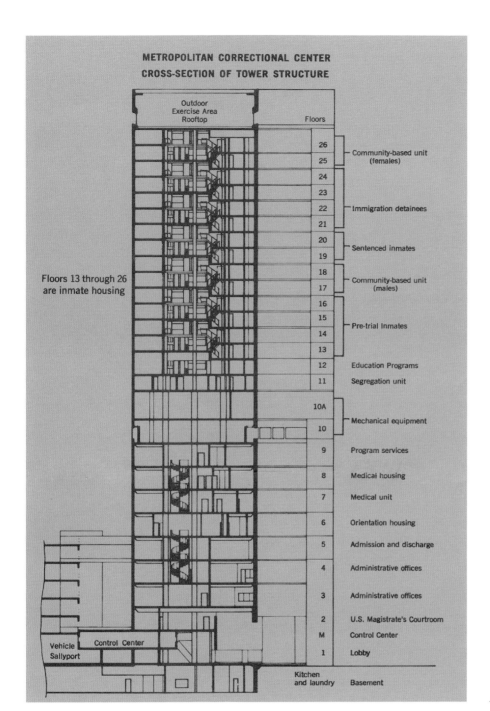

METROPOLITAN CORRECTIONAL CENTER
CROSS-SECTION OF TOWER STRUCTURE

Outdoor Exercise Area Rooftop

Floors 13 through 26 are inmate housing

Vehicle Sallyport

Control Center

Floors	
26	Community-based unit (females)
25	
24	Immigration detainees
23	
22	
21	
20	Sentenced inmates
19	
18	Community-based unit (males)
17	
16	Pre-trial Inmates
15	
14	
13	
12	Education Programs
11	Segregation unit
10A	Mechanical equipment
10	
9	Program services
8	Medical housing
7	Medical unit
6	Orientation housing
5	Admission and discharge
4	Administrative offices
3	Administrative offices
2	U.S. Magistrate's Courtroom
M	Control Center
1	Lobby
Kitchen and laundry	Basement

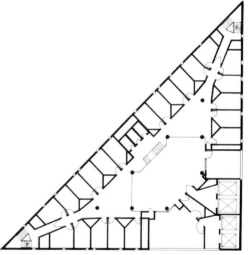

Section of tower and plan of a typical inmate floor.
i59277, i52019, Chicago History Museum.

177

detainees. This small size allowed for separation of men and women, old and young, first-time and repeat offenders, and violent and nonviolent inmates.

Weese and his associates considered several design approaches to the Chicago MCC, which was to include not only facilities for detainees but also a garage that would house the General Services Administration (GSA) motor pool along with a kitchen, laundry, and mechanical facilities for the correctional center. They discarded the possibility of a one- or two-story structure above a block-long garage because of its institutional appearance and 150-foot-long corridors. They also rejected the concept of a mid-rise building with an undulating façade, which was incompatible with what Jack Hartray called the "relatively large-scale, simple, prismatic forms" of Chicago's downtown.

The final design solution was a twenty-seven-story triangular tower at the northwest corner of the site, with a garage extending behind it to the south. The triangular configuration had a number of practical advantages. It eliminated the need for long institutional-like corridors and allowed inmates' rooms to be located at the perimeter of the building around the multipurpose areas at the core. Each room in the facility had a slit-like window 7 1/2 feet high that allowed daylight to penetrate into the entire room. The width of the windows was only 5 inches, the maximum that the Federal Bureau of Prisons would allow without requiring security features, such as bars or alarms. Rather than aligning the windows vertically, Weese opted for random placement, giving the façade an appearance that resembled, according to the architect himself, a giant computer punch card.

Practical considerations were not the only factors that influenced the selection of the triangular design. Aesthetics also played a role. Weese admitted that he had always wanted to design a triangular building because he found the triangle "very sculptural, more interesting than a rectangle or a circle." And it was also "fun to make a new shape."

The upper fourteen floors of the MCC contained housing for inmates. As requested by the Bureau of Prisons, Weese organized these areas into functional or living units. Each unit consisted of two floors and contained a total of forty-four single rooms arranged around the perimeter of the two levels. The units were further subdivided into four 11-room modules with mini-lounges.

Weese placed a multipurpose room containing dining facilities, recreational and exercise areas, visitors' lounges, and facilities for study and rehabilitation at the center midway between the two floors. This split-level arrangement facilitated the simultaneous observation of all common areas by a single corrections officer. Immigration detainees, who did not need the security of a private room and were typically held for only brief periods of time, were housed in sixty-two-bed dormitory units. The total capacity of the Chicago MCC at the time of its completion was approximately four hundred inmates.

Weese's experience in designing sailboats proved invaluable in configuring the individual rooms, which were compact and efficient. Each 7 × 10 foot room contained a single platform bed with drawers for storage underneath, a desk, shelves, and a chair. All furnishings, with the exception of the chair, were entirely built-in. Carpeting eliminated the need for acoustic treatment. Furniture in the common areas was also built-in and arranged in natural groupings to encourage a high level of interaction among detainees. The butcher-block furniture chosen for both the individual rooms and the common areas created a residential quality and was easy to clean and hard to destroy. A bright red, white, and blue color scheme replaced the drab gray and sterile white so frequently found in conventional correctional facilities. The choice of the materials used for the interior furnishings was left to the discretion of the architects, but the Bureau of Prisons did insist that the materials be capable of showing evidence of tampering. For example, acoustical tile had to be applied to a hard surface and rugs had to be glued to the floor.

To maximize security, the tower contained two separate sets of elevator banks. One bank, located entirely within the secure perimeter, connected to the functional units. During the day, detainees used this vertical circulation system rather than conventional corridors to access medical, administrative, educational, and admissions areas in the lower half of the tower. The two elevators of the second bank were for visitors and opened into a secure lobby area on each floor. Before proceeding beyond the lobby, visitors had to pass through another door controlled by a prison official that would not open until the elevator door had closed.

By placing the building's mechanical equipment on the tenth floor, Weese freed the roof for an exercise yard. The rooftop exercise area was landscaped and covered with a steel mesh screen. Locating the mechanical equipment on the tenth floor and then recessing it also allowed the architects to screen it with louvers, maintaining the simple geometry of the building's exterior.

At the base of the building, landscape architect Joe Karr designed a half-acre plaza with a grove of linden trees to the east of the tower that originally provided a green oasis among the Loop's concrete plazas. Unfortunately, the Bureau of Prisons later removed the trees for security purposes.

An arcaded walkway along a narrow alley that intersected the site provided access to the eight-level, 319,000-square-foot garage south of the tower. The garage was recessed from the street in order to emphasize the tower. The dimensions of the structural bays of the garage—25 1/2 × 60 1/2 feet—created long column-free spans and resulted in a capacity of 865 cars.

Post-tensioning the concrete bearing wall of the tower concentrated the loads at the corners of the building and allowed for spans of 100 and 150 feet. This technique was used because it was economical, allowed for random spacing of the windows, and reduced the risk of cracks in the concrete walls. Weese expressed the post-tensioning on the center's exterior by setting off the concrete plug that was used to fill the openings left in the walls on the second and tenth floors for the workmen involved in the post-tensioning process while the walls were being poured. The bronze-tinted glass chosen for the windows blended with the warm tone of the concrete and screened the view of the interior of the building and the inmates from the occupants of nearby high-rise office buildings.

Dedication of the Chicago MCC took place in October 1975. The center was named the William J. Campbell U.S. Courthouse Annex in recognition of the leadership role played by senior federal district judge William J. Campbell in making the facility a reality. In 1977 the Chicago MCC received a National Honor Award from the American Institute of Architects, which applauded it as an "architectural attempt to overcome the traditional barred jailhouse image." According to the AIA jury, "The narrow windows in random pattern indicate a special use, but one does not find an inhumane correctional facility image projected on the community." Following this recognition by the national organization, the MCC also received an Honor Award from the Chicago chapter of the AIA.

The tightly organized space of the MCC was intended as a safeguard against future overcrowding. However, in the 1980s, the Federal Bureau of Prisons added double-bunks to some of the rooms in order to accommodate the growing number of federal inmates.

With time, despite the post-tensioning, cracks caused by moisture penetration of the porous concrete surface appeared in the center's façade. The damage was repaired and a protective coat of paint applied, a solution that transformed the bold and weathered gray concrete into a smooth light tan surface, described by *Chicago Tribune* architectural critic Blair Kamin as "bland as milquetoast." Ben Weese was less disturbed by the change. Because the concrete was originally pigmented rather than natural, he considered the "recoloring" to be justifiable in retaining the building's "prismatic continuity" and integrity.

Job 712
Project Manager: Jack Hartray
Project Designer: Bill Bauhs
Job Captain: Fritz Biederman
Structural Engineer: Severud Associates
Mechanical and Electrical Engineer: Nachman, Uragel & Associates
General Contractor: Turner Construction
Landscape Architect: Joe Karr & Associates

View of typical inmate's room. Hedrich Blessing photograph, HB39636l, ca. 1975, Chicago History Museum.

SELECTED BIBLIOGRAPHY

"Three Models for the Humane Prison That Satisfy the Critics." *Building Design & Construction* (March 1975): 52–54.

"Metropolitan Correction Center, Chicago." *Architectural Forum* (March 1975): 43.

Nory Miller. "The Loop Gets a Stunning Skyscraper Jail." *Inland Architect* 19 (July 1975): 8–13.

Paul Gapp. "An Unusual Landmark for the South Loop." *Chicago Tribune*, October 24, 1976.

Marion B. Wood. "Designing Better Prison Systems." *Chicago Journal*, July 6, 1983.

Blair Kamin. "Jail a Prisoner of Ill-Conceived Renovation Plan." *Chicago Tribune*, October 22, 2006.

View to the north, Willow Street Townhouses. Hedrich Blessing photograph, HB40551H, ca. 1976, Chicago History Museum.

Living room of the Weese townhouse. Kim Clawson photograph, ca. 1982, Chicago History Museum.

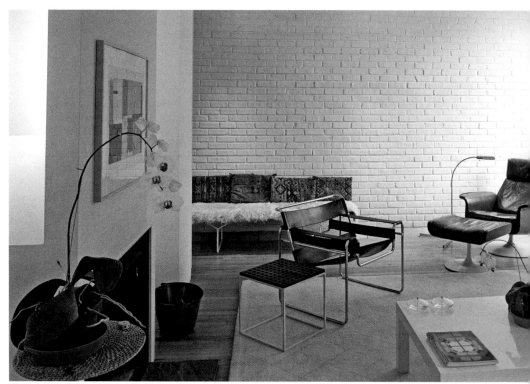

WILLOW STREET TOWNHOUSES

312–318 West Willow Street
Chicago, Illinois, 1973–76

The Harry Weese family initially occupied an apartment on East Superior Street and then moved in the mid-1950s to a one-story second-floor cooperative apartment on North Astor Street on Chicago's North Side. In the 1970s, with daughter Kate the only child still at home, they moved again to a Weese-designed townhouse on Willow Street in Chicago's historic Old Town neighborhood.

Their new home was part of what Weese called "a kind of private redevelopment" that replaced three freestanding frame rooming houses, labeled as "shacks" by one Old Town neighbor, with four new townhouses. As with the earlier 227 East Walton project and the later River Cottages, he acted as both architect and developer.

Eight-inch masonry exterior and party walls and wood joists formed the structural system of the four attached four-story townhouses. The unassuming street façades harmonized in both outward appearance and scale with surrounding structures. The slightly irregular beige brick cladding with matching tinted mortar, Indiana buff limestone trim, and black wrought-iron accents further blended with the other houses in this hundred-year-old formerly working-class but now gentrifying neighborhood.

The plans of the four units varied according to the needs and desires of the individual owners. The more random appearance of the rear façades, which contrasted sharply with the uniformity of those facing Willow Street, reflected this customization. The ground-floor entrances to all four townhouses opened onto a large foyer. A door from the attached garage provided another means of access to the ground level. In the Weese unit, the foyer led to a narrow hallway connecting to a bathroom and a guest room, which doubled as a study and looked out onto the backyard garden. The living room on the second floor of the Weese townhouse faced south, offering views of Willow Street from its two vertical floor-to-ceiling windows. Weese left the common brick walls in the living room exposed and painted them white. The dining room and adjoining kitchen occupied the rear portion of the second level. A focal point of the dining area was a circular Formica-topped dining table with a lighted glass centerpiece designed by Weese. The glass wall to the north allowed diners to enjoy views of the landscaped backyard garden, with its plants, flowering trees, and a piece of sculpture made of

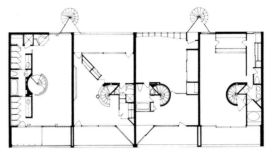

FOURTH FLOOR

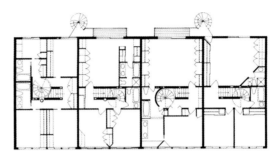

THIRD FLOOR

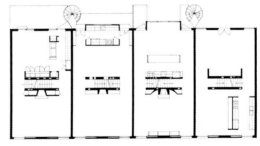

SECOND FLOOR

GROUND FLOOR

Plans. The Weese unit was second from the right. i40551, Chicago History Museum.

Garden of the Weese townhouse, with the sculpture designed by the Weeses' daughter Marcia visible to the lower left. Kim Clawson photograph, ca. 1982, Chicago History Museum.

COR-TEN steel and copper designed by daughter Marcia and placed prominently at the center of a sunken circular paved area.

Unique to the Weese townhouse was its innovative movable kitchen. The fixed south wall of the narrow galley kitchen contained appliances and storage space, while a work island topped with cabinets and open shelves defined the northern boundary of the kitchen. The cabinetry over the island was on ceiling tracks and could be slid up against the wall containing the sink and appliances, turning the island into a buffet for entertaining. This feature recalled an early Weese experiment with a disappearing kitchen in his Barrington Water Tower House of 1948. In that kitchen, a pivoting jackknife worktop and storage unit on rubber-wheeled castors allowed the space to be opened to varying degrees or completely closed to conceal the kitchen appliances.

A central spiral staircase topped by a skylight led to the third and fourth floors of the townhouse. Ribbon windows offered some degree of privacy for the third-floor bedroom facing south onto Willow Street, while sliding glass doors provided access to a small deck off the bedroom on the garden side to the north. The fourth floor contained another bedroom with a large deck overlooking the street. The fourth-floor space on the garden side became a studio for Kitty. Weese installed a slanted skylight across the entire north wall to infuse the space with light and designed a special 4 × 10 foot closet for storage of Kitty's canvases and other art supplies.

After Kitty passed away in 2004, her daughters began making plans to sell the Willow Street townhouse. Before it reached the real estate market, a long-time resident of Old Town who was familiar with the complex but had never seen the interior of the Weese unit requested a showing and made an offer on the spot. The new owners are not empty nesters like Kitty and Harry but share the townhouse with their two teen-age daughters. Yet they feel that the townhouse functions just as well for them as it did for the Weeses and have made only minor changes.

Job 817
General Contractor: R. E. Johnson & Company

SELECTED BIBLIOGRAPHY

"Down to Earth Architect." *Sun-Times Midwest Magazine*, December 12, 1976.

"Architecture Is Alive and Well." *Architectural Review* 162 (October 1977): 242–243.

"Weese Household a Nice Arrangement." *Chicago Tribune*, January 28, 1978.

Kitchen in the Weese townhouse, with the movable wall pulled forward (above) and moved back (below). Kim Clawson photograph, ca. 1982, Chicago History Museum.

Harry Weese's sketch of cross section of vaulted subway station for Washington, D.C., transit system. July 1966. Courtesy of Stanley Allan.

WASHINGTON METRO

Washington, D.C.
Commissioned, 1966
Groundbreaking, 1969
Opening of initial segment, 1976

Jack Hartray characterized the Washington, D.C., Metro project as the "greatest architectural opportunity" of the twentieth century, and Stanley Allan called it the "crown jewel" in the history of the Weese firm's commissions. The Metro established Harry Weese & Associates as the country's foremost architectural designer of rail transit systems and led to the firm's involvement in the planning and conceptual design of systems in cities in North America and overseas, including Miami, Los Angeles, Dallas, Buffalo, Toronto, and Singapore.

Planning for the Washington Metro began in the 1950s, but a pivotal event in its evolution was the establishment of the National Capital Transportation Agency

(NCTA) by President Dwight D. Eisenhower in July 1960. For the next five years the NCTA, under the direction of administrator Darwin Stolzenbach, worked to fulfill its mission—the formulation of a regional transit development program. In September 1965, the U.S. Congress approved the agency's plan for a twenty-five-mile, twenty-five-station rapid rail system primarily within the District of Columbia.

Even before the proposed system received congressional approval, the NCTA made the unprecedented decision to appoint separate architectural and engineering consultants for the project. In most U.S. public work projects of that time, the architects were subcontracted by the engineers and their role was limited to providing aesthetic guidance. In the case of the Washington Metro, however, the architectural and engineering contractors were co-equals and each reported directly to the NCTA.

The rationale behind this decision was to assure high-quality design from both an engineering and an architectural perspective and to circumvent the conflict between

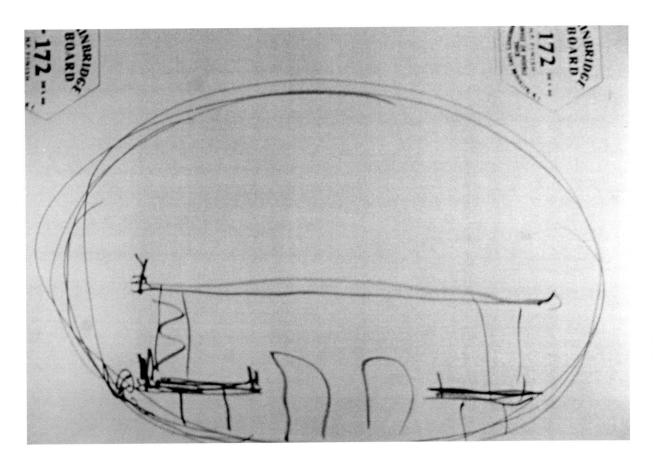

Gordon Bunshaft's sketch of a vaulted station on the back of one of the presentation boards Weese showed at the September 19, 1967 meeting of the Fine Arts Commisions. Courtesy of Charles Atherton.

architects and engineers that had plagued San Francisco's Bay Area Rapid Transit (BART) system, which was designed in the late 1950s and early 1960s. As Stolzenbach recognized in a 1965 letter to William Walton, chairman of the Washington, D.C., Commission of Fine Arts (CFA), "both engineering and architectural talents of a high order must cooperate in the design of this system if it is to be worthy of the Nation's Capital." The wishes of the NCTA were later echoed by President Lyndon B. Johnson in a February 22, 1966, letter to then NCTA administrator Walter J. McCarter in which the president characterized the Metro as an "opportunity to make our Capital a more attractive and inspiring place in which to live and work" and charged the agency to make the system attractive as well as useful and "an example for the Nation."

The NCTA considered only engineering firms with experience in underground construction for the position of general engineering consultant and awarded the contract to DeLeuw Cather & Company, a Chicago-based firm experienced in highway, railroad, tunnel, and bridge

construction. To choose the project's architect, John Rannells, NCTA director of architecture, and Kent Cooper, a Washington architect who had served as project manager on Eero Saarinen's Dulles Airport, drafted a request for proposals, which the agency sent to thirty architecture and planning firms. The deadline for responses was December 31, 1965, only a few weeks after the requests were mailed.

The request for proposals arrived at the office of Harry Weese & Associates on December 15, 1965. Weese spent the next two weeks collaborating with brother Ben and Jack Hartray on a response. The three completed the bulk of the work on the proposal between Christmas and New Years, with Harry communicating daily by phone from Aspen, where he was vacationing with his family. Weese's secretary, Marilyn Levy, mailed the proposal on New Year's Eve.

The four-page, single-spaced letter emphasized the firm's experience in the design of prototypes, citing the systems developed for Purity supermarkets in California and for Cummins Engine Company dealerships nationwide and in Canada. The response also stressed previous collabora-

Partial full-scale mock-up of vaulted train room. Presumably WMATA photograph, photographer unknown, ca. 1969. Courtesy of Stanley Allan.

tions with graphic designers, landscape architects, acoustics experts, and mechanical, structural, and electrical engineers, as well as the interest of Harry Weese & Associates in urban design, exemplified by projects such as the Hyde Park and Southwest Washington urban renewal work. The letter concluded with a statement of the firm's commitment "to devote a considerable portion of our capacity to seeing it [the transit system] conceived, designed, detailed, and monitored over the years it will take to complete." The letter was one of seventeen responses received by the NCTA but, according to John Rannells, it was the only one that

indicated "a seriously detailed understanding of the tasks at hand."

The NCTA scheduled interviews with Weese and four other architectural firms—Whittlesey & Conklin; Keyes, Lethbridge & Condon; John Carl Warnecke; and Cloetheil Woodard Smith. On February 6, 1966, Weese and Stanley Allan, who would become the project manager, met with the seven-member NCTA review board for what Allan later described as a two-hour "stimulating interactive brainstorming session." What impressed the interviewers most about Weese was his interest in the people who would be riding the subway. His concern for comfort, safety, and ease of orientation and his vision of dignified urban structures, durable and handsome materials, and open attractive spaces led the NCTA to recommend Harry Weese & Associates as the architect for the system.

Negotiations were soon underway, and Weese signed a contract with the NCTA in March 1966. Under the conditions of the contract, Weese agreed to open a Washington office; coordinate his firm's work with the NCTA, DeLeuw Cather, and other agencies as required; visit subway systems throughout the world to investigate aspects of rail transit that might be applicable to the Washington subway; and obtain approval from the CFA for a system-wide architectural design concept for the subway stations.

Weese and his associates opened an office on K Street and in late March, Weese, accompanied by wife Kitty, and Allan, traveling with Weese employee Bob Reynolds, embarked on around-the-world trips to survey other subway systems. During the forty-two-day, sixteen-city tour, they visited subways from Rome to Oslo and from Lisbon to Tokyo, making notes, collecting literature and maps, taking photographs, and sketching everything from stations and trains to signage and staff uniforms. In every city they met with transit officials to learn about the characteristics of each system. Throughout the trip they recognized a sense of camaraderie and good will and a willingness to share information, what Stan Allan called "a brotherhood of transit enthusiasm."

An essay written by Weese following his return to Chicago in early May summed up his increasingly mature understanding of the nature and scope of the project that lay ahead. He recognized that nearly every station in the Washington system would be unique and that "despite the greatest desire for prototype, existing underground and surface conditions force the design result." Based on his world tour, Weese recommended what he called the public approach to transit system design, which treated spaces "like public buildings" and sought "a certain dignity and even elegance." During May and June of 1966, Weese and his colleagues began developing an architectural concept to be presented to the NCTA at a meeting scheduled for July 6, and finalized the sketches and statement for the presentation during a nonstop charette held at the Weese's Studio in Barrington over the July 4th holiday. Two days later Weese presented the NCTA with his concept for spacious, column-free, concrete vaults at least twenty-one feet high.

His presentation also included designs for aerial or above-ground stations and open-cut stations—that is, shallow stations that remained uncovered—and outlined key features unifying the design, what Weese would later refer to as elements of continuity. These features included center platforms with entrances and exits on both ends, escalators running directly from the platforms to the street with no intervening mezzanines, indirect lighting on the vaults, entrances in public open spaces such as parks and squares, unified graphics, and the use of consistent materials—exposed structural concrete, granite, bronze, and glass—throughout the system.

The NCTA essentially adopted Weese's proposal, and the firm began applying the principles outlined in the presentation to specific stations. However, DeLeuw Cather was moving in a different direction. Based on stations visited during a trip to Montreal and Toronto with Weese, Reynolds, and NCTA officials, the engineers proposed a clear-span station with a box-shaped cross section supported by precast concrete girders. The economic advantages of this design, in large part owing to the simpler formwork required for construction, appealed to the NCTA.

In November 1966 Weese presented the NCTA with a "Synopsis of Concept Design and Policy" containing dozens of sketches of a variety of possible configurations for the underground subway stations. These designs included variations on the vaulted spaces similar to the original concept submitted in July as well as several options for rectangular train rooms, some column-free, others supported by columns. During the winter, Weese refined the concepts, maximizing space by linking the configuration of the stations with the method of construction. Box-like, cut-and-cover stations had flat walls and ceilings and were supported by long, exposed concrete girders, whereas deeper stations constructed by tunneling through rock had pointed-arch vaults and exposed rock sidewalls, similar to the walls of stations Weese had seen in Stockholm.

Approval of the subway design by the CFA was one of the provisions of Weese's contract. The CFA was an advisory body formed in 1910 on the recommendation of the McMillan Commission to advise the federal government on public buildings and monuments in the District of Columbia. The commission members had seen Weese's initial vaulted design, and Chairman William Walton had declared the approach "thorough and above all imaginative." Prior to the commission's first meeting with Weese on April 18, 1967, members received sketches of several of the station types the Weese office had been working on.

The reaction of CFA members was not favorable. Gordon Bunshaft, a partner in the architecture and engineering firm of Skidmore, Owings & Merrill, and Aline Saarinen, an art and architecture critic and the widow of architect Eero Saarinen, were especially critical of the exposed granite walls of the rock tunnel stations, which

Bunshaft described as "a refined coal mine shaft" and "folk art" and Saarinen characterized as "Hansel and Gretel." In an April 27, 1967, letter to McCarter, CFA Chairman Walton expressed the commission's concern that "continuity of design," rather than variations, should be the overriding factor in the design of the stations—a single form with an emphasis on "simplicity and elegance of detailing."

The next meeting with the CFA occurred on June 20. Weese presented the box design for the rectangular cut-and-cover stations, explained the principle underlying the variations in station design, and introduced the commission to his elements of continuity. But the commissioners again argued for a consistent design for all stations regardless of their method of construction and voted to reject Weese's proposals.

A third meeting between Weese and the CFA on September 19 promised to be as contentious as the first two. Saarinen expressed the commission's wishes for a dignified design in the "spirit of the classical style," and members again voiced their dissatisfaction with the variations in designs for the cut-and-cover and rock tunnel stations. Halfway through the two-hour meeting, Bunshaft, attempting to illustrate what the commission wanted, turned over one of Weese's presentation boards and sketched a vaulted design similar to the one initially submitted by Weese to the NCTA in July 1966 and shown to the CFA that October. Weese refrained from pointing out the similarity between the two and instead praised Bunshaft's concept as "a pretty exciting thing." Former Weese employees involved in the project credit Bunshaft with saving Weese's vision for the grand vaulted spaces that are the dominant feature of the Washington Metro system.

After the meeting with the CFA, Weese, Allan, and Reynolds met for drinks at the Hay-Adams Hotel and then headed to the K Street office, where the three worked into the night converting box sections to vaults. The vaults featured rectangular coffers, which created a more efficient structural system by reducing the weight of the vaults, facilitated poured-in-place concrete construction, accommodated sound-absorbent panels, and reflected the monumentality characteristic of federal architecture. Weese and his colleagues separated the platforms and mezzanines from the surface of the tunnel in order to prevent defacement of the subway walls, a suggestion offered by Bunshaft at the September meeting with the CFA. They also worked with lighting consultant William Lam to refine the indirect lighting of the vaults and with graphics consultant Massimo Vignelli to finalize the signage for the system.

Weese presented the new drawings and a plaster model of a cross section of the vault to the CFA on October 17, 1967. Walton lauded the design as a "magnificent new approach," and the CFA approved Weese's concept. The design also won the approval of the Washington Metropolitan Area Transit Authority, the agency formed in 1967 when the scope of the transit project was expanded to create a ninety-eight-mile regional plan with eighty-six stations in Virginia, Maryland, and the District of Columbia.

Prior to construction, the NCTA erected, on a site adjacent to the future Rhode Island Avenue station, a partial full-scale mock-up of a cross section of a typical below-grade vaulted train room, complete with a segment of a full-size train car. The model measured sixty-four feet in width, thirty feet in height, and seventeen feet in length and was used to study and test various components of the design and construction of the system.

Groundbreaking for the Washington Metro took place in December 1969, and the initial segment of the rail system opened on March 27, 1976. Although there were minor differences among the stations, almost all of the below-grade stations had spacious, concrete vaults with a floating mezzanine that incorporated Weese's elements of continuity and fulfilled the wishes of the CFA for a unified form. The vaults of almost all of the cut-and-cover stations were poured in place, whereas precast concrete liners formed the vaults of almost all of the rock tunnel stations.

Approximately one-half of the stations in the system were above ground. Those completed in the early phase of construction had gull-wing canopies, but three or four other canopy types were subsequently adopted, and even more variations in the design of aerial stations appeared in later years. For example, the city of Alexandria had its own "historic" canopy, and stations of the red line extensions and the orange and blue lines had flat canopies with triangular skylights. Nevertheless, Weese's elements of continuity—granite paving at the edge of the platform, red quarry tile, indirect lighting, consistent signage—remained a unifying feature.

Media reviews of the initial five-mile segment of the Metro system were positive. In 1971, after viewing the drawings and models and getting a preliminary look at the Judiciary Square station then under construction, *Washington Post* writer Wolf von Eckardt described the Metro system as having "a serene kind of beauty" and a "noble spaciousness." *New York Times* architecture critic Paul Goldberger called the Metro "one of the best looking things in the capital" and "one of the few new places in Washington that has true grandeur architecturally." Writ-

Writing in *Inland Architect*, Nory Miller characterized the Metro as "serious civic architecture in the enduring tradition of grandeur, order, harmony, presence" and concluded, "It works, it's beautiful, and . . . they [the riders] *like* it," and *Architectural Record* stated that Weese had "restored to civil engineering the visual grandeur and might characteristic of the great Roman and Victorian engineering feats."

The lack of funding for maintenance of the Metro has created difficulties in recent years. Some stations have been painted gray, loud speakers have been installed in visible places rather than behind acoustic panels as in the original design, and additional graphics and lighting have been introduced. The overall design, however, remains largely uncompromised and appears to have stood the test of time. In a 2000 article in *Praxis*, Megan Miller described the "lofty barrel-vaulted volumes" as "frankly magisterial for an American public works project" and called the Metro's effect "precise, immaculate and colossal" and its appearance "futuristic . . . even in the year 2000."

SELECTED BIBLIOGRAPHY

Stephen Layton. "Metro Debut: Triumph of Men and Machines." *Washington Post*, March 28, 1976.

Nory Miller. "Washington's Metro." *Inland Architect* 20 (June 1976): 7–15.

Wolf von Eckardt. "Metro: Example for the World." *Washington Post*, November 20, 1976.

Paul Goldberger. "Capital Subway: Grace amid Monuments." *New York Times*, February 5, 1978.

Washington Metro. *Architectural Review* 163 (February 1978) 99–102.

Architectural Record 164 (mid-August 1978): 66.

Stanley Allan. *For the Glory of Washington: A Chronicle of Events Leading to the Creation of a System-Wide Architectural Concept for the Design of the Washington Metro Stations.* Chicago: Harry Weese Associates, 1994.

Megan Miller. "Elements of Continuity: The Washington DC Metro." *Praxis* 1:116–125. (2000): 116–123.

William Middleton. "Washington's Magnificent Metro." *Railway Age* (September, 2001).

Zachary Schrag. *The Great Society Subway. The History of the Washington Metro.* Baltimore: Johns Hopkins University Press, 2006.

Rhode Island Avenue
station, with a gull-wing
canopy. Presumably WMATA
photograph. Photographer
unknown. i59914, Chicago
History Museum.

View to East, Frederick E. Terman
Engineering Center, showing the
concrete structure of the lower floor
and the heavy-timber frame and soft
brown brushed stucco infill of the
upper floors. Hedrich Blessing photograph,
HB41250C, ca. 1978, Chicago History
Museum.

FREDERICK E. TERMAN ENGINEERING CENTER, STANFORD UNIVERSITY

Stanford, California, 1974–78

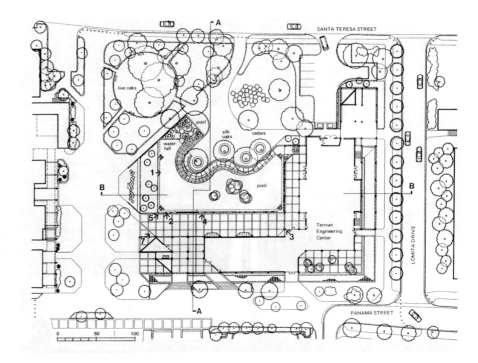

The original Stanford University campus, designed in the late nineteenth century by Frederick Law Olmsted and Shepley, Rutan & Coolidge for clients Leland and Jane Stanford, combined the monumentality of European Beaux-Arts planning with an architectural style reflecting American and regional influences. The buff sandstone Richardsonian Romanesque buildings with their California mission-inspired, sloped red-tile roofs were linked by covered arcades, forming a cloistered inner quadrangle, with the Memorial Church at its center. Access to the campus was via the mile-long Palm Drive.

To provide for future growth, the master plan suggested the addition of up to six more quadrangles extending to the east and west of the "Old Quad," but twentieth-century designers abandoned this concept, resulting in a collection of individual structures rather than the integrated whole envisioned by the original architects. Postwar attempts to provide contemporary interpretations of the original stone architecture using modern materials and design principles, such as the undergraduate library designed by John Carl Warnecke and the law school designed by Skidmore, Owings & Merrill, met with varying degrees of success.

In 1973, electronics company founders William R. Hewlett and David Packard and their wives, all Stanford alumni, endowed a new engineering facility for the Palo Alto campus in honor of Provost Emeritus Frederick Emmons Terman, who served as provost at the university from 1955 to 1965. Rather than selecting the center's architect from a list provided by the university, the dean of the College of Engineering, William M. Kays, initiated a nationwide search, which culminated in the selection of Harry Weese & Associates.

The site chosen for the Frederick E. Terman Engineering Center stood at the junction of the formal campus and its more informal surroundings and contained two silk oak and two cedar trees, forty to fifty feet high, that the university wished to preserve. To comply with this request, Weese designed a seven-story, 152,000-square-foot, L-shaped structure which opened onto an inviting landscape designed by Joe Karr that incorporated the four trees.

The columns and beams of the lower levels of the building, which were partly below grade, were con-

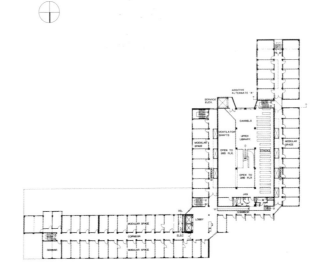

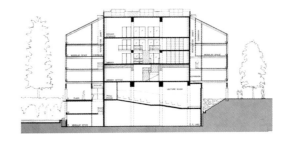

Site plan, plan of entry level and section of the north-south wing. Hendrich Blessing photograph. HB41250, Chicago History Museum

193

View of air well.
Hedrich Blessing photograph,
HB41250H, ca. 1978,
Chicago History Museum.

structed of concrete. The heavy-timber frame of glued laminated fir and hemlock, or glulam, used for the five upper floors of the building was assembled in sections at the site and lifted into place by crane. Infill consisted of soft brown brushed stucco over heavy-gauge sheet metal. At the request of the university, Weese topped the structure with a roof of red mission tile.

Weese configured the building to take advantage of the mild climate of the San Francisco Bay Area. Offices, smaller classrooms, and modular spaces that could be easily adapted to meet future requirements were located along the double-loaded corridor of the slender east-west wing, a configuration that brought both cross ventilation and an abundance of light into these perimeter spaces. Larger facilities requiring greater temperature and humidity control, such as laboratories, studios, the lecture hall, and the three-level library, were placed in an enclosed concrete core at the center of the wider north-south wing and mechanically cooled. Additional modular spaces arranged around the perimeter of this wing were naturally ventilated.

Operable glazed French doors, extending from floor to ceiling but recessed to shield them from excessive

direct light, gave access to a small balcony for each of the offices located along the building's perimeter. Adjustable louvered cedar shutters that moved on a standard hanging track commonly used in barns could be slid over these openings to control the amount of sunlight and air entering the offices. When open, the shutters allowed both light and breezes into the interior. Closed, they blocked the sun but could still provide natural ventilation through open windows.

To enhance ventilation, Weese inserted air wells alongside the corridors to funnel breezes through the building. Air rising up through these open vertical shafts escaped through operable skylight vents in the roof. The air shafts doubled as light shafts, allowing light filtering in through the skylights to penetrate to the lower levels. These energy conservation features eliminated the need for air-conditioning systems in the naturally ventilated portions of the building, and the extensive perimeter glazing, the skylights, and the light wells maximized the use of daylight and reduced electricity costs.

The two lower levels of the center were below the entry level on the street side of the L-shaped building but

View of landscaped
courtyard with sunken
reflecting pool, and circular
islands planted with
weeping Maytens trees.
Hedrich Blessing photograph,
HB41250Q, ca. 1978,
Chicago History Museum.

opened onto the sunken landscape on the inner angle of
the complex. A large reflecting pool contained three circular islands planted with weeping Maytens trees, which contrasted with the rectilinear geometry of the building. The
concrete curbs surrounding the islands provided seating
for students choosing to wade through the shallow water.
A sinuous wall held in place by large wooden beams rose
fourteen feet from the pool level back up to grade level and
formed a series of terraces that served as planters.

The preserved silk oak and cedar trees shaded a paved
area at the grade level at the top of the wall. Recirculated
water pumped up from the reflective pool fed a semicircular pool. Water spilled from the pool down through a series
of concrete bowls set into a heavily planted slope and back
into the reflective pool at the bottom.

In 1978, the Chicago chapter of the American Institute of Architects recognized Weese's design with a Distinguished Building Award. The jury commented on Weese's
efforts to take advantage of the site and described the
building's character as "sympathetic to its region."

The San Francisco–based firm of Tanner Leddy Maytum
Stacy subsequently designed a 12,000-square-foot addition to
the Terman Engineering Center, which opened in 1996. This
low rectangular building, known as the Charles B. Thornton
Center for Engineering Management, stands to the south
of the Terman Center. Although the Weese building retains
much of its original character, the landscape has been substantially altered, and many important design elements, notably
the islands and wooden retaining wall, have been eliminated.

Job 841
Associate Architect: John Weese
Landscape Architect: Joe Karr & Associates
Structural Engineer: Nishkian, Hammill & Associates
Mechanical Engineer: Kasin Guttmann & Associates
Electrical Engineer: Cammisa & Wipf
General Contractor: F. P. Lathrop Construction

SELECTED BIBLIOGRAPHY

"Glulam Rates High Marks in Schools." *Glulam Report* (Spring
1977).
Allan Temko. "Finding Form Once Again on the Farm." *San
Francisco Chronicle*, February 20, 1978.
"Frederick E. Terman Engineering Center, Palo Alto, California."
Architectural Record 174 (February 1986).

Page from sketchbook used by Harry Weese during an initial visit to the site for the Union Underwear Corporate Headquarters. Chicago History Museum, i51994.

UNION UNDERWEAR CORPORATE HEADQUARTERS

1 Fruit of the Loom Drive
Bowling Green, Kentucky, 1978–80

In the late 1970s, Ben Heineman, then chairman and CEO of Northwest Industries, chose his friend Harry Weese to design a new corporate headquarters for the holding company's Union Underwear subsidiary.

The site of the planned facility was an eighty-acre wooded, rolling Kentucky bluegrass landscape five miles southeast of downtown Bowling Green, Kentucky, and six miles from the company's existing offices and manufacturing plant. The new headquarters building was to house those functions as well as Union Underwear personnel being relocated from New York City. The client requested a relatively modest but architecturally impressive structure capable of projecting a new and attractive image. The building was to accommodate 350 employees within approximately 80,000 square feet at a cost of approximately $5.5 million and was to be occupied as soon as possible. Other program requirements included a canteen-type food service, barrier-free circulation, a dignified interior décor, an energy-conscious heating and cooling system, and extensive indoor and outdoor landscaping.

On a trip to the site Weese recorded his impressions in an artist's sketchbook, filling its pages with a continuous stream of words and phrases such as "abundance of the earth," "flowering," "harvest," "gathering," "blanketing," and "quiet cover." As Stanley Allan later recalled, Weese returned to the office on a Friday afternoon and worked almost nonstop through Sunday night. "On a 30-foot roll of 18-inch tracing paper, he drew the design for the entire building—site plan, landscaping, floor plans, elevations, details, structure, materials, perspectives and even a logo."

Weese's configuration of the building and his efforts to preserve the beauty of the site and protect the natural

Aerial view. Gray Construction Company photograph, ca. 1980.

setting reflected those initial reactions. His careful siting allowed the structure to become a part of the gently rolling terrain without the need for extensive cut and fill. During the preparation of the site, the contractor struck the opening to an underground cave. Ever the innovator, Weese proposed drawing air from the cave to naturally cool the building, but mold and humidity concerns thwarted his plans.

Weese placed the headquarters building at the top of a ridge above two tree-lined parking areas, one to the northeast and the other to the southwest. Concrete tunnels led from these parking areas to a lower-level, reinforced-concrete employees' lobby that had stairs and elevators to the upper-level offices. This lower level also housed mechanical rooms and the loading/receiving dock.

The visitors' entrance, on the main floor, led to a reception area and lobby that served as a conference and waiting room and a space for product displays. This area also contained the canteen. Most of the 58,000-square-foot main floor consisted of open offices separated by partitions. The building's interior was a continuous open space flooded by light from thirteen skylights. A dramatic two-story atrium, extending from north to south, bisected the space and contained a pair of meandering, recirculating streams, each of which flowed from a common point at the center of the building into ponds at the perimeter. Landscape architect Joe Karr lined the streams were with mature trees and large, interestingly weathered stones that had been collected from the site, and planted ficus trees and hundreds of small shrubs and groundcover plants among the rocks. In addition to the recirculated water, the streams fed by rainwater that accumulated in two inverted skylights and drained down into the streams via a metal funnel and chain.

Weese discretely grouped private offices for the advertising staff and senior executives under the central portion of a floating mezzanine. The 19,000-square-foot mezzanine contained additional private offices for Union Underwear executives and conference space. Several of the mezzanine offices had exterior decks formed by punching openings in the mansard roof.

One of the most unusual features of the Union Underwear headquarters was the structural system. An exposed

View of the atrium showing
interior stream and tree-like
columns. Balthazar Korab
photograph, 49601, ca. 1980.

heavy-timber frame supported the exterior walls, which were clad in cement asbestos panels trimmed with cypress wood. An unbroken ribbon of insulated solar cool glass formed the upper part of the wall. The terne-coated stainless-steel roof, which was expected to turn to a mellow tan over time, sloped inward to meet a flat roof twenty feet above the main-floor level. Thirty-six steel "tree" columns or "trunks" that split into four prongs or "limbs" supported the middle portion of the flat roof. Painted deep blue, these structures resembled inverted umbrellas. Laminated yellow pine beams connected the limbs. White fir decking with tongue-and-groove joinery spanned the spaces between the exposed wood roof joists.

Heineman sold Northwest Industries to Farley Industries in 1985, and Union Underwear was renamed Fruit of the Loom after its famous trademark. Berkshire Hathaway acquired the company in 2002 and now uses the Weese-designed building as the Fruit of the Loom world headquarters.

Job 1009
Contractor: James N. Gray Construction
Structural Engineer: Engineers Collaborative
Mechanical and Electrical Engineer: Waldron, Batey & Wade
Landscape Architect: Joe Karr & Associates

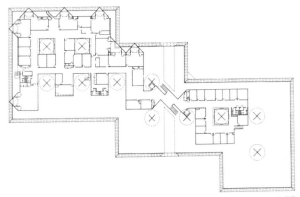

MEZZANINE

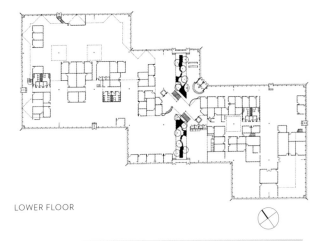

LOWER FLOOR

Plans. Chicago History Museum, i52028, i52029.

View of exterior, showing the cement asbestos panels trimmed with cypress wood and the mansard roof clad with terne-coated stainless steel. Balthazar Korab photograph, 49585, ca. 1980.

199

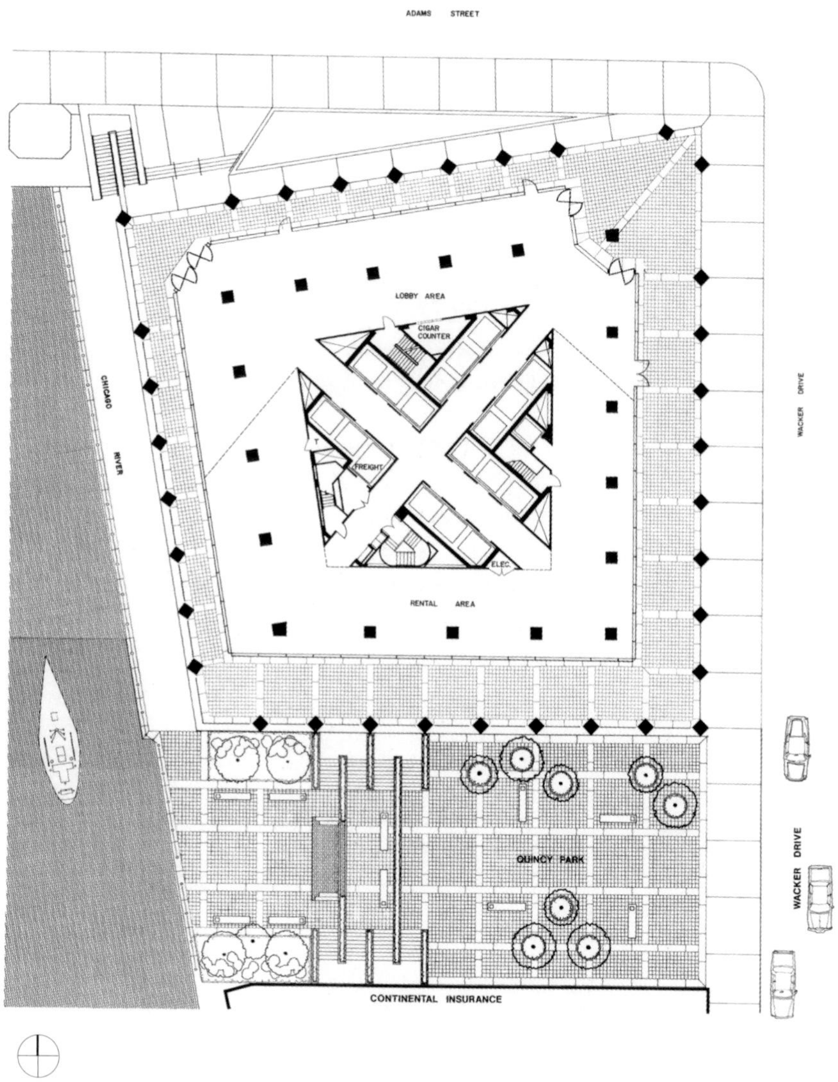

Site plan, showing
trapezoidal configuration
of the building and Quincy
Park to the south. i59320,
Chicago History Museum.

200 SOUTH WACKER DRIVE

Chicago, Illinois, 1978–81

Although the $60 million, forty-story riverside office tower at 200 South Wacker Drive was a speculative project, clients John A. Buck II and Wesley Irvine Jr. and their equity partner, Urban Investment and Development Corporation, were nevertheless seeking a "high-quality building with an interesting architectural statement, a unique overall design, with an appealing lobby and other public areas and an efficient floor plan." Other criteria included a design that complemented the riverfront location and distinguished the structure from its neighbors, which included the Sears Tower, where Buck and Irvine worked as leasing agents for Chicago developer Cushman & Wakefield.

In the 1970s, the Continental Insurance Company owned the site of the future 200 South Wacker Drive building, an irregular 25,000-square-foot parcel fronting the river at Wacker Drive and Adams Street in Chicago's South Loop. Young John Buck recognized the potential of the property, which he passed daily on his way to the Sears Tower, and arranged a meeting with Continental Insurance executives through Cushman & Wakefield's New York office. The Continental chairman initially refused Buck's request for a free option, but when the persistent Buck returned six months later with $257,000, Continental's new chairman granted him a two-year option, with the first year free.

Buck recruited his associate Irvine to join the project, and the two began searching for an architect to design the tower they planned to build. When the firms they initially contacted quoted fees of $20,000 to $50,000 for schematic drawings, an acquaintance at the Chicago architectural firm of Perkins & Will suggested that they speak with Harry Weese. Weese and Buck developed an instant camaraderie, and Weese agreed to design the building for $1,000, with the understanding that he would receive a more customary fee if the project became a reality.

Buck also secured Continental Insurance as the lead tenant for his planned tower. In order to accommodate the needs of the insurance firm, which planned to lease sixty percent of the available space, and attract other large tenants, the building needed a large floor plate. A square or rectangular building with a tight core would have been the most efficient approach to design. However, because

View to the northeast from above the Chicago River revealing the building's configuration as a trapezoid divided diagonally into triangles. Hedrich Blessing photograph, HB42361B, ca. 1981, Chicago History Museum.

View of pedestrian arcade.
Hedrich Blessing photograph,
HB44285D, ca. 1981, Chicago
History Museum.

of the small, irregularly shaped site created by the diagonal path of the river at this location, such conventional configurations would not provide the 21,000 square feet per floor required by Continental. Weese and project architect Norm Zimmerman explored other options and found that only a trapezoidal building filling almost the entire site would meet the space requirements of the principal tenant.

The trapezoidal plan and the stipulation that no interior space be more than forty feet from the window wall necessitated an asymmetrical core, which was split diagonally to form four triangular quadrants. Aligned along these cuts were three banks of six elevators, rotated forty-five degrees from the expected orientation. The diagonal orientation of the plan became apparent on the exterior roofline where the building split into two triangles, a southeast section with a height of thirty-two stories and a northwest portion that rose seven stories higher. The hypotenuse of the northeast section was sheathed in a glass curtain wall. The southeast portion contained a triangular, three-story atrium topped with a skylight that extended from the roof of the building down to the thirtieth floor. As a result of these two design features, a high percentage of office space in the upper portion of the building was close to windows and enjoyed expansive views.

The building's concrete frame was sheathed in white-painted aluminum. By rotating the concrete support columns at the building's perimeter by forty-five degrees and running the glazing flush with their outer corner, Weese reduced contact of the supports with the tinted glazing to a width of only six inches.

At street level, visitors encountered pedestrian arcades formed by the outer columns and the angled clear glass walls of the recessed lobby. Because of these arcades, which completely surrounded the building, the developers were able to take advantage of floor-area-ratio (FAR) bonuses in Chicago's zoning code and build a substantially higher building than they would have been allowed otherwise.

The thirty-foot-high lobby contained two mezzanine levels with cantilevered balconies overlooking the river and 8,900 square feet of commercial space. Granite cladding covered the columns, floors, and core walls of the lobby. The natural light flooding the space created an ideal environment for the plants that originally cascaded from the balconies. Two below-grade levels housed mechanical equipment and loading docks and provided 20,000 square feet of additional commercial or retail space.

Working in the wake of the 1973 oil crisis, the Weese firm designed 200 South Wacker Drive to be both elegant and energy efficient. Glazing was limited to only forty

View of lobby. Hedrich Blessing photograph, HB44285B, ca. 1981, Chicago History Museum.

Quincy Park adjacent to 200 South Wacker Drive. Joe Karr photograph, August 1995.

percent of the façade and consisted of thermopane heat-absorbing glass. Weese's engineers selected air-conditioning and ventilating systems that minimized energy consumption. Dampers automatically shut off air-conditioning to floors not in use, and heat captured from energy-efficient fluorescent lights warmed the perimeter areas. As a result of these energy conservation features, energy usage at 200 South Wacker totaled 50,000 BTUs per square foot per year, twenty-five to thirty percent lower than the energy usage in most Chicago buildings of that time.

Buck and Irvine's equity partner rejected plans by Joe Karr for an elegant $1 million riverside park that featured an upper deck with a Spanish Steps–like staircase leading to the river. Quincy Park, the park that was eventually constructed to Karr's designs immediately south of 200 South Wacker, was smaller and less costly but still offered a welcome oasis from busy South Wacker Drive. Office workers accessed the park by means of a curved granite staircase that led from the street level to a brick-paved seating area. A fifteen-foot waterfall defined the east boundary of the park, and curved granite-block walls framing the waterfall camouflaged the lower Wacker Drive loading docks. This riverside park and the building's river walkway not only

fulfilled the client's request for a design that complemented the riverfront site but also advanced Weese's longstanding desire to transform Chicago's largely neglected river from a liability to an amenity.

Job 947
Project Architect: Norm Zimmerman
Landscape Architect: Joe Karr & Associates
Construction Manager: Schal Associates
Structural Engineer: Gillum-Colaco
Mechanical/Electrical Engineer: Environmental Systems Design
Curtain Wall Construction: Antoine-Heitmann Associates

SELECTED BIBLIOGRAPHY

Gary Washburn. "His Determination Towers over Chicago." *Chicago Tribune*, August 13, 1978.
"Strike Up the Music along the Riverside." *Inland Architect* 23 (July 1979): 24.
"Tower Makes Best of Riverside Site." *Engineering News Record* (May 15, 1980): 24.

BROWN-FORMAN DISTILLERS CORPORATION

INTERNATIONAL BUILDING
(WAREHOUSE D), 1979–81

THE FORESTER CENTER
(WAREHOUSE A), 1987–89

850 Dixie Highway
Louisville, Kentucky

View to southwest of the Brown-Forman International Building, formerly Warehouse D (in foreground), and the Forester Center, formerly Warehouse A (in background). i52017, Chicago History Museum.

Owsley Brown II, chairman of Brown-Forman Distillers Corporation and great grandson of its founder, compared the adaptive reuse of two former warehouses into office buildings to a sonnet—"You have to work in a very fixed framework."

The Brown-Forman whiskey storage warehouse designated Warehouse D, located in the company's distillery facility in the historic California industrial district of Louisville, Kentucky, was one of the oldest distilling warehouses in the area, dating back to the turn of the twentieth century. At one time, Brown-Forman had used it to age barrels of Old Forester Kentucky Bourbon, America's first bottled bourbon, but in 1979 the company commissioned Harry Weese & Associates to convert the structure into offices for the company's import and export divisions and the marketing and computer services departments.

Owsley Brown was president of Actors Theatre and first met Weese in the 1960s when the architect transformed two historic buildings in downtown Louisville into a performance space for the theater company. (see entry). When Brown-Forman needed additional space in the late 1970s, Brown and his brother brought Weese back to Louisville to assist in the conversion of Warehouse D into a contemporary office facility.

Harry Weese & Associates was responsible for the overall concept, space planning, and interior design of the former warehouse, and Joseph & Joseph Architects of Louisville, a firm that had longstanding ties to Brown-Forman, served as the architects of record, taking responsibility for the structural, mechanical, and electrical systems and overseeing construction. Because Warehouse D had just been listed on the National Register of Historic Places, its exterior appearance could not be changed, but Weese dramatically altered the interior. He reduced the building to

a masonry shell by removing the wooden barrel ricks that filled the interior and instead inserted a rough-sawn heavy-timber frame. To take advantage of the existing staggered window pattern, Weese accordingly staggered the floors above the second level in a split-level pattern, resulting in four floors on the east side and five on the west.

To bring light into the interior of the deep structure, Weese left the center of the building's interior open, creating a large atrium extending from the ground floor to a skylight rooftop. Offices on the east and west sides of this atrium overlooked a ground-level garden designed by landscape architect Joe Karr, who also designed an exterior garden for the area between Warehouse D and adjacent production facilities.

Kitty Weese supervised the interior design, selecting the office furniture and even stipulating the size and placement of the artwork. When the renovation was complete, Warehouse D was renamed the International Building in recognition of the import and export divisions housed there and the growing importance of international markets and foreign suppliers to Brown-Forman.

Although Brown labeled the conversion of Warehouse D a success, not all of the Brown-Forman employees were

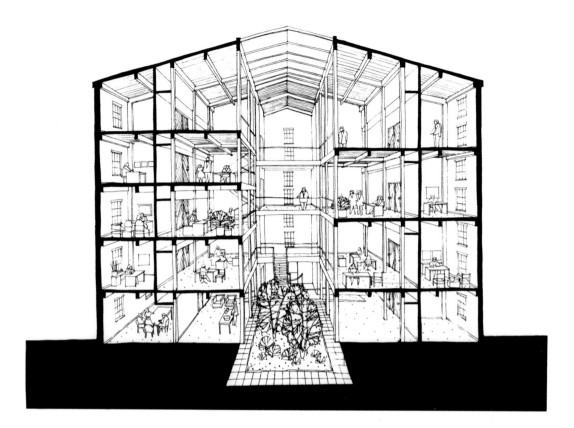

Perspective section of the Brown-Forman International Building. i52018, Chicago History Museum.

pleased with the open office arrangement overlooking the central court. Members of the secretarial staff complained of feeling insecure and exposed. To ease their discomfort, Brown-Forman added louvered screens to shield work stations and improve employees' sense of well-being. Excessive sunlight entering the building posed another problem, which was resolved by the installation of Mylar screens.

In 1987, Brown-Forman was once again in need of additional space. This need coincided with the move of the company's whiskey aging and storage operations to a distillery three miles south of the main complex, which left the twelve-story, 120,000-square-foot building known as Warehouse A empty and unused. The Brown brothers reassembled the team of Harry Weese & Associates and Joseph & Joseph Architects, which had designed the building for the Browns' grandfather in the mid-1930s, to convert the vacant warehouse into a corporate office building.

Warehouse A, a reinforced-concrete structure faced in brick, was considerably larger than Warehouse D but had substantially smaller windows, and significant portions of the exterior walls had no windows at all. The interior of Warehouse A was divided into six 2-story floors of whiskey storage space separated by seven-inch-thick concrete slabs. Concrete columns eighteen inches square supported the floors.

To qualify for historic preservation investment tax credits, the Browns had to retain the existing windows, which, because the building was a warehouse and did not require much light on the interior, were quite small. Weese solved the dilemma of bringing light into the deep interior recesses by carving out the building's interior to create a central skylit atrium which took the form of an inverted ziggurat that widened as it ascended to the roofline.

Each floor was just over sixteen feet in height and was illuminated by two rows of windows. The area between the concrete slabs and the new floors installed above them provided space for pipes and wiring. The exposed concrete columns and capitals preserved the industrial character of the building.

Under the direction of Karr, the atrium became a lush garden with forty-foot bamboo trees that formed a green canopy when viewed from above. Other landscape features included a terraced waterfall and planters ringing the atrium at each level. Brown characterized the interior of Warehouse A with its prism-shaped skylight, plants, and waterfall as "most ingenious" and added that "it never fails

View of interior of
the Brown-Forman
International Building.
Hedrich Blessing photograph,
HB49618l, ca. 1981 Chicago
History Museum.

View of atrium of the Brown-Forman Forester Center. Hedrich Blessing photograph, HB49618E, ca. 1989, Chicago History Museum.

to please." Karr also transformed an unsightly area north of the entrance to Warehouse A into an attractive forecourt garden by installing a circular recessed seating area; planting honey locust trees, low evergreens, and perennials; and allowing ivy to grow up the building's brick façade.

Following the renovation, Warehouse A became known as the Forester Center. As in the past, it continued to be distinguished by its rooftop water tank, which was shaped like a quart bottle of Old Forester and was visible from inside through the skylight in the building's atrium.

WAREHOUSE D (INTERNATIONAL BUILDING)
Job 1015
Project Architect: David Munson
Structural Engineer: Joseph & Joseph Architects

Mechanical and Electrical Engineer: Kaestner Lynch Associates
General Contractor: Dahlem Construction
Landscape Architect: Joe Karr & Associates
Interior Design: Design Unit

WAREHOUSE A (FORESTER CENTER)
Job 8858
Structural Engineer: Joseph & Joseph Architects
Mechanical Engineer: Hesse & Warford Engineers
General Contractor: Parco Construction
Landscape Architect: Joe Karr & Associates

SELECTED BIBLIOGRAPHY

"Brown-Forman Corp. Forester Center Renovation." *Design Cost & Data* (September/October 1990): 12–14.
Dena Crosson. "100-Proof Conversion." *Historic Preservation* (January/February 1991): 58–59.

View of interior garden with terraced waterfall in the atrium of the Brown-Forman Forester Center. Hedrich Blessing photograph, HB49618D, ca. 1989, Chicago History Museum.

WOLF POINT LANDINGS

West bank of Chicago River between Fulton Street
and Grand Avenue east of Canal Street
Chicago, Illinois

FULTON HOUSE

345 North Canal Street
Chicago, Illinois, 1979-81

RIVER COTTAGES

357, 359, 365, 367 North Canal Street
Chicago, Illinois, 1988

Harry Weese had recognized the residential potential of the North Branch of the Chicago River even before city officials and Loop business leaders announced plans for the beautification and revitalization of the riverbank in the late 1970s. By that time, Weese was already the owner of a small parcel of land on the west bank of the North Branch just south of Kinzie Street that eventually became the site of the four townhouses known as the River Cottages. In 1977, Weese formed a partnership, Wolf Point Landings Associates, with Denver real estate consultant John B. Wogan Jr., husband of Kitty Weese's Design Unit partner Jackie Green Wogan, and the two began making plans to transform a stretch of former industrial property and unused railroad land along the west bank of the North Branch extending from Fulton Street to West Grand Avenue into an exciting and viable neighborhood with residences, restaurants, shops, and a marina. Weese and Wogan christened the development Wolf Point Landings

View to the northeast of the North American Cold Storage warehouse, which was nearly windowless prior to its conversion to Fulton House. McShane-Fleming Studios photograph, 1979, i59678, Chicago History Museum.

in reference to the early pioneer settlement that was once located near the site. Early promotional materials for the complex optimistically compared its potential impact to that of Boston's Quincy Market and San Francisco's Ghirardelli Square.

The partners' first purchase was a parcel of land between Canal Street and the river, between Kinzie and Fulton streets just north of Weese's parcel. This land contained the North American Cold Storage warehouse. The conversion of the sixteen-story warehouse into Fulton House, a residential condominium, became the first project, and the only one to be completed by the partnership, of a four-phase master plan formulated by Weese for Wolf Point Landings.

Within a few months after this initial purchase, Weese and Wogan acquired a vacant lot immediately south of the warehouse, known as the Milwaukee Road property, which was originally intended for use as a parking lot for Fulton House residents. Weese later proposed an eight-story, ninety-six-unit condominium called River House for that site. Weese and Wogan financed the purchase of both Fulton House and the Milwaukee Road property through the Continental Illinois Bank of Chicago.

The three subsequent phases of the project targeted locations north of Kinzie Street on land referred to as the SMI property, which constituted approximately six acres. Weese and Wogan acquired the rights to develop this site through a land sale contract with the owner, who retained title. Phase two was to have included Kinzie Terrace, a long, twenty-six-story condominium structure with 428 units; the Galleria, a two-story, 120,000-square-foot commercial and retail component at the base of Kinzie Terrace; and a small-craft marina east of Kinzie Terrace. Phase three was to be Wolf Tower I, a slender, forty-story, 320-unit residential building between Kinzie Terrace and Kinzie Street with commercial space and Galleria shops on the first two levels. The fourth and final phase of the project was to be a twin of Wolf Tower called Wolf Tower II located between Kinzie Terrace and Grand Avenue. An esplanade lined with linden trees was to have paralleled the river along the entire five-block length of Wolf Point Landings.

To determine the demand for residential units at this location and obtain input to help guide the direction of the development, Wogan's firm, Counselors in Real Estate, commissioned a survey of more than three thousand Chicago residents and daytime Loop workers. Few people

FACING PAGE
"Grand Marina Proposal," a perspective drawing by Gene Streett, showing Weese's master plan for Wolf Point Landings. From left to right along the river in this view are River House, Fulton House, Kinzie Street, Wolf Tower I, Kinzie Terrace, Wolf Tower II, and Grand Avenue. Of these structures only Fulton House was completed. River Cottages were eventually built on the small green patch of land between Fulton House and Kinzie Street. i59322, Chicago History Museum.

View to the northwest,
Fulton House. Photograph
ca. 1981, i59679, Chicago
History Museum.

lived in the Loop or the areas immediately adjacent to it in the late 1970s, but Weese's experience at Printers Row, a project he had spearheaded in the South Loop a few years earlier, suggested to him that demand was rising quickly. The survey was needed to convince lenders and investors of this fact. Survey responses suggested that the demand for downtown housing over the following two years was likely to exceed the number of available residential units by seven fold.

Phase one of Wolf Point Landings, the retrofitting of the 1908 cold storage warehouse for residential use, officially began when Chicago Mayor Jane Byrne shattered a champagne bottle against the east wall of the warehouse on July 12, 1979. The project proved to be much more challenging, time-consuming, and expensive than anticipated. The building had to "thaw" for six months before renovation could begin. Cracking of the seventy-year-old bricks during the thawing process necessitated the addition of steel reinforcement rods secured by masonry stars on the exterior walls. Workers had to remove thick layers of insulation made of cork, horsehair, and other materials from the inner surface of the walls, and had to disassemble an elaborate steel-pipe network that once carried ammonia and brine refrigerants. Because of the risk that the flame torches used to sever the piping might ignite strips of cork insulation still clinging to the walls, Chicago firefighters were present at the site throughout the process. Workers on scaffolds had to break through the ten- to twelve-inch-thick masonry walls to create openings for oversized windows and sliding balcony doors.

The façade of the building had served as a surface for advertisements, and the rubber-based billboard paint that had accumulated on the walls over the years proved difficult to remove. When a mixture of high-pressure water and acid used to prepare the walls for the sealer failed to loosen the paint, workers had to resort to a light sandblasting, a process that was undertaken reluctantly because of the potential damage sandblasting can cause to the hard exterior surface of brick. Any paint still adhering to the walls had to be removed by hand. Strict quality-control standards maintained during these processes minimized defacement of the masonry.

Once the paint was removed, the crew applied a clear sealer to the brick exterior, followed by a second sealer containing various amounts of pigment. Weese mixed color samples by hand in the field in an attempt to match the original color, which varied due to the wide range of bricks used in the construction and subsequent repair of the building and variations in the weathering rates of the different exposures.

Although Weese lobbied for residential loft spaces with minimal improvements similar to those in the Printers Row development in the South Loop, the more conventional floor plans preferred by Wogan and the bank prevailed. The 104 condominiums offered sixteen different layouts priced from $83,300 to $325,000. Floors three through thirteen each contained eight one-bedroom units, and the fourteenth and fifteenth floors featured eight duplex apartments with two-story living rooms, their upper levels lit by the round windows in the building's entablature. The eight penthouse units on the sixteenth floor retained the same basic configuration as the typical apartment units on the lower eleven floors but were customized to suit individual owner's tastes.

Weese and Wogan reserved 20,000 square feet on the lower level and the first two floors of the building for commercial use. Plans for this space included a discotheque, restaurant, tea room, and the Wolf Tap. A planned additional amenity was to be a special Weese-designed sailboat, the Wolf-30, for use by the residents. Because the boat had a folding mast, the bridges over the Chicago River would not have to be raised to allow the craft to pass under them. The Wolf-30 never came to be, but Fulton House residents did have access to a pontoon boat used initially to taxi potential buyers along the river.

Marketing efforts for Wolf Point Landings focused on the development's proximity to the city's major retail, business, government, and financial centers and its cultural and recreational attractions. Advertisements for the project emphasized the panoramic views of the river and surrounding cityscape from Fulton House's windows and balconies. As construction progressed, sales agents accumulated a waiting list of six hundred names, and the preconstruction marketing program generated thirty-five immediate sales. But by the time the models opened in October 1980, mortgage rates had soared to twenty-three percent and interest in the property had evaporated. By May 1982, only fifty-five units had been sold. But even if the real estate market had remained strong, the numerous delays, unanticipated difficulties, and the cost of converting the structure would have eroded any possible profits.

In an effort to rescue the project, Weese and Wogan offered half of the condominium units, which were originally intended solely as residences, to commercial buyers as office condominiums. Within four months, four sold, with two additional sales pending. In April 1983, an investment group purchased the thirty-six unsold properties designated for residential use with plans to offer them as rental units. The undisclosed sales price allowed the partnership to make a substantial payment on the debt to the Conti-

FACING PAGE

View looking southwest
from Kinzie Street bridge
to the River Cottages.
Robert Bruegmann
photograph, 2009.

nental Bank, but Wogan's unwillingness to invest any additional money into the project created difficulties between the partners.

In 1984, Jeffrey Grossman, head of the Lincolnwood-based venture capital firm North American Group, learned of Weese's predicament and came forward, ostensibly to save the project. Weese teamed up with Grossman to form Wolf Point Ventures, Ltd., and the new partnership purchased the property held by Wolf Point Landings Associates, which was then dissolved. Grossman was to reimburse Weese for payments Weese had made to Continental Bank to maintain the Milwaukee Road property adjacent to Fulton House, and in return Weese gave Grossman an option to develop the privately financed SMI property. In May 1985, Weese and Grossman announced plans for a 266-slip marina, with groundbreaking scheduled for the following month and completion by the end of September. But this project would never materialize, and Weese would never receive any significant payments from Grossman. Weese claimed that Grossman fraudulently obtained his signature on a document that transferred the right of ownership of the SMI property to Grossman, who arranged an immediate sale of the property. Although lawsuits were filed, Weese was never able to recoup any of the money or land he had lost to Grossman. Grossman was later convicted for other fraudulent business deals.

Although Harry Weese never realized his grand plan for the North Branch of the Chicago River, his efforts toward residential development along the river continued, albeit on a much smaller scale. In the mid-1980s, he announced plans for four multilevel residences that he called the River Cottages on the small site between Fulton House and Kinzie Street he had purchased independently in the 1970s, and that was never included in the Wogan or Grossman ventures.

Weese traced his inspiration for the River Cottages to waterside homes he had seen along the Danube River in Hungary during travels in Europe in the mid-1950s. His contemporary interpretation of these unusual residences incorporated numerous nautical references, such as porthole windows and cross bracing that suggested a schooner's rigging and sails. Glazing was limited on the west, or street, side of the townhouses, but the east side facing the river featured patios or balconies at each level and spaces for private boat docks. The sloping walls of the east façade echoed the design of the never-realized Kinzie Terrace.

The River Cottages were clustered in groups of two on either side of an open court. The two upper floors and rooftop deck of the townhouse to the north of the court extended over it to connect with the two townhouses to the south. The River Cottages contained up to six levels of living space and ranged in size from 2,200 to 4,200 square feet. Residents accessed the garages, which were located at grade level, from Canal Street. Parts of the complex were zoned for commercial use, although none of the buyers chose to operate a business.

Listing prices for the River Cottages ranged from $350,000 to nearly $600,000. Buyers would be purchasing a shell—exterior walls, roofs, doors, windows, plumbing and electrical stubs, and heating/air-conditioning units without ducts to distribute the air. Perhaps the project's strongest selling point was the Weese name, which was well known and well respected at the time. Many potential buyers were fascinated by the project and there were multiple offers for each of the cottages, but most failed to close, largely because of the time and expense required to finish the interiors. It was three to four years before buyers materialized for all four townhouses, but all the original owners still occupied the River Cottages in 2009.

With the River Cottages, Harry Weese almost realized his dream of living in a waterfront house in Chicago where he could dock his boat just outside his door. He initially reserved the cottage to the south for his private use, but his wife, Kitty, was reluctant to move from the Weese-designed townhouse on Willow Street in Chicago's Old Town, and Weese never completed the plans for the cottage or moved into the property.

WOLF POINT LANDINGS MASTER PLAN
Job 246.21-38

RIVER COTTAGES
Job 246.34/8909
Mechanical and Electrical Engineer: Key Mechanical
Structural Engineer: Seymour Lepp & Associates
Contractors: Gerhardt F. Meyne and Sumner Sollitt

SELECTED BIBLIOGRAPHY

"1st Phase Work Begins at Wolf Point Landings." *Chicago Tribune*, July 13, 1979.

"Condo Conversion List Now Includes a Giant Icebox." *Chicago Tribune*, September 30, 1979.

Elizabeth Brenner. "Condo Project on River 'To Fill Development Gap.'" *Chicago Tribune*, November 15, 1979.

"Building's Frozen Assets Thaw; Become Tasteful Base for Reuse." *Dodge Construction News* (November 17, 1980): 8, 10, 12.

"Architect Turns Chicago River into Backyard." *Chicago Sun-Times*, April 22, 1990.

"Weese Drops Anchor at River Cottages." *Chicago Magazine*, 1990.

Aerial view showing
the towers in the center,
Mitsui townhouses in the
foreground, and Temple
townhouses at the left
overlooking the temple
compound. Photographer
unknown. i59268, Chicago
History Museum.

UNITED STATES EMBASSY HOUSING

2-1-1 Roppongi, Minato-ku
Tokyo, Japan, 1979–82

Harry Weese spent the summer of 1937 bicycling through Europe with a friend from his grammar school days in Kenilworth. Among his lasting impressions from this trip were the half-timber houses near Rouen in Normandy with their stuccoed walls and thatched roofs. Eight years later while serving in the Pacific during World War II, Weese was struck by the similarities between Japanese rural architecture and the buildings he had seen in Normandy. More than three decades later, these traditions would inspire Weese's design for the United States Embassy Housing complex in Tokyo.

Since the 1950s, U.S. State Department personnel assigned to the U.S. embassy in Tokyo had lived in a three-building complex designed by architect Antonin Raymond and structural engineer Paul Weidlinger and located on the former Mitsui estate, a twelve-acre property on a high ridge in central Tokyo adjacent to a Buddhist shrine and a Shinto cemetery. By the late 1970s, these structures were aging and no longer sufficient to accommodate all of the U.S. diplomats and civil service personnel stationed in Tokyo. The State Department's Office of Foreign Buildings Operations, the same agency that had commissioned Weese to design the United States Embassy in Accra in the 1950s, decided to replace the outdated complex with a new, expanded housing development and in 1978 awarded the commission for the project to Harry Weese & Associates.

After an initial site visit, Weese returned to Chicago and worked with a design development team in his office to create a concept for the embassy housing complex. The plan developed by Weese and his team distributed 173 housing units among five buildings—three staggered fourteen-story tower blocks containing 131 apartments and two townhouse clusters containing a total of 42 multilevel three- and four-bedroom units. The compact housing arrangement left sufficient space on the site for recreational facilities, which included a swimming pool, gymnasium, and tennis courts.

The towers represented a merger of the techniques and aesthetics of European modernism with local traditions. The fireproof steel framing system consisted of two-story X-braces to resist seismic forces. The X-bracing also permitted the use of smaller beams and columns, which allowed for greater flexibility in the placement of windows. Walls were white stucco.

The decision to use stucco—a material common in Japan but never before utilized in high-rise construction in that country because of fears that aging, violent weather, or an earthquake might cause it to fail—met with opposition from Ohbayashi-Gumi, the local contractor. Ohbayashi-Gumi questioned its dependability, arguing that no stucco building over three stories existed in Japan, and proposed several alternatives, including precast panels, lightweight concrete boards, and aluminum curtain walls, but Weese prevailed. Flexible neoprene joints specially designed for this project separated the stucco panels. It was Weese's belief that these joints could absorb building displacement during earthquakes by allowing the top floors of the towers to move by more than one inch. The contrast of the black neoprene with the white stucco created a Mondrian-like effect and also recalled the half-timber tradition of rural Japan.

Site plan showing three towers at center, Mitsui townhouses to west, and Temple townhouses to north, and plan of a typical floor of one of the tower blocks, United States Embassy Housing, Tokyo. i52001 and i52002, Chicago History Museum.

Tokyo's vulnerability to typhoons and high temperatures accounted for the sliding aluminum shutters, or brise-soleil, installed on the windows and doors to protect against sun, rain, and strong winds. The shutters also lowered energy consumption by reducing the heat entering the units.

The Japanese are especially sensitive to the impact of shadows cast by tall buildings on neighboring residential structures, and Tokyo's sunshine/shadow code limited the time that shadows could be cast on residential properties to two hours. To comply with this regulation and to preserve views and exposure to sunlight of adjacent residential properties, the Weese designers lowered the height of the towers from 246 feet as originally planned to 145 feet and reduced the number of units each tower contained.

Tokyo's restriction against timber structures in the city center necessitated the use of reinforced concrete in place of the timber frames originally proposed for the townhouses. The townhouses, like the towers, had stucco-clad walls. Pitched roofs topped the units in both clusters. Weese characterized the 14 Mitsui townhouses at the western edge of the site as "four-story Corbusier-style dwellings." Pilotis, or columns lifted the building off the ground, leaving open spaces for carports at grade level and three levels of living space above. A "village lane" separated the 28 three-story Temple townhouses on the northern boundary into two rows arranged back to back. A two-story underground garage below the Temple townhouses provided parking for tower and Temple townhouse residents.

In configuring the complex, the designers took care to create a maximum sense of privacy for individuals living with their coworkers in a crowded urban center. In the towers, zigzag corridors eliminated the need for the long, monotonous, institutional-like hallways often found in tall buildings, and the glazing at each end varied the vistas from the corridors. With the exception of six single-level units designed for the handicapped, the tower apartments were stacked duplexes, with entrances that alternated between the lower and upper level. Consequently, only half of the occupants of each floor shared the same hallway.

The landscape design for the complex by Hakone Ueki enhanced the sense of an oasis in the busy and densely populated city. The balconies or terraces included in each apartment and townhouse unit allowed residents to enjoy the traditional Japanese gardens with their ponds and stones. Weese said he hoped that the balconies and terraces would become landscaped in the tradition of Rome, Milan, and Tokyo with "potted plants, laundry, and other evidence of humanity." Trees original to the site were saved and reused.

The close cooperation and mutual respect between Harry Weese & Associates and local contractors contributed to the completion of the project in only thirty-one months. Both the office of Foreign Buildings Operations and the embassy staff members who lived there judged the housing complex to be a great success, and it became a prototype for U.S. embassy housing facilities elsewhere. William L. Slayton, a deputy assistant secretary in the U.S. State Department at the time of the project, called Weese's work "a superb site plan and some of the most exciting buildings produced by the State Department and, I might add, by Harry."

Job 1008
Project Manager: Stanley Allan
Project Coordinators: Vincent Ziolkowski and Harry Kugasaki
Working Drawings and General Contractor: Ohbayashi-Gumi Ltd.
Structural Engineer: Kimura Structural Engineers
Mechanical Engineer: P. T. Morimura & Associates

SELECTED BIBLIOGRAPHY

William L. Slayton. "In Search of Good Design: Selecting an Architect." *Inland Architect* 28 (March/April 1984): 30–36.
"Housing for the United States Embassy in Tokyo." *Japan Architect* (September 1983): 7–15.
Harry Weese. "Image Recollected." *Japan Architect* (September 2, 1983): 16.
Toshihiko Kimura. "On the Structure of the United States Embassy Housing Development in Tokyo." *Japan Architect* (September 1983): 18–21.
Hiroshi Watanabe. "Evaluation: America's Presence in Tokyo—A Japanese Viewpoint." *Architecture* 73 (July 1984):75–81.

Section of Mitsui townhouses. i52003, Chicago History Museum.

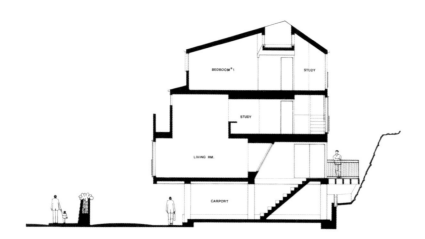

"Village lane" between
Temple townhouses.
Photographer unknown. i59267,
Chicago History Museum.

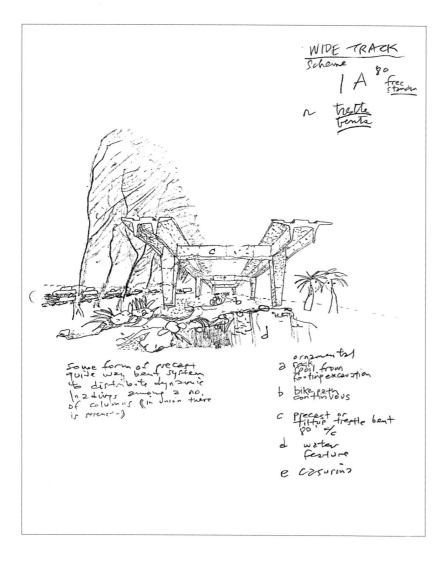

WIDE TRACK
Scheme
1 A 80 free standing
2 trestle bents

Some form of precast guide way bent system to distribute dynamic loadings among a no. of columns (in union there is strength)

a ornamental rock spoil from footing excavation
b bike path continuous
c precast or tilt-up trestle bent 80 o/c
d water feature
e casurino

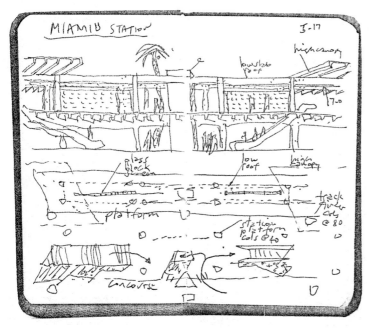

MIAMIB STATION   I-17

MIAMI-DADE COUNTY TRANSIT SYSTEM

Dade County, Florida, 1984

The Washington Metro established Harry Weese & Associates as experts in transit design and led to numerous additional transit-related commissions, both in the United States and abroad. Soon after the opening of the first segment of the Metro in 1976, the Weese firm became the principal architectural consultant for the Miami-Dade County heavy rail system, which became known as the Metrorail.

Planning for the Metrorail had begun in 1954 with the Miami Urban Area Transportation Study, but work could not start until 1972 when voters approved a bond issue that provided local funding. In 1973, the Metro-Dade Office of Transportation Administration (OTA), the agency charged with coordinating the transportation projects approved under the bond issue, retained a team headed by Kaiser Engineers of Oakland, California, to conduct preliminary planning and engineering studies for the Metrorail system. Final design began in 1976 when the OTA named Kaiser Transit Group, a five-member joint venture led by Kaiser Engineers, as general architectural and engineering consultant for the project. Kaiser selected Harry Weese & Associates as the general architectural consultant. Weese named Douglas A. Tilden, a veteran of the Chicago office and the Washington Metro project, to lead the effort in the firm's Miami office.

In contrast to his experience in Washington, where the architects and engineers had joint leadership, in Miami Weese and his design team found themselves in a five-way venture. Kaiser Engineers had already developed a design concept during the early planning and study phase of the project between 1973 and 1976 and apparently considered Weese's role to be limited to executing the proposed station designs. Weese, however, perceived his role as the designer of all elements visible to the public—the guideway, the stations, the station sites, and the rail vehicle itself. On one of Weese's first trips to Miami, he chartered a helicopter to review plans for the system from the air. He had little tolerance for expensive and long-drawn-out planning exercises, preferring instead to rely on his long experience, urban design expertise, and intuition to lay out the twenty-mile system. As with buildings, Weese maintained that the first step in planning transit systems was to gain a clear understanding of urban realities and possibilities. He believed that the initial surveying for

Weese's sketch, dated July 20, 1977, for the Miami Metrorail system, showing key elements of his proposed design, including a) the use of the oolitic limestone spoil as ornamental landscaping material; b) the incorporation of continuous bike paths along the route; c) a structural system of precast concrete columns, beams, and double T girders; d) water features; and e) casuarina (Australian) pines, an invasive species that was never actually used in this project. Courtesy of Douglas Tilden.

Weese's sketch of a typical Metrorail station illustrating the basic configuration of a center-platform station consisting of a central elevator flanked by an escalator and a stairway ascending from the ground-level concourse to the platform. The structural system, which was fully independent of the guideway, was arranged in forty-foot bays, with the columns supporting the platform and the roof centered on the quarter points of the guideway's structural module. Courtesy of Douglas Tilden.

View of University station. This Station, designed by the Weese office, illustrates the kit-of-parts approach to station design made possible by the use of consistent precast concrete structural components. Steven Brooke photograph, 2008.

infrastructure projects could be done quickly from high above. Once the situation was grasped, the basic lines of the transit system could then be laid down in short order. In his vision, documented in a sketch from July 1977, the system would run through a continuous, handsomely landscaped linear park.

Knowing that an above-ground rail system would have significant urban impact and consequences throughout the Miami metropolitan area, Weese then turned to the designs for the guideway, the elevated structure that would support the system's six-car trains. In doing so he came into direct conflict with the engineers. In contrast to Kaiser's proposal for a heavy structure that was closely related to highway construction, Weese envisioned a lighter structure of precast concrete columns, beams, and girders with post-tensioned sway bracing. Sarosh Dhondy of Carr Smith Associates, a structural engineer who shared Weese's vision for structural members that were light in appearance and consistent in their assembly, developed and championed the double T girders that were eventually used for the guideway.

Weese's approach to the guideway supports contrasted sharply with typical practice. The usual approach was to divide the distances between each station into equal girder lengths. As a result, the girder length was different for each segment of the route, leading to longer casting times, higher costs, and greater building complexity. Instead, Weese proposed using more than three thousand girders with a consistent length of eighty feet and adding a limited number of mid-run girders of unique "make-up" length where needed. By maximizing standard girder lengths and having them cast locally, it was possible to reduce both costs and construction time.

Weese also struggled with the engineers' proposal for a minimum distance between the inbound and outbound tracks. As he pointed out, fifteen of the twenty stations in the system had center train-boarding platforms between the two guideways. The engineers' approach would have resulted in repeated widening and narrowing of the distance between tracks as it widened at the stations and narrowed in-between. Seeking simplicity and visual consistency, Weese lobbied for a constant, wider distance between guideways. His proposal, which ultimately prevailed, also permitted far greater amounts of sunlight to penetrate to the areas below the tracks.

Kaiser had proposed running the tracks at ground level, within fenced rights-of-way, except at cross streets where the tracks would have risen up and over the intersections and then descended back to ground level. This concept would have eliminated Weese's linear park concept and led to an irregular rise and fall in track height. "We did not come to Miami to create a roller coaster," Weese stated, ultimately bringing the OTA and Kaiser Engineers around to his point of view with the assistance of city and county planning officials. In the end, with only a few exceptions, Weese achieved his vision for an all-elevated, visually consistent guideway structure of uniform height traversing a series of linear parks designed by a number of landscape architects coordinated by Steve Trudnak in the Weese office. At one point Weese had proposed the insertion of arbors covered with flame vine and bougainvillea between the guideway girders to soften the structure's appearance and provide shade for those walking or riding bicycles below the guideway's alignment. This proposal was not adopted, but ficus ivy was planted at the base of all guideway columns and trained up their full heights, providing some of the same effects and protecting the columns from graffiti artists.

Having achieved control of the project's major structural component, Weese set about locating his pavilion-like stations (twenty in all) along the guideway alignment. He and his team leaders created station design guidelines that laid out the "elements of continuity," those architectural and structural component assemblies that would give the project a visual and operating consistency but allow the architects of the individual stations some flexibility. The Weese office itself designed the University station as an example of what could be done.

In one final aspect of the design Weese crossed the traditional boundary between transit engineering and architecture by insisting that he and his team play a key role in the design of the rail vehicles. Weese proposed cars with colorful high-gloss finishes like those he had seen in Europe, along with spacious windows and locally inspired interior design motifs. The federal government intervened, however, requiring Miami and Baltimore to jointly purchase their train fleets from the last, and failing, U.S. fabricator of such vehicles, according to Douglas Tilden, who says that these cars, with their 1940s-era design and corrugated exterior stainless-steel panels, were the last vehicles this manufacturer would produce.

Weese's influence on the Miami Metrorail was vast. His eight-year involvement as the general architectural consultant yielded, according to Tilden," structures of straightforward simplicity, purpose-built, avoiding an unconscionable piling on of 'architecture' all too often seen today in transit system design." As with the Washington Metro, his solution was cost-effective and as maintenance-free as possible. And, as with Washington, Weese and his design team insisted that architecture is structure and structure is architecture.

Job CH487

Harry Weese & Associates for overall design coordination and two stations, other firms for remaining 16 stations.

Project Leader: Douglas A. Tilden

Team Members: Doug Tachi, Ron Pales, Pedro Montorro, Rene Rodriguez, Steve Trudnak, Karl Landesz, and Tim Werbstein

Structural Engineer: Carr Smith & Associates

Civil Engineer: Post, Buckley, Schuh & Jernigan

Mechanical and Electrical Engineer: Kaiser Engineers

Lighting Consultant: Marlene Lee

Landscape Architect: Stresau Smith & Stresau with various local firms resonsible for specific parts of the system

SELECTED BIBLIOGRAPHY

Beth Dunlop. "But Stations Lack a Certain Romance." *Miami Herald*, May 20, 1984.

Night view of University station, illustrating the open pavilion approach to station design that Weese and his design team considered appropriate for a Miami climate of clear sunlight, balmy breezes, and frequent misty rainfall. Steven Brooke photograph, 2008.

BIBLIOGRAPHIC ESSAY

Although Harry Weese was one of the most widely published architects of his era, there have been surprisingly few attempts to collect his work in a systematic way and assess his place in history. By far the most ambitious effort during his lifetime was a special issue of the Japanese architectural magazine *Process Architecture*, number 11, put out in 1979. *Harry Weese: Humanism and Tradition*, published in Tokyo with text in Japanese and English, included a foreword by the architect; text by Carleton Knight; short descriptions of a set of buildings, mostly compiled directly from the firm's publicity materials; numerous illustrations; some commentary by Douglas Schroeder, Laurence Booth, and George Hinds; and a "Chronological List of Major Works." Unfortunately there is not a great deal of biographical information, the descriptions are often cursory, and the catalog is far from complete or reliable. A second book that deals with a portion of the work is a volume compiled by Kitty Baldwin Weese entitled *Harry Weese Houses* (Chicago: Chicago Review Press, 1987). This valuable collection of materials contains illuminating commentary on Harry Weese and his approach to architecture.

A good introduction to the architect's ideas and working methods can be found in a short essay by Wolf Von Eckardt entitled "Harry Weese" in *A Guide to 150 Years of Chicago Architecture* edited by Robert Bruegmann, Sabra Clark, Paul Florian, and Cynthia Weese (Chicago: Chicago Review Press, 1985), a publication that accompanied an exhibition at the Museum of Science and Industry in Chicago. For the Baldwin Kingrey store, there is *Baldwin Kingrey: Midcentury Modern in Chicago 1947–1957* by John Brunetti (Chicago: Wright, 2004).

Among the more significant periodical publications on Harry Weese the man and his work are "Harry Weese," *Architectural Review*, May 1957; "The Office of Harry Weese and Associates," *Inland Architect*, September 1957; a half-dozen pages on Weese in *Life*, October 6, 1958; "Current Work of Harry Weese," *Architectural Record*, May 1963; Andrea O. Dean, "Harry Weese of Chicago," *AIA Journal*, May 1978; Rick Kogan, "Can Harry Weese

Change Our Town? An Architect Bucks the Brass," *Chicago Daily News Panorama* magazine, February 18–19, 1978; M. W. Newman, "A Salute to Harry Weese, Still Ahead of the Times," *Chicago Sun-Times*, November 8, 1992; Blair Kamin, "Weese's Legacy," *Chicago Tribune*, August 24, 1997; Herbert Muschamp, "Harry Weese, 83, Designer of Metro System in Washington," *New York Times*, November 3, 1998; and Stan Allan, "A Man of Many Words and Works," *Inland Architect*, 1998.

Weese himself wrote prodigiously in *Inland Architect* and in many other magazines and newspapers, but these writings have never been collected. Among his essays for various publications were "Housing Patterns and What Makes Them," *Architectural Record*, July 1958; "Random Thoughts on Architectural Control and Their Effects on Cities," *AIA Journal*, March 1961; "The Chicago Civic Center as Public Architecture," *AIA Journal*, 1969; "What's Next for Chicago?" *Commerce*, October 1974; "Let's Spare Chicago's Splendid 'L'," *Chicago Tribune*, August 27, 1978; "The Continuing Search for a Postmodern Architecture," *CRIT/ASJ*, Spring 1979; "Salvaging the Built Environment," *The Executive*, February 25,1981; and "A Springboard to Reality," *Form and Function* (Finland), February 1984.

Starting in the 1980s Weese started writing regularly for *Inland Architect*. Listed here are just a few of the many pieces he contributed to that magazine: "Beyond Burnham," April 1980; "Growing Up with Frank Lloyd Wright," June 1981; "Chicago Front and Center. How Would Burnham Have It in 1992?" July/August 1982; "Pluralism's Poses," July/August 1982; "Chicago's Manifest Destiny: A Destination Resort," March/April 1983; Special take-out section, "1992 and Beyond," March/April 1983; "A Pallid Primer of 'Plannese'," July/August 1983; "Troubled Allies at O'Hare," November/December 1983; "The Last International Exposition in the Twentieth Century," March/April 1984; "Architecture and the Fin de Siecle," March/April 1984; "Expo 1992," May/June 1984; "A Planner's Premise or the World According to Weese," November/December 1985; and "Wabash Galleria," November/December 1987.

There are also several important interviews with Weese. A discussion with Paul Heyer appears in Paul Heyer's *Architects on Architecture: New Directions in America* (New York: Walker Publishing, 1966). In the library of the Art Institute of Chicago there is a typescript of an interview William Marlin conducted around 1975 that may have been intended as the basis for a book that was never written. Betty J. Blum from the Architecture Department at the Art Institute conducted the most extensive oral interview with Weese in March 1988 as part of the superb collection of interviews of Chicago architects available in the Burnham library at the Institute and online at *http://www.artic.edu/aic/libraries/caohp/weeseh.html*. Although the transcription and editing are excellent, by the time of the interview Weese's memory seems to have started to falter. In addition, the library has compiled and put up on the Web oral interviews with Ben Weese, Jack Hartray, Ezra Gordon, and other members of the firm who talked about their work with Harry Weese.

Most of the archival materials from Weese's architectural firm went to the Chicago History Museum. This material was still being processed in 2008. His notebooks and a good many personal items went to the Art Institute of Chicago. The largest collection of materials relating to Columbus, Indiana, can be found at the Columbus Indiana Architectural Archives. The MIT Museum has Weese's original thesis drawings. The Cranbrook Archives has a well-organized collection of materials related to Weese's early career and his stay at that institution. Other materials remain in the hands of members of the family.

CATALOG OF
MAJOR WORKS

The following list is an attempt to compile information about major new buildings and important renovations by Harry Weese, Harry Weese & Associates and Harry Weese Associates. Unfortunately the existing records are somewhat scattered and sometimes conflicting. The major source of information for this effort was a set of two ledger books in the possession of James Torvik. Apparently compiled by the firm starting in the 1980s, this chronological list presumably drew much of its information from earlier lists.

In this compilation the entries are arranged chronologically by the date when building construction was finished. The name of the project is usually the name as it was recorded in the firm's ledger books, although variants and later names are sometimes noted. The addresses given are current addresses, except in the case of private houses where for reasons of owner privacy, no addresses have been indicated. The date refers to the completion of construction, although for very protracted projects there is also an indication of the date design began. The final component is a set of notes compiled by the author in 2009 including, whenever known, the status of the building during the years 2007-09 when the book was in the final stages of preparation.

1936
Shack Tamarack, Glen Lake, Mich., for Harry E. Weese. Standing. See entry on Glen Lake Houses.

1939
Cottage Two, Glen Lake, Mich., for Harry E. Weese. Standing. See entry on Glen Lake Houses.
Pritchard House, Glen Lake, Mich., for Richard Pritchard. Standing. See entry on Glen Lake Houses.

1940
Harker House, Evanston, Ill., for Mildred Harker. Standing. Remodeled.

1941
Simplicity House, Highland Park, Ill., for Alexander A. Newton.
Weese House, Barrington, Ill., for Robert P. Weese. Standing.

1942
Red House, Barrington, Ill., for Mr. and Mrs. Harry E. Weese. Demolished 1983.

1948
Ottawa Bank, 245 Central Ave., Holland, Mich., for Ottawa Savings and Loan Association. With Brewster Adams and John van der Meulen. Standing 2009.
Water Tower House, Barrington, Ill., for Harry M. Weese. Standing. Remodeled.

1949
Camp Windego, Wild Rose, Wis., for Girl Scouts of Evanston. Camp no longer in operation. Buildings standing?

1950
Benner House, Champaign, Ill. Standing 2009.

1951
Loomis Courts Housing, Loomis Blvd. and 14th Pl., Chicago, Ill., for Chicago Housing Authority. With John Van der Meulen and Brewster Adams. Loewenberg and Loewenberg associated architects. Standing 2009, undergoing restoration.
Richard House, Davenport, Iowa, for Jim and Pat Richard.
Stendler House, Champaign, Ill., for Celia Stendler. Standing 2009.
Zim House, Champaign, Ill., for Herbert Zim. Standing 2009.

1952
Barrett House, Kenilworth, Ill., for Roger Barrett. Library addition to house Lincolniana.
Kohlhase House, Barrington, Ill., for Frank A. Kohlhase. Standing 2009.
Welch House, Barrington, Ill., for William and Jane Welch. Standing 2009.
Yellow House (Lot 18 house), Barrington, Ill., for Harry M. Weese. Standing 2009.

1953
Bassett House, Columbus, Ind., for Kirk and Bernie Bassett. Standing 2009.
Lauther House, Columbus, Ind., for Edgar and DeLora Lauther. Standing, remodeled 2009.

1954
Drucker House, Wilmette, Ill., for Robert Drucker. Standing 2009.

1955
Camp Wild Rose scout house, St. Charles, Ill., for Girls Scouts of Chicago. Camp still operates. Building standing?
Picher House, Belvedere, Calif. Apparently demolished 1973.

1956
227 East Walton, Chicago, Ill., for group headed by Harry Weese and John Baird. Standing. See entry in this book.
Lillian C. Schmitt Elementary School, 1057 27th St., Columbus, Ind., for City of Columbus. Standing. See entry in this book.

1957
Johnson House, 5617 Kenwood Ave., Chicago, Ill., for Gale Johnson. Standing. See entry in this book.
Weese "Studio," Hawthorne Ave., Barrington, Ill., for Harry M. Weese. Standing. See entry in this book.

1958
Allen House, Wayne Township, Ill., for Thomas E. Allen. Standing 2009.
Robie House renovations, 5757 South Woodlawn Ave., Chicago, Ill., for Webb & Knapp. Standing 2009.

State Bank of Clearing, 5235 West 63rd St., Chicago, Ill., for Clearing Industrial District, Inc. Standing but empty 2009.

United States Embassy, Accra, Ghana, for U.S. State Department. Standing. See entry in this book.

1959

Bartholomew County Home for Aged, 2025 Illinois St., Columbus, Ind., for Bartholomew County. Standing 2009.

Irwin Union Bank-Eastbrook Plaza, Town Square, Hope, Ind., for Irwin Union Bank and Trust Company. Standing 2009.

1960

Columbus Village (three stages), 1560 28th St., Columbus, Ind., for Mayor's Housing Committee. First commission 1951. Standing 2009.

Hamilton Cosco office building and research, 2525 State St., Columbus, Ind., for Hamilton Cosco. Standing 2009.

IBM Branch Office, 340 W. Washington Ave., Madison, Wis., for International Business Machines Corporation. Not standing.

Lincoln Center, 2501 25th St., Columbus, Ind., for City of Columbus. Standing 2009.

University of Chicago Pierce Hall, 5514 S. University Ave., Chicago, Ill., for University of Chicago. Standing 2009.

1961

IIT Fraternity House, 3361 S. Wabash Ave., Chicago, Ill., for Illinois Institute of Technology. Now Alpha Sigma Phi, Standing 2009

Irwin Union Bank-Everroad, Everroad Shopping Center, 25th St. and National Rd., Columbus, Ind., for Irwin Union Bank and Trust Co. "Dead Horse" Bank. Standing 2009

Northside Junior High School, 2700 Maple Ave., Columbus, Ind., for City of Columbus. Standing. See entry in this book.

Purity stores, Palo Alto and elsewhere, Calif., for Purity Stores, Inc. First commission 1953. Various locations, primarily in California.

1962

Arena Stage, 1101 Sixth St., S.W., Washington, D.C., for Washington Drama Society. Standing, now embedded in larger complex. See entry in this book.

Camp Juniper Knoll dining hall, Elkhorn, Wis., for Girl Scouts of Chicago. Camp still operates. Building standing?

Drake University married student dorms, Des Moines, Iowa, for Drake University. Standing 2009.

Drake University mens dormitory, Des Moines, Iowa, for Drake University. Standing 2009.

East End Apartments, Chicago, Ill., for East End Associates.

Hyde Park Shopping Center, Chicago, Ill., for Webb & Knapp. Standing, remodeled. See entry on Hyde Park A & B Urban Renewal Project.

Kedvale Square, 18th and 19th St. and Keeler Ave., Chicago, Ill., for Lawndale Redevelopment Corporation. Standing 2009.

Old Town Apartments, Chicago, Ill., for Old Town Apts. & Eugenie Ln. Apts Trust. Standing 2009.

1963

Armstrong (Goltra) House, Vail, Colo., for Pauline Armstrong. Not standing 2009.

Butternut Springs cottage, Elkhorn, Wis., for Girl Scouts of Chicago. Camp still operates. Building standing?

Cornell College dormitories, Mt. Vernon, Iowa, for Cornell College. Pauley and Dows Halls for women. Standing 2009.

Hyde Park A & B townhouses, Chicago, Ill., for Webb & Knapp. Commission 1956. With I. M. Pei. Standing. See entry in this book.

Jens Jensen Elementary School, 3030 West Harrison St., Chicago, Ill., for City of Chicago Board of Education. Standing 2009.

Midland Manufacturing Plant, Skokie, Ill., for Midland Manufacturing Company.

Reed College Library addition, Portland, Ore., for Reed College. Standing 2009.

St. Thomas Episcopal Church, 226 Washington St., Menasha, Wis., for St. Thomas Episcopal Church. Standing 2009.

1964

Brittingham Project (Sampson Plaza), West Washington and Proudfit Aves., Madison, Wis., for Sampson Enterprises Inc. Standing 2009.

Morton Arboretum Library, Lisle, Ill., for Morton Arboretum. Standing 2009.

Newlin residence, Columbus, Ind., for George and Elizabeth Newlin. Standing 2009.

Northern Baptist Theological Seminary, 660 East Butterfield Rd., Lombard, Ill., for Northern Baptist Theological Seminary. Standing 2009.

Otter Creek Country Club, 11522 East Rd., Columbus, Ind., for Bartholomew County. Standing 2009.

Tangeman House, Muskoka Lakes, Ontario, for Dr. and Mrs. Robert Tangeman. Standing. See entry in this book.

1965

Cornell College women's dormitories, Mt. Vernon, Iowa, for Cornell College. Now Tarr Hall. Standing 2009.

First Baptist Church of Columbus, 3300 Fairlawn Dr., Columbus, Ind., for First Baptist Church. Standing. See entry in this book.

Illinois Center for the Visually Handicapped, 1151 South Wood St., Chicago, Ill., for State of Illinois Public Works. Now Illinois Center for Rehabilitation and Education. Standing 2009.

Reed College Community Center, Portland, Ore., for Reed College. With Zimmer Gunsul Frasca. Renovated 1997; standing 2009.

1966

10 West Hubbard St., Chicago, Ill., for 10 Hubbard Corporation. Formerly offices of Harry Weese & Associates. Standing 2009.

Hyde Park LR #14 (Kenwood Gardens), Kenwood and Kimbark avenues. south of 55th St., Chicago, Ill., for Kenwood Associates. Standing 2009.

IBM Building, 611 East Wisconsin Ave., Milwaukee, Wis., for Northwestern Mutual Life Insurance Company. Standing. See entry in this book.

Orchestra Hall renovations, 220 South Michigan Ave., Chicago, Ill., for the Orchestral Association. Standing 2009.

Reed College gymnasium, Portland, Ore., for Reed College. Now Watzek Sports Center. Renovated 2001; standing 2009.

1967

Auditorium Theater renovations, 70 East Congress Pkwy., Chicago, Ill., for Auditorium Theater Council. Standing 2009.

Beloit College Science Building and Library, Beloit, Wis., for Beloit College. Demolished.

Chicago Teachers Union apartment building, 55 West Chestnut St., Chicago, Ill., for Chicago Teachers Union Tower Corporation. Now John Fewkes Tower. Standing 2009.

Cornell College Chapel, Mt. Vernon, Iowa, for Cornell College. Now Alee Chapel. Standing 2009.

Cornell College Commons, Mt. Vernon, Iowa, for Cornell College. Standing 2009.

Cornell College mens dormitories, Mt. Vernon, Iowa, for Cornell College. Now Rorem Hall. Standing 2009.

Interama-Caribbean Pavilion, Miami, Fla., for Inter-American Center Authority. Not built.

Rochester Institute of Technology Library and General Studies Building, Rochester, N.Y., for Dormitory Authority of New York. Standing 2009.

1968

Air India housing, Bombay (Mumbai), India, for Air India. Built. Standing?

Cummins Engine Company offices, laboratories, factory buildings, 1900 McKinley Ave., Columbus, Ind., for Cummins Engine Company. First commission 1951. Standing 2009.

Seventeenth Church of Christ, Scientist, 55 East Wacker Dr., Chicago, Ill., for Seventeenth Church of Christ, Scientist. Standing 2009. See entry in this book.

University of Colorado physics complex, Boulder, Colo., for University of Colorado. Standing 2009.

1969

Channel Square, 325 P St., S.W., Washington, D.C., for Southwest Housing Renewal Company. Standing 2009.

Latin School, 59 West North Blvd., Chicago, Ill., for Latin School of Chicago. Standing. See entry in this book.

Lavatelli House, Snowmass, Colo., for Leo and Celia Lavatelli. Not standing 2009.

Shadowcliff, Ellison Bay, Wis., for Ben W. Heineman. Standing. See entry in this book.

Milwaukee Performing Arts Center, 929 North Water St., Milwaukee, Wis., for Milwaukee Performing Arts Center. now Marcus Center for the Performing Arts. Standing, remodeled, 2009.

1970

Chicago Botanic Garden maintenance building, Glencoe, Ill., for Chicago Horticultural Society. Now Construction Building. Standing 2009.

Crow Valley Country Club, 4315 East 60th St., Davenport, Iowa, for Crow Valley Golf Club. Standing 2009.

Formica Building, Fourth and Walnut sts., Cincinnati, Ohio, for Towne Properties. Standing 2009.

Time-Life Building, 541 North Fairbanks Ct., Chicago, Ill., for Time Inc. Standing. See entry in this book.

University of Colorado Psychology/Biology Building, Boulder, Colo., for University of Colorado. Commission 1963. Standing 2009.

University of Wisconsin South Lower Campus Academic Complex and Art (Elvehjem) Center, Madison, Wis., for University of Wisconsin. Commission 1963. Standing 2009.

United States Embassy Housing I, Accra, Ghana, for U.S. State Department. Standing 2009.

1971

Bank Street College of Education, 610 West 112th St., New York, N.Y., for Bank Street College of Education. Commission 1964. Standing 2009.

Carleton College Fine Arts Building, Northfield, Minn., for Carleton College. Standing 2009.

Fort Lincoln Urban Renewal, Bladensburg Rd. at Banneker Dr., Washington, D.C., for National Capital Housing Authority. Only low-rise completed. Standing 2009.

IBM Systems Manufacturing Building, Endicott, N.Y., for International Business Machines Corporation.

University of Illinois at Chicago Physical Education Building, Chicago, Ill., for University of Illinois. Standing 2009.

University of Vermont Fine Arts Center, Burlington, Vt., for University of Vermont. Masterplan, not built.

1972

Actors Theatre, 316 West Main St., Louisville, Ky., for Actors Theatre of Louisville. Standing. See entry in this book.

Arena Stage Kreeger Theater, Washington, D.C., for Washington Drama Society. Standing 2009. See entry in this book.

Forest Park Community College, 5600 Oakland Ave., St. Louis, Mo., for Junior College District of St. Louis. Commission 1965. Now St. Louis Community College in Forest Park. Standing 2009.

Given Institute of Pathobiology, 100 East Francis St., Aspen, Colo., for University of Colorado, Denver. Standing. See entry in this book.

University of Illinois at Chicago Education and Communications Building, Chicago, Ill., for University of Illinois. Standing 2009.

1973

Commonwealth Fullerton Apartments, 345 West Fullerton St., Chicago, Ill., for Commonwealth Realty. Standing 2009.

Crown Center Hotel, 1 East Pershing Rd., Kansas City, Mo., for Crown Center Redevelopment Corporation. Standing. See entry in this book.

First National Bank, Wilkinson and Second sts., Dayton, Ohio, for First Dayton Development Corporation. Standing 2009.

Metropolitan Correctional Center (William J. Campbell U.S. Courthouse Annex), 71 West Van Buren St., Chicago, Ill., for General Services Administration. Standing. See entry in this book.

University of Delaware Solar House, Wilmington, Del., for University of Delaware. Built?

1974

180 North LaSalle, Chicago, Ill., for Romanek-Golub and Company. Standing 2009.

Drake University Fine Arts Building, Des Moines, Iowa, for Drake University. Commission 1967. Standing 2009.

Drake University Olmstead Student Center, Des Moines, Iowa, for Drake University. Standing 2009.

John Knox Home, 1210 Colonial Ave., Norfolk, Va., for John Knox Limited Partnership. Standing 2009.

Lake Village, Lake Park Ave. and 47th St., Chicago, Ill., for Lake Village Associates. Standing 2009.

Northwest Medical Arts Building, 1100 West Central Rd., Arlington Heights, Ill., for seven doctor tenants. Standing 2009.

Oak Park Civic Center, 123 Madison St., Oak Park, Ill., for Village of Oak Park. Standing. See entry in this book.

University of Illinois at Champaign-Urbana Levis Center, Champaign, Ill., for University of Illinois. Commission 1969. Standing 2009.

University of Massachusetts, Boston Library, Boston, Mass., for University of Massachusetts. Standing 2009.

1975

Baird House, Aspen, Colo., for John Baird. Standing 2009.

Credit Card Center, Des Moines, Iowa, for Amoco Oil.

Credit Card Center, 3700 Wake Forest Rd., Raleigh, N.C., for Amoco Oil. Standing 2009.

Dundale Square apartments, 6600 Chesapeake Blvd., Norfolk, Va., for Dundale Square Limited Partnership. Standing 2009.

Goose Lake Prairie Visitors Center, 5010 North Jugtown Rd., Morris, Ill., for State of Illinois Capital Development Board. Standing 2009.

Grace Street Elderly Housing, 635 West Grace St., Chicago, Ill., for Grace Street Associates. Standing 2009.

Hubachek Retreat, DeKalb, Ill., for F. B. Hubachek.

Mercantile Bank, 1101 Walnut St., Kansas City, Mo., for New York Life Insurance Company. Converted to residential. Standing 2009.

Williams College Sawyer Library, 55 Sawyer Library Dr., Williamstown, Mass., for Williams College. Slated for demolition 2009. See this entry in book.

Taylor House, Winnetka, Ill., for Mr. and Mrs. William J. Taylor Jr.

Trans Union offices, 90 Half Day Road at Tri-state Expressway. Lincolnshire, Ill., for Trans Union. Standing 2009.

1976

Alabama Capitol renovations, Montgomery, Ala., for State of Alabama.

Cornell College Science Building, Mt. Vernon, Iowa, for Cornell College. Now West Science Center. Standing 2009.

Euclid Place, Lake Street and Euclid Ave., Oak Park, Ill., for Euclid Place Associates. Incorporates Frank Lloyd Wright's Francisco Terrace. Standing 2009.

First Plaza, Copper, Second, Third and Tijera Streets, Albuquerque, N.M., for First Albuquerque Properties. Standing 2009.

Lake Michigan College, 2755 East Napier Ave., Benton Harbor, Mich., for Lake Michigan College. First commission 1966. Standing 2009.

New Trier High School Gymnasium, Winnetka, Ill., for New Trier Township High Schools. Standing 2009.

Roberts House, DeKalb, Ill., for Thomas Roberts. Standing 2009.

Southern Illinois University School of Medicine, North Rutledge St. north of Miller St., Springfield, Ill., for Illinois Building Authority. Standing 2009.

Terminal on the Square renovation, 1000 Botetourt Gardens, Norfolk, Va., for Norfolk Redevelopment & Housing Authority. Now Fred Heutte Center. Standing 2009.

Willow Street Townhouses, 312–318 West Willow St., Chicago, Ill., for Quincy White Company. Standing. See entry in this book.

Washington Metro, Washington, D.C., for Washington Metropolitan Area Transit Authority. Commission 1966. First segment opened 1976; work continued to 1994. Standing. See entry in this book.

1977

Bank of Wheaton, 211 South Wheaton Ave., Wheaton, Ill., for Bank of Wheaton. Standing 2009.

Hinsdale Retirement Homes, Washington Square Apartments, 10 North Washington, Hinsdale, Ill., for Hinsdale Retirement Homes Inc. Standing but empty 2009.

Marriott Hotel, 540 North Michigan Ave., Chicago, Ill., for 540 North Michigan Square Venture. Standing 2009.

Middletown Civic Center, Main St. and Manchester Blvd., Middletown, Ohio, for City of Middletown. Standing 2009

SUNY at Buffalo Law School and Library, Amherst, N.Y., for State University Construction Fund. Now O'Brian Hall. Standing 2009.

1978

Bolingbrook Office Building, Bolingbrook, Ill., for Exchange National Bank of Chicago.

Stanford University Frederick E. Terman Engineering Center, Stanford, Calif., for Stanford University. Standing. See entry in this book.

1979

Prairie Convention Center, Washington, Adams and 9th sts., Springfield, Ill., for Springfield Metropolitan Exposition and Auditorium Authority. Standing 2009.

Steelcase Showroom, Merchandise Mart, Chicago, Ill., for Steelcase, Inc. Showroom removed.

1980

1100 Lake Shore Drive, Chicago, Ill., for Turner Development Corporation. Standing 2009.

Miami-Dade County Transit System, Miami, Fla., for Miami-Dade County. Standing 2009. See entry in this book.

Grand Rapids Convention Center, Grand Rapids, Mich., for City of Grand Rapids; County of Kent.

Mayo Clinic Harwick Building II, 205 Third Ave., S.W., Rochester, Minn., for Mayo Foundation. Addition to Harwick I. Standing 2009.

Museum Square, 401 K St., N.W., Washington, D.C., for Bush Development Company. Standing 2009.

One Pershing Square, Kansas City, Mo., for Pershing Square Redevelopment Company.

Union Underwear Corporate Headquarters, 1 Fruit of the Loom Dr., Bowling Green, Ky., for Union Underwear. Standing. See entry in this book.

Northwest Industries interiors, Sears Tower 61st and 62nd floor, Chicago, Ill., for Northwest Industries.

1981

200 South Wacker Dr., Chicago, Ill., for Buck-Irvine Associates. Standing. See entry in this book.

Baym Residence, Aspen, Colo., for Gordon Baym. Standing 2009.

Brown-Forman Warehouse D renovations, 850 Dixie Hwy., Louisville, Ky., for Brown-Forman. Standing. See entry in this book.

Brown, Colma Denant law offices, 444 W. Michigan Ave., Kalamazoo, Mich., for Brown, Colma Denant. Standing 2009.

Fulton House, Chicago, Ill., for Fulton House Associates. Standing. See entry on Wolf Point Landings in this book.

Kansas City Music Hall, 301 West 13th St., Kansas City, Mo., for City of Kansas City.

Neiman Marcus store at Oakbrook Mall, Oak Brook, Ill., for Neiman Marcus. Standing 2009.

Transportation Building renovation, 600 South Dearborn St., Chicago, Ill., for Transportation Associates. Standing 2009.

University of Chicago Court Theater, 5535 South Ellis Ave., Chicago, Ill., for University of Chicago. Standing 2009.

1982

75 East Wacker Dr. renovations, Chicago, Ill., for The Hayman Company. Standing 2009.

Riyadh Airport Community, Riyadh, Saudi Arabia, for Kingdom of Saudi Arabia. Commission 1975. Presumably standing 2009.

St. Louis Post Office and Custom House renovations, St. Louis, Mo., for General Services Administration. Standing 2009.

United States Embassy Housing, 2-1-1 Roppongi, Minato-ku, Tokyo, Japan, for U.S. State Department. Standing 2009.

Niagara Frontier Transit System planning and design, Buffalo, N.Y., for Niagara Frontier Transportation Authority.

1983

Carbondale Public Library, 405 East Main St., Carbondale, Ill., for City of Carbondale. Standing 2009.

Donohue Building renovations, 711 South Dearborn St., Chicago, Ill., for Printers Row Redevelopment Corporation. Standing 2009.

Grandview condominium, Peoria, Ill., for Kenneth E. Pickens.

1984

South Cove, Harbor Isle Dr., New Buffalo, Mich., for New Buffalo Harbor Inc. Standing 2009.

1985

411 East Wisconsin, Milwaukee, Wis., for Winmar Company. Standing 2009.

1986

Terminals Building renovations, 537 South Dearborn St., Chicago, Ill., for Community Resources Corporation. Standing 2009.

United States Embassy Housing II, Accra, Ghana, for U.S. State Department.

Willowlake Center, Army Trail Rd., Bloomingdale, Ill., for DKR Development. Standing 2009.

1987

Singapore Transit planning, Singapore, for Singapore Transit.

1988

Carmel Plaza I, 200 K St., N.W., Washington, D.C., for Bush Development. Standing 2009.

Quincy Park–200 South Wacker Drive, Chicago, Ill., for the John Buck Company. Commission 1978. Standing 2009. See entry on 200 South Wacker Drive.

River Cottages, Chicago, Ill., for Larrabee-Dickens Corporation. Standing 2009. See entry on Wolf Point Landings in this book.

Union Station renovation, Washington, D.C., for Union Station Redevelopment Corporation. Harry Weese & Associates restoration architects, Benjamin Thompson & Associates, architects for retail spaces. Standing 2009.

1989

Midway Airport transit station, Chicago, Ill., for Chicago Transit Authority. Standing 2009.

Raffles Hotel renovations, Singapore, for Raffles Hotel.

Swiss Grand (Swissôtel), 323 East Wacker Dr., Chicago, Ill., for MAT Associates. Standing 2009.

1990

Grand Central Terminals renovations, New York, N.Y., for Metropolitan Transportation Authority with Beyer Binder Belle. Standing 2009.

Adams/Wabash station renovations, Chicago, Ill., for Chicago Transit Authority. Standing 2009.

East St. Louis Courthouse renovations, 750 Missouri, East St. Louis, Ill., for General Services Administration. Apparently now Melvin Price Federal Building and Courthouse. Standing 2009.

Hotel Intercontinental renovations, Chicago, Ill., for various hotel operators. Radisson renovations (1978), Forum renovations (1989) and Intercontinental renovations (2000) with Gensler. Standing 2009.

Mormon Temple restoration and renovation, Salt Lake City, Utah, for Church of Jesus Christ of Latter-Day Saints. Standing 2009.

Wildermuth Library, Gary, Ind., for Gary Public Library. Standing 2009.

1991

Zaiser House, Naples, Fla., for Len Zaiser. Standing 2009.

1992

Amoco Research Center, Naperville, Ill., for Amoco Oil. Standing 2009.

Chinatown Square, Archer Ave. and Cermak Rd., Chicago, Ill., for Chinese American Development Corporation. Commission 1985. Standing 2009.

Los Angeles Metro planning and station design, Los Angeles, Calif., for MRTC. Harry Weese & Associates work 1984–1992.

1993

Field Museum renovations, Chicago, Ill., for Field Museum. Multiple projects 1967–93. Standing 2009.

Newberry Library renovation and bookstack addition, 60 West Walton St., Chicago, Ill., for Newberry Library. Multiple projects from 1959 to 1993. Standing 2009.

1994

Scattered site housing, Chicago, Ill., for the Habitat Company.

Mt. Carmel High School priory and classroom addition, 6410 S. Dante St., Chicago, Ill., for Mt. Carmel High School. Standing 2009.

1995

Buckingham Foundation Renovations, Grant Park, Chicago, Ill., for Buckingham Fund. Standing 2009.

Chicago State University student union and residence, Chicago, Ill., for Chicago State University. Standing 2009.

Mormon Temple restoration and renovation, Washington, D.C., for Church of Jesus Christ of Latter-Day Saints. Standing 2009.

1996

Metra (Chicago & North Western) trainshed renovation, 111 North Clinton St., Chicago, Ill., for Regional Transportation Authority. Standing 2009.

Park Evanston Building, 1630 Chicago Ave., Evanston, Ill., for the John Buck Company. Standing 2009.

Mormon Temple restoration and renovation, Logan, Utah, for Church of Jesus Christ of Latter-Day Saints. Standing 2009.

1997

Mormon Temple restoration and renovation, Manti, Utah, for Church of Jesus Christ of Latter-Day Saints. Standing 2009.

Frances Xavier Warde School renovations and Gymnasium addition, 751 N. State St., Chicago, Ill., for Holy Name Cathedral. Standing 2009.

St. Isaac Jogues parish center and classroom addition, 306 West Fourth St., Hinsdale, Ill., for St. Isaac Jogues Parish. Standing 2009.

1998

Fenwick High School fieldhouse and renovations, 505 Washington Blvd., Oak Park, Ill., for Fenwick High School. Standing 2009.

1999

Veterans Administration cemetery plan and shelters, Joliet, Ill., for Veterans Administration. Standing 2009.

North Bridge mixed-use development. Area bounded by Grand Ave., Ohio, Rush, and State sts., Chicago, Ill., for the John Buck Company. With Gensler. Only partly constructed. Standing 2009.

2002

North Avenue Collection, 939 West North Ave., Chicago, Ill., for Centrum Properties. Standing 2009.

INDEX

[Page numbers in *italic* refer to captions. Buildings cited are Weese designs unless otherwise indicated in parentheses. Buildings are indexed by city location.]

Aalto, Alvar, 19, 20, 31, 44, 53, 74, 75, 172
Accra, Ghana
    U.S. embassy in, 39, 96–99, 228
    U.S. embassy housing, 230, 232
Adams, Brewster, 24, 35, 38, 40, 87
Adler, Dankmar, 134
Albuquerque, New Mexico, First National Bank, 62, 231
Allan, Stanley Nance, 46, 62, 72, 184, 187, 188, 196, 218
American Institute of Architects, 20, 45, 51, 73, 91, 140, 148, 154
    Distinguished Building Award, 166, 195
    Firm of the Year Award, 62
    National Honor Award, 179
Amherst, New York, SUNY Buffalo Law School and Library, 231
Anchorage, Alaska, library design (unbuilt), 63–64, *65*
Anderson, Don, 112
Anderson, H. E., 159
Anderson, Lawrence B., 16
Antoine-Heitmann Associates, 204
apartment buildings
    Weese's, 39, 59, 62, 85–86
Architectural Record, 43, 48
Architectural Review, 43
Arlington Heights, Illinois, Northwest Medical Arts Building, 230
Armour Research Foundation, 33–34
Aspen, Colorado, 29, 44
    Baird House, 231
    Baym House, 231
    Given Institute, 57, 155–59, 230
Asplund, Gunnar, 19, 74, 75
Ayers, Thomas, 73

Bacon, Edmund, 20
Bailey, James, 123
Baird, John, 59, 68, 85, 86
Baldwin, Benjamin, 20–21, *22,* 26–27, 84
Baldwin, Kitty, 27, 28. *see also* Weese, Kitty (Baldwin)
Baldwin Kingrey, 31–32, *32, 33,* 34
Barnes, Edward Larrabee, 24–25, 33, 74, 132, 165
Barrington, Illinois
    Kolhase House, 228
    Red House, 228
    Studio, *42,* 43, 44, 75, 92–95, 228
    Water Tower House, 33, 44, 183, 228
    Weese, Robert House, 228
    Welch House, 228
    Yellow House, 228
Bauer, Catherine, 20

Bauhs, Bill, 59, 159, 175, 179
Beaux-Arts tradition, 15
Bechtel, 59
Bell, Robert E., 45, 124, 154
Belluschi, Pietro, 72
Beloit Wisconsin. Beloit College, 46, 76, 230
Belvedere, California, Picher House, 228
Bemis Foundation, 23–24
Bennett, Edward, 27
Bennett, Marshall, 68
Benton Harbor, Michigan, Lake Michigan College, 231
Berry, Raymond D., 136
Berryman, Nancy, 60
Bertoia, Harry, 20, 22, 31
Biederman, Fritz, 179
Bilandic, Michael, 68
Bingham, Barry, Sr., 160
Blessing, Charles, 34
Bloomingdale, Illinois, Willowlake Center
Bohlin Cywinski Jackson, 170
Bolingbrook, Illinois, Bolingbrook Office Building, 231
Bolt, Beranek & Newman, 109, 141
Bombay, India, Air India houses, 51, 230
Booth, Laurence, 59, 61, 70
Boston, Massachusetts, University of Massachusetts, 57, 230
Boulder, Colorado, University of Colorado, 230
Bouwkundig Weekblad, 48
Bowling Green, Kentucky, Union Underwear, 62, 196–99, 231
Bowman brothers, 30
Brassert, Herman A., 14
Breuer, Marcel, 24
Brown, Owsley, II, 163, 205
Brown, Pamela, 163
Buchan, George, 113
Buck, John A, II, 200
Buffalo, New York, Niagara Frontier Transit, 231
Bullfinch, Charles, 15
Bunshaft, Gordon, 24, 25, *185,* 187–88
Burchard, John Ely, 23
Burke & Associates, 159
Burlington, Vermont, University of Vermont Fine Arts Center, 230
Burnham, Daniel, 12, 27, 53, 66, 67, 68–70
Burnham & Hammond, 20
Byrne, Jane, 68

Cammisa & Wipf, 195
Campbell, Sendler, 163

Carbondale, Illinois, Carbondale Public Library, 231
Carr Smith Associates, 222, 223
Cartwright, Kevin, 55
Century of Progress fair, 15
Champaign, Illinois
    Benner House, 228
    Stendler House, 228
    University of Illinois Levis Center, 230
    Zim House, 228
Chermayeff, Serge, 27, 46
Chicago, Illinois
    10 West Hubbard Street offices of Weese & Associates, 48–49, 124–26, *127,* 229
    1100 Lake Shore Drive apartments, 62, 231
    200 South Wacker Drive office tower, 62, 200–204, 231
    227 East Walton Street apartment building, 39, 75, 85–86, 228
    Adams-Wabash elevated station renovations, 232
    architectural tradition, Weese in, 74, 75
    architecture criticism of 1970s, 70–71
    Auditorium Theater restoration, 53, 134–37, 230
    BASIS group designs for, 26–27
    Buckingham Fountain renovations, 232
    Campbell U.S. Courthouse Annex/Metropolitan Correction Center, 57, 176–79, 230
    Chicago Public Library Public Library, 27
    Chicago State University student union and residence, 232
    Chicago Teachers Union (See Fewkes Tower)
    Chinatown Square, 232
    Commonwealth Fullerton Apartments, 230
    Donahue Building, 231
    Diana Court (Michigan Square) Building (Holabird & Root), 62–63
    East End Apartments, 229
    Fewkes Tower, 75, 230
    Field Museum renovations, 232
    Frances Xavier Warde School, 232
    Fulton House (See Wolf Point Landings)
    Glessner House (Richardson), 53
    Grace Street Elderly Housing, 231
    Hyde Park A & B, 38, 114–19, 229
    Illinois Center for the Visually Handicapped, 229
    Illinois Institute of Technology fraternity, 229
    Jens Jensen School, 229
    Johnson House, 90–91, 228
    Kedvale Square, 229
    Lake Village East, 59, 230
    Latin School, 51, 142–45, 230
    Loomis Court (Chicago), 35, 38, 230
    Loop elevated, 68
    Marriott Hotel, 62–63, *64,* 231
    Metra (Chicago and Northwestern) train shed renovations, 232
    Metropolitan Correctional Center (See Campbell U. S. Courthouse Annex)
    Mt. Carmel High School addition, 232
    Midway Airport, 232
    Navy Pier proposal, 67–68
    Newberry Library renovations, 232
    North Avenue Collection, 232
    North Bridge Development, 232
    Northwest Industries offices, Sears Tower, 231
    Old Town Apartments, 229
    Orchestra Hall, 230
    post-World War II, 34
    preservation movement, 53
    Printers Row project, 59–61

Quincy Park, (See 200 S. Wacker Drive)
River Cottages (See Wolf Point Landings)
Robie House renovations, 228
Scattered Site Housing, 232
Seventeenth Church of Christ, Scientist, 51, 73, 138–41, 230
Soldier Field preservation, 68
State Bank of Clearing, 229
Steelcase Showroom, 231
Swiss Grand Hotel (Swisshotel), 232
Terminals Building (See Printers Row)
Time-Life building, 51, 75, 150–54, 230
Transportation Building (See Printers Row)
University of Chicago Court Theater, 231
University of Illinois at Chicago, 230
Weese's commitment and civic engagement, 30, 56, 59, 73, 76, 77
Weese's designs and recommendations, 34–35, 38, 43, 46, 66–70
Willow Street Townhouses, 54, 55, *180,* 181–83, 231
Wolf Point Landings, 72, 210–14
World's Fair (1992), 68–71, 73, 76
church designs
    First Baptist (Columbus, Indiana), 48, 50, 73, 128–33
    Seventeenth Church of Christ, Scientist (Chicago), 51, 73, 138–41
    St. Thomas Episcopal (Neenah, Wisconsin), 46–48, 75
Cincinnati, Ohio, Formica Building, 230
city planning
    BASIS design group, 26–27
    building height, 43
    design and zoning controls, 52–53
    Riyadh, Saudi Arabia, *57,* 57–59
    urban renewal movement in 1950s, 35, 38, 114–15
    Weese's Cranbrook fellowship, 20, 22
    Weese's designs and philosophy, 34–35, 38, 43, 52–53, 55–56, 66–71, 77, 114–19
    Weese's early studies, 19
Clap, Mr., 15
Clawson, Kim, 126
Clay, Grady, 72
Cohen, Stuart, 70
Columbus, Indiana
    architectural significance, 37
    Bartholomew Country Home for the Aged, 229
    Bassett House, 228
    Columbus Village apartments, 36, 229
    Cummins Engine Company, 230
    First Baptist Church, 48, 50, 73, 128–33, 229
    First Christian Church (Saarinen), 36
    Hamilton Cosco, 229
    Irwin Union Bank-Eastbrook, 229
    Irwin Union Bank-Everroad, 229
    Lauther House, 228
    Lillian Schmitt Elementary School, 36, 87–89, 228
    Newlin House, 229
    Northside Junior High School, 36, 40, 75, 100–101, *103,* 228
    Otter Creek Country Club, 229
    Weese's designs, 36–37
Condit, Carl, 70
Cooper, Kent, 185
Le Corbusier, 15–16, 27, 75
Corley, John, 73
COR-TEN steel, 152
Cosentini Associates, 149, 154, 170
Cranbrook Academy of Art, 20, 84
Crombie Taylor Associates, 136, 137
Cummins Engine Foundation, 36, 37, 87, 88

Dade County, Florida, Miami-Dade County Transit System, 220–23, *224*

Dahlem Construction, 208

Dakin, James , 162

Daley, Richard J., 60

Dart, Edward, 45, 75

Davenport, Iowa

    Crow Valley Country Club, 230

    Richard House, 228

Davidson, Cynthia, 71, 72

Dayton, Ohio

    First National Bank, 230

DeGolyer, Robert S., 16

DeKalb, Illinois

    Hubachek Retreat, 231

    Roberts House, 62, 231

DeLeuw Cather & Company, 185, 187

Design Unit, 53–54, 113, 145, 148, 149, 208

Des Moines, Iowa

    Amoco Oil Credit Card Center, 231

Drake University, 48, 229,230

Deutsche Bauzeitung, 48

Devine, Tom, 154

Dhondy, Sarosh, 222

Dimmitt, Donald, 31

Doxiadis, Constantinos, 56

Dring, Bill, 49, 175

Dunlop & Company, 101

Dunlop Construction, 89

Dwight Building Company, 170

Dzienicki, Andrew, 149

Eames, Charles and Ray, 21, 25, 26, 29, 31

East St. Louis, Illinois, East St. Louis Courthouse renovations, 232

Eckardt, Wolf von, 188

Eckbo, Garrett, 37, 72

Edilizia Moderna, 48

Eldridge & Son, 166

elevators, double-decker, 152

Elkhorn, Wisconsin

    Butternut Springs cottage, 229

    Camp Juniper Knoll, 229

Ellison Bay, Wisconsin

    Shadowcliff, 51, 53–54, 147–49, 230

embassy design

    Accra, Ghana, 39, 96–99

    contextual considerations, 96–97

embassy housing

    Tokyo, Japan, 62

Emerson, William, 15

Endicott, New York, IBM Systems Manufacturing Building, 230

energy-efficient design, 57, 203–4

Engineers Collaborative, 109, 123, 132, 141, 145, 149, 159, 199

Entenza, John, 53

Environmental Systems Design, 204

Evanston, Illinois

Harker House, 228

Park Evanston Building, 2332

Fichandler, Zelda, 104, 105, 109

Fitzgerald, Joseph, 68

Fox, Frances, 38

Fredericks, Marshall, 22

Fuller, Buckminster, 15, 56

furniture

    Museum of Modern Art competition, 26

    Weese's aspirations, 28, 30

    Weese's designs, 33–34, 84, *84*

Gaines, Theodore, 59

Gary, Indiana, Wildermuth Library, 232

Gensler, 73, 126

Georgel, Andre, 149

Gersh, Joe, 80

Gidwitz house (Chicago) (Rapson and van der Meulen), 35, 36

Giedion, Sigfried, 70

Gillum, J. D., 166

Gillum-Colaco, 204

Girard, Alexander, 31

Glen Lake, Michigan, 23, 29

    Cottage Two, 81–83, 228

    Pritchard House, 23, 82, *83,* 228

    Shack Tamarack, 17, 80–81, 82–83, 228

Glencoe, Illinois, Chicago Botanic Garden maintenance building, 230

Goldberg, Bertrand "Bud," 45, 75

Goldberger, Paul, 188

Goltz, Milton, 113

Gordon, Ezra, 41, 42, 99, 109

Grand Rapids, Michigan, 230

Gray Construction, 199

Green, Jackie, 54

Gregory, Donald, 22

Griffin, Walter Burley, 12

Gropius, Walter, 15, 24

Grossman, Jeffrey, 214

Grotell, Maija, 20, 22, *22*

Gruen, Victor, 165

Hakone Ueki, 218

Hall, Donald J., 165

Hall, Joyce C., 165

Hansen, Paul, 149

Hartmann, William, 16, 30, 53

Hartnack, Karl, 45, 49

Hartray, John F. "Jack," Jr., 41, 45, 46, 49, 55, 61, 76, 77, 128, 132, 152, 154, 178, 179, 184, 185

Hasbrouck, Bill and Marilyn, 60

Haskell, Douglas, 36

Hatfield Electric, 101

Hazen, Joseph, 150, 151

Heineman, Ben, 54–55, 147, 196

Hesse & Warford Engineers, 208

Hickey, Tom, 61, 149

Highland Park, Illinois, Simplicity (Newton) House, 228

Himmel, Ivan, 59

Hinsdale, Illinois

    St. Isaac Jogues parish center and classroom addition, 232

    Washington Square Apartments (Hinsdale Retirement Homes) 231

Hoffmann, Hans, 21

Hogan, Charles, 37

Holabird & Root, 31

Holland, Michigan, Ottawa Bank, 38, 228

Holloway, Perkins, Eisman, 166

hotel designs, 62–63, *64,* 165–67

Hunt, Richard, 72

Hutchinson, Louise, 91

Inland Architect, 40, 43, 49, 70, 71, 227
interior design, Kitty Weese's. *see* Design Unit
International Exposition (1937), 19
International Style, 15
Irvine, Wesley, Jr., 200
Izenour, George C., 136, 137

Jacobs, Jane, 35, 117
Jahn, Helmut, 73
Jefferson National Expansion competition, 33
Jensen, Jens, 12
Johnson, D. Gale, 90
Johnson, Lyndon B., 185
Johnson, Norman, 166
Johnson, Philip, 53
Johnson & Company, 183
Joliet, Illinois, Veterans Administrations Cemetery, 232
Jory, Jon, 162
Joseph & Joseph Architects, 205, 206, 208

Kaestner-Lynch, 163, 208
Kahn, Louis, 45–46
Kaiser Engineers, 220, 223
Kalamazoo, Michigan, Brown, Colma, Denant, 231
Kamin, Blair, 179
Kansas City, Missouri
    Crown Center Hotel, 57, 165–67, *167,* 230
Kansas City Music Hall, 231
    Mercantile Bank Building, 57, 231
    One Pershing Square, 231
Kapnick, Harvey, 68
Karn, Jerry, 65, 72
Karn Charuhas Chapman & Twohey, 72
Karr, Joe/Karr & Associates, 49–50, 51, 170, 175, 178, 179, 193, 195,
    197, 199, 204, 205, 206, 208
Kasin Guttmann & Associates, 195
Kays, William M., 193
Keck, George Fred, 15, 24, 30, 36
Keck, William, 15, 30
Keith, Sally, 16
Kenilworth, Illinois, Barrett House, 228
Kepes, Georgy, 24
Kerekes & Kerekes, 109
Key Mechanical, 214
Kiley, Daniel/Kiley and Partners, 37, 50, 123, 132, 166
Kimura Structural Engineers, 218
King, Donald W., 155–56
Kingrey, Jody, 30–32
Kiriazis, Judith, 71
Klement, Vera, 60
Klimek, Carl, 170
Klint, Klaare, 31
Kornacker, Frank, 41, 89, 99, 109
Kravolec & Best, 99
Kugasaki, Harry, 218

Lam, William, 123, 132, 188
Landesz, Karl, 223
landscaping
    Kiley's, 37
    Weese's childhood neighborhood, 12–13
    Harry Weese & Associates design, 49–50, 51
    Weese on, 56
Lapota, Matthew, 24
L'Architecture d'Aujourd'hui, 48

Larrabee Dickens Corporation, 55
Lathrop Construction, 195
Lee, Marlene, 223
Leers Weinzapfel Associates, 89, 101
Lepp & Associates, 214
Levi, Julian, 114
Levin, Jack, 117
Levy, Marilyn, 46
Lewis, Samuel R., 85
Lewis & Associates, 89, 101, 109, 123, 132, 141, 145
Life magazine, 43
Lin, Maya, 72
Lincolnshire, Illinois, TranUnion offices, 231
Lisec, Michael, 59, 140, 141
Lisle, Illinois, Morton Arboretum Library, 229
Little, Robert, 24
Loewenberg & Loewenberg, 35
Logan, Utah, Mormon Temple Restoration, 232
Lombard Illinois, Northern Baptist Theological Seminary, 229
Loo, Ai Ling "Eileen," 16
Los Angeles, California, Los Angeles Metro Planning, 232
Louisville, Kentucky
    Actors Theater, 57, 160–63, 230
    Brown-Forman building, 62, 205–8, *209,* 231
Lustig & Associates, 145

MacKinnon, Cyrus, 160
Madison, Wisconsin
    Brittingham Project (Sampson Plaza), 229
    IBM Branch, 229
    University of Wisconsin, *50,* 51, 75, 76, 230
Maher, George, 12, 26
Maher, Philip, 26
Manchester Guardian, 48
Mangum, Edward, 104
Manti, Utah, Mormon Temple restoration, 232
Markelius, Sven, 19, 23
Marlin, William, 71
Marshall & Brown, 166
Mass, Marvin, 152
Massachusetts Institute of Technology, 15–17, 19–20
materials of construction, 75
    COR-TEN steel, 152
Mathsson, Bruno, 31
McHarg, Ian, 50
McKim, Mead & White, 15
Meyerson, Martin, 26–27
Meyne, Gerhardt F., 214
Miami, Florida, Interama, 230
Miami-Dade County Transit System, 220–223. *224,* 231
Middletown, Ohio, Civic Center, 62, *63,* 75, 231
Mies van der Rohe, Ludwig 15, 24, 30, 75
Miller, Dolores, 46, 108, 109
Miller, J. Irwin, 36, 37, 87, 111
Miller, Megan, 191
Miller, Nory, 49, 71, 191
Miller, Walt, 46
Miller & Associates, 132, 137, 141, 154
Milles, Carl, 19, 20, 22
Milwaukee, Wisconsin
    411 E. Wisconsin, 232
    IBM Building, 121–23, 229
    Performing Arts Center, 50, 230
Mitchell, Wallace, 20, *22*
mobile homes, 43–44

modernist design
    development in 1950s, 38
        furniture, 30, 31–32
        postmodernist rejection of, 70–71
        Weese's early exposure, 15–16
        Weese's place in, 74, 75
Moholy-Nagy, László, 24
Montgomery, Alabama, Alabama Capitol renovations, 231
Montorro, Pedro, 223
Morgensen, Borge, 31
Morimura & Associates, 218
Morris, Illinois, Goose Lake Visitors Center, 231
Mount Vernon, Iowa, Cornell College, 48, 229–231
Munson, David, 73, 208
Muskoka Lakes, Ontario, Tangeman House, 36, 111–13, 229

Nachman, Uragel & Associates, 179
Naess & Murphy, 45
Nagle, James, 61
Nagle Hartray, 145
Nagle Hartray Danker Kagan McKay Penney Architects, 145
Naperville, Illinois, Amoco Research Center, 232
Naples, Florida, Zaiser House, 232
National Institute of Arts and Letters, 48
Neenah, Wisconsin, St. Thomas Episcopal Church, 46–48, 75, 229
Netsch, Walter, 75
Neumann, Hans, 37–38, 45, 46
Neutra, Richard, 29
New Buffalo, Michigan, South Cove, 232
New York, New York
    Bank Street College of Education, 230
    Grand Central Terminal renovations, 232
Newman, M. W., 71, 75
Newman, Oscar, 117
Newton, Alexander, 26
New York world's fair (1939), 23
Nimmons & Fellows, 12
Nishkian, Hammill & Associates, 195
Nivola, Constantino, 72
Norfolk, Virginia
    Dundale Square Apartments, 231
    John Knox Home, 59, 230
    Terminal on the Square, 231
Norman, Harold W., 136
Northfield, Minnesota, Carleton College Fine Arts Building, 230

Oak Brook, Illinois, Neiman Marcus store, 231
Oak Park, Illinois
    Euclid Place, 231
    Fenwick High School, 232
    Village Hall, 57, 75, 172–75, 230
Ohbayashi-Gumi, 217, 218
Olmsted, Frederick Law, 193
Owings, Nathaniel, 30

Paepcke, Elizabeth, 155, 156
Paepcke, Walter P., 24, 29, 155
Pales, Ron, 223
Parco Construction, 208
Paul, Gene, 128
Pei, Ieoh Ming, 16, 24, 38, 44, 74, 115, 116
Peoria, Illinois, Grandview condominiums, 231
Perkins, Larry, 33
Perkins & Will, 33
Pingusson, Georges-Henri, 28

Portland, Oregon, Reed College, 229–230
Post, Buckley, Schuh & Jernigan, 223
postmodernism, 48, 70–71, 76
Power Construction, 145
prefabricated structures
    mobile homes, 43–44
    Weese's early designs, 22
    Weese's later efforts, 67–68
preservation
    Auditorium Theater (Chicago), 53, 134–37
    Weese's investments, 59–60
    Weese's philosophy, 27, 48–49, 56, 61, 77
Prestini, James, 30, 31
Price, Martin, 113
Prince, Philip, 159
prison design, 57, 176–79
Pritchard, Richard, 23
public housing
    Weese's designs and philosophy, 35
    Weese's work in 1950s, 35, 38
Purity Stores, 37, *37*

Quinn, Kathryn, 62

radiant heating and cooling, 85–86
Raleigh, North Carolina, Amoco Oil Credit Card Center, 231
Rannells, John, 185
Rapson, Ralph, 20, 22, 25, 26–27, 35, 36, 38, 74
Raymond, Antonin, 217
Rebori, Andrew, 30
Red House, 26, 29–30
Repp & Mundt, 101, 132
residential design
    early Weese commissions, 26, 33, 90–91
    Weese & Associates in 1960s, 51, 111–13
Reynolds, Robert, 46, 49, 59, 187, 188
Richardson, Ambrose, 24, 26–27, 34
Richardson, H. H., 15, 53
Riyadh, Saudi Arabia, *57*, 57–59, 231
Robbins, Clarence E., 101
Robin, Ron, 99
Roche Prize, 20
Rochester, New York, Rochester Institute of Technology, 230
Rodriguez, Rene, 223
Rosati, James, 72
Rose, James, 37
Ruderman, James, 154
Rudolph, Paul, 44

Saarinen, Aline, 187–88
Saarinen, Eero, 17, 21–22, 25, 26, 33, 36, 39, 52, 74, 128
Saarinen, Eliel, 17, 20, 36
Saarinen, Loja, 22
Saether, Kolbjorn, 100
Saether & Associates, 101
Safdie, Moshe, 56
Salt Lake City, Utah Mormon Temple restoration and renovations, 232
San Francisco, California, 53
Sasaki, Hideo, 72
Sawyer, John, 168–69
Schal Associates, 204
school designs
    in Columbus, Indiana, 36, 40, 87–89, 100–101, *103*
    Stanford University, 62, *192*, 193–95

University of Massachusetts, 57
University of Wisconsin, *50,* 51, 75, 76
Weese & Associates in 1960s, 48, 50–51, 142–45
Williams College, 57, 76, 168–70, *171*
Schweiker, Paul, 30
Seegers, Arnie, 61, 170
Sekler, Eduard, 40
Selzer-Ornst, 123
Sepeshy, Zoltan, 20
Severud, Fred N., 136
Severud Associates, 179
Severud-Perrone-Sturm-Bandel, 170
Shepley, Rutan & Coolidge, 193
Shryock, Gideon, 162
Singapore, Raffles Hotel renovations, 232
Singapore transit planning, 232
Skidmore, Owings & Merrill, 16, 24, 26–27, 30, 136
Skokie, Illinois, Midland Manufacturing, 229
Slayton, William L., 218
Smithson, Alan, 38
Smithson, Peter, 38
Snowmass, Colorado, Lavatelli House, 230
Snyder Construction, 137
Soleri, Paolo, 56
Sollitt, Sumner, 136, 214
Sollitt Construction, 141
South Dearborn Renovation Associates, 60
Spachner, Mrs. John V., 136
Spillman, Pat Y., 37
Springfield, Illinois
    Prairie Convention Center, 231
    Southern Illinois University School of Medicine, 231
St. Louis, Missouri
    Forest Park Junior College, 50–51, 230
    St. Louis Post Office and Custom House renovations, 231
Stanford, California, Terman Engineering Center, Stanford University,
    62, *192,* 193–95, 231
Stockton, Walter T., 16
Stolzenbach, Darwin, 184, 185
Strengell, Marianne, 20, 22
Stresau Smith & Stresau, 223
Sullivan, Louis, 53, 75, 134
Swann, Lily, 21–23
Swei, Houng-Lin, 132

Tachi, Doug, 223
Tague, Robert Bruce, 26–27
Tangeman, Robert and Clementine, 36, 111–13
Tanner Leddy Laytum Stacy, 195
Tengbom, Ivar, 19
Testa, Angelo, 31
Tester & Son, 109
theater designs
    Actors Theater (Louisville), 57, 160–63
    Arena Stage (Washington, D.C.), 38, 46, 104–9
    Auditorium Theater renovation, 53, 134–37
Thornton, Charles H., 64
Thuermer, Angus MacLean, 98
Tigerman, Stanley, 70
Tilden, Douglas, 149, 220, 222, 223
Tokyo, Japan, U.S. embassy housing complex, 62, *216,* 217–18, *219,* 231
Torvik, James, 73
Train, Jack, 41transportation
    automobile, 52, 53
    Chicago Loop, 68

Miami-Dade County Transit System, 220–23, *224*
    public transportation, 56
    see also Washington Metro system
Trudnak, Steve, 222, 223
Tull, Donald E., 128
Turner Construction Company, 149, 154, 179

Vail, Colorado, Armstrong (Goltra) House, 229
van der Meulen, John, 35, 36, 37–38, 40
van Eyck, Aldo, 38
Vietnam Veterans Memorial, 72
Vignelli, Massimo, 188
Vrechek, George, 60, 62, 73

Waldron, Batey & Wade, 199
Walton, William, 187, 188
Warnecke, John Carl, 193
Washington, D. C.
    Arena Stage, 38, 46, 104–9, 229–230
    Carmel Plaza, 232
    Channel Square, 230
    Federal Triangle, 65–66, 72
    Fort Lincoln Urban Renewal, 230
    Kreeger Theater, *104,* 109
    Metro system. *see* Washington Metro system
    Museum Square, 231
    Southwest urban renewal project, 38
    Union Station, 232
Washington Metro system
    above-ground stations, *190, 191*
    contracting system, 184–85
    credit for successful design, 51–52
    critical reception, 188–91
    design features, 187, 188
    design process, 187–88
    full-scale mock-up, *186,* 188
    groundbreaking, 188
    origins, 184
    request for proposals, 185–86
    selection of architectural firm, 186–87
    significance of, 51, 52, 76, 77, 184
    station cross section, *184*
Watson & Co., 99
Webb & Knapp, 38, 115
Weese, Benjamin (brother), 12, 15, 23, 24, 25–26, 32–33, 39–40, 46,
    48, 53, 57, 61, 70, 75–76, 100, 152, 170, 185
Weese, Cynthia (sister-in-law), 61
Weese, Harry, *4, 22, 42, 155*
    awards and honors, 20, 22, 45, 48, 51, 62, 73, 91, 98, 108, 132, 137,
        140, 148, 154, 166, 179, 195
    Baldwin Kingrey and, 31–32, *33,* 34
    Baldwin partnership, 26
    Barnes and, 25, 33
    BASIS group, 26–27
    at Bemis Foundation, 23–24
    Burnham and, 66, 67, 68–70
    childhood, 12–15
    civic engagement, 30, 56, 73, 77
    in classical tradition of architecture, 74–75
    Columbus (Indiana) designs, 36–37
    commitment to Chicago, 30
    at Cranbrook, 20–23, 84
    critical appraisal of work of, 74–77, 226–27
    design characteristics, 75
    design philosophy, 55–56, 74

drawings and watercolors, *17, 21, 25,* 29, *29, 33*
Eames and, 25
early commissions, 26, 33
education, 15–20
European travels, 19, 34, 39
first awareness of architecture, 14
first practice, 32–33
furniture design, 26, 28, 30, 31, 33–34, 84, *84*
home and family, 44, 53–55, 92–93, 94, 181
Inland Architect and, 71–72
interviews with, 227
later years, 73–74
major works, 79, 228–32. *see also specific project (indexed by city)*
managerial style, 40, 42
marriage, 28
Pei and, 16, 38, 44, 115, 116
personal qualities, 42–43, 44, 48, 61
political and social thought, 16, 35, 52–53, 55–57, 74
postmodernist movement and, 70–71, 76
preservation philosophy, 27, 48, 56, 77
public speaking, 53
range of building types addressed in career of, 39, 75, 79
real estate investments, 39, 48, 55, 59–61, 72
Saarinen (Eero) and, 22–23, 25, 39
sailing, 25–26, *54,* 55
at Skidmore, Owings & Merrill, 24, 30
social life, 16, 44
super-high building designs, 64–65
thesis, *18,* 19–20
urban design for Chicago, 34–35, 43, 66–70
Vietnam Veterans Memorial competition, 72
working methods, 23, 38, 39, 45, 46, 61
World War II and, 27–30, 84
    see also Harry Weese, Architect & Engineer; Weese & Associates
Weese, Harry Ernest (father), 12, 13, 14–15, 25, 80
Weese, Horace Greeley (grandfather), 13
Weese, Jane (sister), 12
Weese, John (brother), 12, 24, 32, 195
Weese, Kate (daughter), 28, *42,* 44, 53
Weese, Kitty (Baldwin), 28, *29,* 31, 39, 44, 53–55, 74, 92–93, 148
    see also Design Unit

Weese, Marcia (daughter), *42,* 44, 53, 54, *182*
Weese, Marjorie (mother), 12, 81
Weese, Robert P. (uncle), 91
Weese, Shirley (daughter), *42,* 44, 53
Weese, Sue (sister), 12, 24, 82, 83
Harry Weese, Architect & Engineer
    first hires, 37–38
    first office, 32–33
Harry Weese Associates, 73
Harry Weese & Associates, 38
    designs of 1970s, 52, 55, 57–61, 62–66
    growth in 1950s, 38–44
    growth in 1960s, 45–52
    problems of later years, 61–62, 72–73
    staff and associates, 40–42, 45–46, 49–50, 61, 72
    Weese's separation from, 73
    West Hubbard Street offices, 48–49, 124–26, *127*
    work environment, 45, 46, 49, 61
Weese Seeger's Hickey Weese, 61
Weidlinger, Paul, 217
Werbstein, Tim, 223
West, Clifford, 22
Williamstown, Massachusetts, Williams College, 57, 76, 168–70, *171*
Wogan, John B., Jr., 210, 211, 213
Wood, Elizabeth, 35
Woodland, George, 19
World War II, 27–30
Wright, Frank Lloyd, 12, 14, 23–24, 25
Wurster, William, 42

Yale, Weese at, 17–19
Yamasaki, Minoru, 64
Yellow House, 33
Yost, Morgan, 36
Younger, Dwen, 99

Zeckendorf, William, 38, 115
Zetlin, Lev, 64
Zimmerman, Norm, 59, 73, 163, 166, 203, 204
Ziolkowski, Vincent, 218